Stimulation
in Early Infancy

Stimulation in Early Infancy

Edited by

ANTHONY AMBROSE

*Centre for Advanced Study
in the Developmental Sciences,
Minster Lovell, Oxford*

*Proceedings of a C.A.S.D.S. Study Group on "The
Functions of Stimulation in Early Postnatal Develop-
ment" held jointly with the Ciba Foundation, London,
November 1967, being the first study group in a
C.A.S.D.S. programme on "The Origins of Human
Behaviour"*

ACADEMIC
PRESS

1969

LONDON
NEW YORK

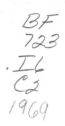
ACADEMIC PRESS INC. (LONDON) LTD.
24-28 Oval Road,
London NW1

U.S. Edition published by
ACADEMIC PRESS INC.
111 Fifth Avenue,
New York, New York 10003

Library of Congress Catalog Card Number: 74-109025
Standard Book Number: 12-055950-1

PRINTED IN GREAT BRITAIN BY
The Whitefriars Press Ltd., London and Tonbridge

Contents

Early Stimulation: Effects and Mechanisms

Mother-Infant Interaction: Effects and Biological Functions

Early Stimulation and Cognitive Development

CHAIRMAN'S CONCLUDING OBSERVATIONS
D. A. HAMBURG

Membership

Study Group on The Functions of Stimulation in Early Postnatal Development held at the Ciba Foundation, London, November 13th–17th, 1967.

Lord ADRIAN
Trinity College,
University of Cambridge

M. D. S. AINSWORTH
Department of Psychology,
Johns Hopkins University,
Baltimore

P. P. G. BATESON
Sub-department of Animal
Behaviour, University of
Cambridge

J. S. BRUNER
Center for Cognitive Studies,
Harvard University,
Cambridge

M. DAVID
Centre de Santé Mentale,
Paris

V. H. DENENBERG
Department of Biobehavioral
Sciences, University of
Connecticut, Storrs

D. G. FREEDMAN
Committee on Human
Development, University of
Chicago

B. E. GINSBURG
Department of Biobehavioral
Sciences, University of
Connecticut, Storrs

D. A. HAMBURG
(Chairman II)
Department of Psychiatry,
Stanford University,
Palo Alto

J. KAGAN
Department of Social Relations
Harvard University,
Cambridge

S. LEVINE
(Chairman I)
Department of Psychiatry,
Stanford University,
Palo Alto

ix

Centre for Advanced Study in the Developmental Sciences

The Centre for Advanced Study in the Developmental Sciences is being established near Oxford, England. It is an international Centre for promoting the growth of knowledge about the development of human behaviour and the factors that influence it. It is controlled by the Developmental Sciences Trust, which is a charitable educational trust founded in 1967 under the chairmanship of Lord Adrian.

The Centre's activities relate to all those sciences and disciplines that can contribute to greater knowledge of the biological, social and psychological principles that govern the development and functioning of human behaviour over the life-cycle. The aims of the Centre are, first, to stimulate and co-ordinate research in directions where it is most needed and to foster among scientists and teachers in these fields a developmental and multi-disciplinary perspective on human nature; second, to encourage the application of knowledge from the developmental sciences by those, in all sectors of society, engaged in coping with or preventing human problems.

The Centre will implement its aims by means of a number of problem-oriented programmes. For each of these it will organize international study groups and training courses, provide facilities for sabbatical or study leave, and publish books and reports on research findings. The Centre will also provide a specialist library in the developmental sciences, run an information service, and provide facilities for other organizations concerned with human development to hold study groups.

The Centre is due to open at Minster Lovell Mill in September 1970. The 3-year preparatory period has been occupied with the building of suitable premises, setting up the administrative and financial organization, and planning the scientific programme. At the same time a preliminary programme of five international study groups was undertaken, with the generous collaboration of the Ciba Foundation, London, on the general theme of the origins of human behaviour. Groups of leading scientists came together, each for five days, to examine in depth the effects of biological and environmental factors on the origins and early development of a number of aspects of behaviour that are basic to the effective functioning of human beings. The present volume represents the proceedings of the first of these study groups.

Developmental Sciences Trust

Preface

The research papers and discussions in this volume are the outcome of a multidisciplinary study group, the members of which were drawn from Behaviour Genetics, Developmental Neurology, Developmental Psychology, Ethology and Animal Behaviour, Neurophysiology, Paediatrics, and Psychiatry. The purpose of this wide-ranging group was to explore the variety of ways in which stimulation from the environment in the earliest phases of life can affect the development of behaviour, with special reference to the effects on the infant of his interaction with his mother. There was no intention of making a comprehensive review of what is now known in this field. The group set out to examine the implications of a number of new lines of research which show promising signs of increasing our understanding of the role of early environmental influences in the normal development of the individual.

The nine prepared papers concern studies not only of humans but also of rodents and of birds. The animal studies were presented first in the expectation that the findings and some of the methods used to obtain them would be of interest, not only in their own right, but in provoking questions about human infants which had not previously been given close attention. A special feature of this study group, as of all those to be planned by the new Centre, was the opportunity provided for discussion in depth. Not only was each paper followed by lengthy discussion, extensive time was provided for the group to explore issues of its own choosing. What transpired is reported under the headings of four general discussions and two ad hoc papers (by Kagan and Hamburg).

In editing the material, especially that of the discussions, a primary consideration has been to make it structured, concise and readable. This has entailed not only a good deal of re-ordering of contributions, but also some loss of the tone of feeling within the group which rapidly developed and persisted throughout its five days' work. This was one of spontaneity, informality, respect and friendship. Such a tone, together with the diversity of membership and its constructively critical outlook, gave rise to a working atmosphere that was most productive. In particular, since the research or theory under consideration at any one time was nearly always new to certain of the members, numerous important issues taken for granted by some were opened up for re-examination and clarification by the group. Furthermore, the possibility of bridging operations between the different approaches to, and different ideas about, the problem-area was always just in the background as an exciting prospect. In view, however, of the dangers both of extrapolation from one evolutionary level to another, and of generalizing from research findings based on use of some limited theory or method, that possibility was rightly treated with the utmost caution. There was, nevertheless, a continual sense of optimism and anticipation in the group, which was related among other things to a common belief in the potential value of interdisciplinary communication in stimulating new and fruitful ideas for future research.

I acknowledge with gratitude the editorial assistance received from Miss Rena Fenteman. Her persistent care, and her timely advice stemming from long experience, greatly facilitated my own task and made the outcome much more readable. I also thank Mrs. Olga Maratos and Mrs. Caroline Garland for their help with checking material, and Mr. W. Hill for preparing the index. Any errors that remain are my own responsibility.

I regret that, following the study group, publication of these proceedings has been subject to so much delay. The group was held at a time during the Centre's preparatory phase when increasing demands of all kinds, both upon my time and on that of the minimal staff available, caused repeated hold-ups in the progress of the editorial work. I wish to emphasize that I regard such delay as highly undesirable and that, once the Centre becomes operational from 1970 onwards, it is planned that publication of proceedings should be achieved within nine months of each study group.

Centre for Advanced Study in the   ANTHONY AMBROSE
Developmental Sciences, London
November 1969

Early Stimulation: Effects and Mechanisms

Infantile Stimulation: a Perspective[1]

SEYMOUR LEVINE[2]

Stanford University

IT IS CERTAINLY fitting and proper that, for the first study group of the new Centre for Advanced Study in the Developmental Sciences, the subject should be the influences of infantile stimulation. I shall try to introduce and give perspective to research concerned with the effects of infantile stimulation on many aspects of the organism's functioning. However, when one attempts a historical perspective, there is a problem about where to look for a beginning. As in most areas of research, it is very difficult to identify the specific origins of the notions which have proved fruitful. Ideas, in some ways, have no beginning. Yet there is now an abundant research literature on the effects of infantile experience on later behaviour. Running through this literature as far back as one can trace, there is some hint, suggestion, or experimental fact which can be seen to have generated the notion that those events which occur early in development markedly affect subsequent behaviour throughout the life history of the organism.

There seems to be little question, however, that the most profound influence leading to an ontogenetic approach to behaviour stems from Freudian theory (1949). This has given rise to numerous human studies which attempt to reveal early environmental influences on later personality development (e.g. Ainsworth, 1962). In an indirect way Freudian theory is also responsible for the large body of experimental literature dealing with the effects of infantile stimulation. In particular it led to one of the first demonstrations, performed in 1956 by Levine *et al.*, of the

[1] The work on which this chapter is based was supported by Research Grant No. 02881 from the National Institute of Child Health and Human Development and a Research Grant from The Leslie Fund, Chicago.

[2] During his work the author was maintained by Research Career Development Award K3-MH-19, 936 from the National Institute of Mental Health.

influence on later behaviour of both handling and shocking the pre-weanling rat. In spite of the fact that the study eventually bore little relationship to certain hypotheses concerning the effects of infantile "trauma" in particular, it did stimulate continuing research into an important developmental problem, namely, the effects on the growing organism of stimulation of varying kinds applied at one or another phase of infancy.

It is not my purpose to review all the evidence now available on the effects of infantile stimulation on a whole range of dependent variables. One of the most striking facts is that what appear to be *minimal* changes in the early environment have proved to have profound effects on the subsequent performance of the developing organism. Although there are many variables the effects of which have yet to be clarified, one cannot avoid the conclusion that those events which occur during sensitive periods in the organism's development have profound bio-logical consequences. One needs only to survey the extensive reports from Denenberg's laboratory (e.g. Denenberg, 1962) to be continually impressed by the behavioural consequences of infantile stimulation. Our own research (Levine, 1966), which has focused primarily on the effects of early experience on neuroendocrine function, has also demon-strated that minimal environmental changes can affect the central nervous system in such a way as to produce a markedly different pattern of neuroendocrine activity, with the consequence of differences in ACTH regulation and subsequent steroidogenesis.

In 1962 we proposed (Levine, 1962a) a classification of the experi-mental manipulations imposed on the organism during infancy. "This classification was based on the actual manipulations imposed on the organism and was categorized into either physical or mechanical, and non-mechanical or environmental. If the technique employed in the laboratory consists of imposing upon the animal stimulation from an external source, such stimulation would be classified as physical, for example, electric shock, loud sound, extreme temperature variations, mechanical rotation, handling, etc. Such experiences are usually brief, occurring at regular intervals, and in general fairly intense. In contrast, if the environment is experimentally structured so that the nature of the environment involved changes in general living conditions including housing, feeding, and contact with other animals in the environment, these may be considered as environmental and would include such experiences as restriction of free environment, alterations in feeding and drinking, in group living and competition, etc. The environmental experiences are usually constant and long acting and vary markedly in their degree of severity." This system of classification, although not without its problems, appears to be appropriate for the experiments that have been undertaken in subsequent years. Research has tended to concentrate more upon certain kinds of manipulations than upon others. Handling and shock still appear to be the major physical stimuli imposed upon the developing organism. More recently there has been a growing emphasis on maternal variables which fit into the category of environmental stimuli.

The number of dependent variables investigated is almost legion, ranging from the influence of infantile stimulation on brain chemistry (Tapp and Markowitz, 1963), to that on social-seeking and novelty-seeking behaviour (Denenberg and Grota, 1964), with almost every variant in between. It is, in fact, somewhat disturbing to find that so many aspects of the organism's function are influenced by infantile stimulation. It is undoubtedly possible that there are many aspects which are not influenced by preweaning stimulation. It does appear, however, that the major effects observed as a consequence of infantile stimulation occur in situations where emotional factors are of major importance. Thus, where learning seems to be affected, it is usually under conditions of aversive stimuli (Levine, 1956). Learning an approach response seems to be less affected by infantile stimulation (Spence and Maher, 1962). It appears that infantile stimulation does not affect cognitive function *per se*, but that it has a major role in altering some characteristic of the organism which is related to emotional reactivity.

Denenberg (1964) has theorized that, up to a certain point, increasing amounts of stimulus input in infancy act to reduce emotional reactivity in a monotonic fashion. In a series of experiments he and his co-workers have demonstrated that, as the amount of handling is increased during infancy, so emotional responsivity in adulthood appears to be generally reduced. Further, an additional aspect of this theory states that there exists an optimum amount of early stimulation which results in efficient performance in adulthood, and that stimulation leading to very high or very low emotional reactivity results in impaired performance, albeit by different processes. From this it follows that an inverted-U function should be obtained between the amount of infantile stimulation and adult performance on tasks which involve some noxious element and which are of moderate difficulty. The data obtained certainly appear to support this theoretical notion. However, this theory is at best descriptive, defined either in relation to the performance of the organism or in relation to the independent criteria of open field behaviour. It gives little insight into the actual mechanisms involved in the modification of the organism resulting from infantile stimulation.

Although several hypotheses have been offered to account for the effects of infantile stimulation on later emotional behaviour and on physiological responses to stress (Bovard, 1958; Levine et al., 1956; Levine and Mullins, 1966), so far the most compelling evidence implicating any single factor as a possible mediator of the effects of infantile stimulation has been reported by Schaefer (1963) and his associates. Observing that most young mammals, especially rats, cannot regulate body temperature, Schaefer suggested that the infant rat rapidly loses body heat unless this is regulated by the mother. He therefore hypothesized that a drop in body temperature was the critical factor in mediating the effects of infantile stimulation. The crucial experiment reported by Schaefer to support his position consisted of handling pups in an incubator designed to maintain normal body temperature. Rats handled under these conditions did not differ from nonhandled controls as measured by adrenal ascorbic acid depletion responses to cold stress at 14 days of age. Infant rats handled at room temperature, however, differed significantly from both the incubator-handled and the control animals.

Although Schaefer emphasizes body temperature as the critical factor, his results could also be interpreted as indicating that cold offspring alter the behaviour of the mother. Thus it would be the disturbance in the mother-infant relationship which produced the differences, rather than any specific effect of body temperature. A recent study by Young (1965) indicated that lactating females showed a distinct preference, on retrieval tests, for warm as opposed to cold pups. In an experiment (the results of which have not yet been published) in our laboratory we observed that removing the pups from the nest had the same effect on the adult corticosterone response to stress, whether the pups were maintained at room temperature or at nest temperature. Further, these animals did not differ from rats that were left in the nest while the mother was removed. All groups differed significantly from undisturbed controls. Thus, although the experimental data do not entirely support the hypotheses presented by Schaefer, they do force one to consider a whole set of new dimensions. These arise from the possibility that a major determinant of the effects observed as a function of infantile handling may be mediated by what occurs in the mother-infant interaction following the procedures imposed upon the newborn organism. The study by Young, previously described, which has been repeated and confirmed in our own laboratory, leads to the conclusion that the mother-infant relationship is indeed affected in some manner as a function of the experimental manipulations used in the infantile stimulation studies.

Recently we have conducted a series of studies (Levine and Thoman, 1967) in which mother-infant relationships have been disturbed. Using corticosterone response to stress either at weaning or in adulthood, we demonstrated that manipulation of the mother can produce profound permanent effects on neuroendocrine activity and behaviour in the offspring. Here again we have no knowledge as to how a change in the environment of the newborn, through alteration in the mother-infant relationship, produces the long-term effects observed. However, it is to be noted that a single stressful experience administered to the mother, such as ether stress when the offspring is 3 days of age, permanently alters both avoidance conditioning and the steroid response to a brief exposure to ether in the offspring when it reaches adulthood. We shall make an attempt, later in this study group, to specify a possible physiological mechanism to account for these effects.

So far we have discussed infantile stimulation with some degree of deference and with the obvious implication that there is something unique about infantile stimulation as opposed to stimulation at any other period in the organism's life. Several investigators have demonstrated (Levine, 1956; Seitz, 1954; Spence and Maher, 1962; Wolf, 1943), in the rat, that stimulation in the preweaning period has consequences that are different from those of equivalent stimulation in adulthood. This perhaps is the crudest demonstration of a critical period in respect of the effects of experience at one point in life on later performance. The concept of critical period, and its usefulness for infantile stimulation studies, has been discussed in detail by Denenberg (1964) and by Levine (1962a). The conclusion reached by Denenberg concerning the critical period hypothesis is as follows: "Experimental research with the mouse and rat, investigating stimulation between birth and weaning, has established that the critical period hypothesis is not sufficient to account for the findings. In instances where the data are consistent with the hypothesis further study has found that the critical period is a complex function of the parameter of stimulus intensity. Research to date indicates that, in the rat and mouse at least, there may be as many critical periods as there are combinations of independent variable parameters and dependent variable measures."

It is apparent that many psychophysiological processes are altered by infantile stimulation. Brain neurochemistry (Tapp and Markowitz,

1963), neuroendocrine activity (Levine, 1966), EEG activity (Meier, 1961), the response to pathogens (Ader and Friedman, 1965), rates of survival to severe stress (Levine and Otis, 1958), and the response to brain lesions (Levine, 1962b) have all been modified as a result of infantile stimulation. In general, it appears that one of the consequences of stimulating organisms during infancy is a permanent change in emotional reactivity. As yet, however, we are far from understanding the processes whereby these alterations are achieved. It is hoped that the material generated in this study group will give us some insight into possible mechanisms whereby certain kinds of experience early in ontogeny result in the most profound and permanent changes in the multitudes of functions which the organism uses to adapt to the environment.

REFERENCES

ADER, R. and FRIEDMAN, S. B. 1965. Social factors affecting emotionality and resistance to disease in animals. V. Early separation from the mother and response to a transplanted tumor in the rat. *Psychosom. Med.* **27**, 119–122.

AINSWORTH, M. D. 1962. The effects of maternal deprivation: a review of findings and controversy in the context of research strategy. *Public Health Papers*, **14**, Deprivation of maternal care: a reassessment of its effects. World Health Organization, Geneva.

BOVARD, E. W. 1958. The effects of early handling on viability of the albino rat. *Psychol. Rev.* **65**, 257–271.

DENENBERG, V. H. 1962. The effects of early experience. In E. S. E. Hafez (Ed.), *The behaviour of domestic animals*. Baillière, Tindall & Cox, London. Pp. 109–138.

DENENBERG, V. H. 1964. Critical periods, stimulus input, and emotional reactivity: a theory of infantile stimulation. *Psychol. Rev.* **71**, 335–351.

DENENBERG, V. H. and GROTA, L. J. 1964. Social-seeking and novelty-seeking behaviour as a function of differential rearing histories. *J. abnorm. soc. Psychol.* **69**, 453–456.

FREUD, S. 1949. *An outline of psychoanalysis*. Norton, New York.

LEVINE, S. 1956. A further study of infantile handling and adult avoidance learning. *J. Personality* **25**, 70–80.

LEVINE, S. 1962a. The effects of infantile experience on adult behavior. In A. J. Bachrach (Ed.), *Experimental foundations of clinical psychology*. Basic Books, New York. Pp. 139–169.

LEVINE, S. 1962b. The psychophysiological effects of infantile stimulation. In E. Bliss (Ed.), *Roots of behavior: genetics, instinct, and socialization in animal behavior*. Hoeber, New York. Pp. 246–253.

LEVINE, S. 1966. Infantile stimulation and adaptation to stress. In R. Levine (Ed.), *Endocrines and the central nervous system*. ARNMD Symposium. Williams & Wilkins, Baltimore. Pp. 280–291.

LEVINE, S. and MULLINS, R. F., JR. 1966. Hormonal influences on brain organization in infant rats. *Science, N.Y.* **152**, 1585–1592.

LEVINE, S. and OTIS, L. S. 1958. The effects of handling during pre- and post-weaning on the resistance of the albino rat to deprivation in adulthood. *Canad. J. Psychol.* **12**, 103–108.

LEVINE, S. and THOMAN, E. B. Maternal factors influencing subsequent adreno-cortical activity in the offspring. Presented at Symposium on Postnatal Development of Phenotype. Liblice, Sep. 1967.

LEVINE, S., CHEVALIER, J. A., and KORCHIN, S. J. 1956. The effects of early shock and handling on later avoidance learning. *J. Personality* **24**, 475–493.

MEIER, G. W. 1961. Infantile handling and development in Siamese kittens. *J. comp. physiol. Psychol.* **54**, 284–286.

SCHAEFER, T. 1963. Early "experience" and its effects on later behavioral processes in rats: II. A critical factor in the early handling phenomenon. *Trans. N.Y. Acad. Sci.* **25**, 871–889.

SEITZ, P. F. D. 1954. The effects of infantile experience upon adult behavior in animal subjects: I. Effects of litter size during infancy upon adult behavior in the rat. *Am. J. Psychiat.* **110**, 916–927.

SPENCE, T. and MAHER, B. A. 1962. Handling and noxious stimulation of the albino rat. II. Effects of subsequent performance in a learning situation. *J. comp. physiol. Psychol.* **55**, 252–255.

TAPP, J. T. and MARKOWITZ, H. 1963. Infant handling: effects on avoidance learning, brain weight, and cholinesterase activity. *Science, N.Y.* **140**, 486–487.

WOLF, A. 1943. The dynamics of the selective inhibition of specific functions in neurosis: a preliminary report. *Psychosom. Med.* **5**, 27–38.

YOUNG, R. D. 1965. Influence of neonatal treatment on maternal behavior: a confounding variable. *Psychon. Sci.* **3**, 295–296.

Discussion

Relevance of Rodent Handling Studies for Research on Humans

HAMBURG: Are studies done mainly with rodents relevant for human and nonhuman primates? Certainly study of the rat is an interesting aspect of biology in its own right, and it has completely sound justification apart from its implications for human problems. Still, we are concerned with human problems. We ought to be able to get some leads about where to look in man, what kinds of research would be interesting and fruitful, in the light of certain major trends in the rodent evidence.

Early Stimulation and its Effects

BATESON: It would help if those people studying rats could be more specific about the kinds of stimulation used in their experiments. They talk about "early stimulation" as though *everything* that stimulates the young animal will have long-term effects on adult behaviour. This seems dubious. In fact removing the rat from its nest, shocking it, and the other procedures used are all very different forms of stimulation. We need more careful definition of the things that produce the effects observed.

LEVINE: Four kinds of stimulation used by us are as follows. Handling, as we define it, is simply picking an animal up from the nest, moving it to another area and then putting it back. This usually starts within 24 hours after birth and continues for periods varying from 2 days to 21 days. We have also used electric shock over a wide range of intensities, and also cold, though not extensively. In yet other experiments all that was done was simply to change the animal husbandry conditions. Instead of feeding the animals outside the cage they were fed inside the cage; the same was done for drinking. These various kinds of change, whether intense or only very minimal, all tend to produce essentially the same kind of effect.

DENENBERG: It is important also to point out that these forms of stimulation can have major effects of two different kinds. One is the immediate physical impact which directly affects the infant's physiology. The other is the impact on processes of social interaction with the mother. When, after stimulating the young animal, you put it back in the nest with its mother, the mother acts differently towards it. The infant is a changed animal: it is colder or warmer or, if it has been shocked, it has urine over it. In some of our experiments we have found very complex social interactions between the young and its mother or its peers. In others, however, the major variation was due to the physical stimulation itself. We can handle our rats, not give them back to the mother, and still get a corticoid response half an hour later. So the two kinds of impact, although obviously overlapping to some significant extent, should be kept conceptually distinct.

BATESON: Does the physical stimulation produce a long-term effect as well as a short-term one?

DENENBERG: We don't know because we don't put them back to the mother, we kill them. If we handle the rat in the standard way and then put it back with the mother, wait half an hour, and then take it out and kill it, we get a corticoid response identical in value to that obtained when a handled animal is not put back with the mother for half-an-hour. The long-term consequences may not be the same but we certainly get a change in the animal's physiology without having to give it back to the mother. That is why I say that we can directly change the animal.

BRUNER: This presumably refers to the effects of extreme stimulation.

What about the lower or middle parts of your inverted-U curve regarding the response you get to stimulation? Surely there has to be
some sort of comparison between the various parts of the curve before
you can decide what is producing the major physiological effect. There
is an interesting parallel between your inverted-U effects and the
effects obtained in the Yerkes–Dodson function. In this, with the right
amount of drive the behaviour is fine; if there is too little, the organism
does not become activated; if there is too much, the behaviour can't
be held together sequentially. It would be interesting to explore in your
work what kind of response pattern gets built up in the middle range
of stimulation. This level of stimulation might make the organism
respond more adequately to stress in contrast to a great dose of stimulation which might produce a breakdown of behaviour.

LEVINE: The difficulty is in deciding what constitutes an adequate
response. If, for example, I take nonhandled animals and try to classically condition an emotional response of freezing, they acquire that
response infinitely faster than animals which have been handled, because the response system I am asking the animal to use is one which
in any case it uses much more frequently than does a handled animal.
Again, if I take an open field situation and look at the patterns of
behaviour, why is it that one animal is exploring and the other animal
is running out of the situation? Our quantification defines what we are
seeing in the qualitative aspects of the animals' behaviour. This is
critical. The kinds of conclusion one comes to are dependent upon the
nature of the situation in which one is requiring the animal to function.
This is why we always have to define the nature of the adequacy or
inadequacy of the organism's performance in terms of what it is that
is being performed.

Differences between Handled and Nonhandled Animals

KAGAN: Will you give us a brief, clinical, sketch of what the handled
animal is like in contrast to the nonhandled animal?

LEVINE: Let us suppose we have all our animals in a rack of cages.
Some cages contain handled animals, that is, those that have had brief
handling during days 1 to 3; others contain nonhandled animals. The
first thing you observe as you walk into the laboratory is that all the
handled animals are in the front and all the nonhandled animals are
at the back. Now suppose you feed them as we do by giving them
celery. You observe that the handled animals have eaten up the celery;
15 minutes later the nonhandled animals haven't touched it. If you
handle the animals, pick them up, the handled animals create no prob-

lem; one can pick them up, even after an interval of several weeks since the initial handling. The nonhandled animals are much jumpier, more skittish, and hyperactive. If you put these animals in some apparatus, any kind, say a shuttle box, but without electric shock, initially the handled animals will move back and forth over the barrier; the nonhandled animals will either stay in a corner or they will skip very fast and then stay in a corner. If you shock the animals, one animal will jump this way and the other animal will jump that way. In consequence one animal will learn because the adaptive response is jumping this way, the other animal will not learn because the maladaptive response is jumping that way. If, however, I lower the shock level in my avoidance box, one animal doesn't move at all and the other animal jumps this way; now he learns better as the case may be. This is where I refer to shifting the function by shifting the stimulus parameters that you use in adulthood. You can't simply determine whether the animal is better or not better. It always has to be defined in terms of what you are requiring the organism to do.

BRUNER: One might say that at a particular level of shock stimulation you get some kind of swamping-out of all kinds of delay patterns and all sorts of exploratory scanning patterns. Do your experiments suggest that there is a swamping-out of scanning, in which the animal can't get close enough to look over the situation? The way it has been stated so far has made it seem as if it is mainly steroid chemistry that gets the results.

LEVINE: No, not steroid chemistry. I am talking strictly descriptively about what the organism is doing. Something is changing physiologically—I would call it "arousal". In handled and nonhandled animals the threshold for arousal is different. Where an optimal level of arousal is necessary for function, the handled animal takes less stimulus to reach that optimal level. With the nonhandled animal, by the time the optimal level of arousal is reached the animal is already swamped and is simply making random, non-adaptive responses.

FREEDMAN: You describe the differences between handled and nonhandled rats in terms of arousal, but surely the nonhandled rats are scared.

LEVINE: They are not always scared: for example, when put in a situation where the stimulus to which they respond is not very novel.

DENENBERG: It is important to distinguish between scared or emotional behaviour and exploratory behaviour. In our factor analysis these are two independent dimensions. The handled animal will explore the environment, the nonhandled will not. It is not that the animal which is exploring is not emotional; an animal can be emotional and also explore.

The Rationale of Rodent Handling Experiments

PRECHTL: I am still puzzled about your experiments because even rats have a natural history. How do you visualize the relationship between the types of stimulation that you give in your experiments and those received by the rat in the course of its natural history? What is the rationale of your handling procedure? Is this a stimulation that would normally occur, or is it something that is completely out of the natural range of the rat's stimulations?

LEVINE: Perhaps I have glossed over this because our work did not start up as a study of the effects of handling. Initially I was much concerned with notions of development in psychoanalysis. We began by asking questions about the effects of noxious stimulation. We asked what would happen if a newborn animal, an experimental rat in our case, was presented with reasonably intense noxious stimulation. What would be its subsequent response to noxious stimulation in adulthood? I was concerned with the rat analogue of what I perhaps misinterpreted analytic theory to be saying. In our initial experiment we set up a two-group design and subjected each group of animals to different treatments for 3 minutes each day from the day of birth. The experimental group was placed on a very small platform in a chamber and given a small amount of electric shock. The control group was placed on the same platform but not given electric shock. We soon realized, however, that this control group was not a proper control because we were still taking the animals out of their cage. We needed a completely non-treated group. Now, in adding such a group to our design, our assumption was that since it would be having the best of all possible worlds—living with a warm, nutrient, moist mother, not being disturbed and having all the comforts of life—it would essentially not be affected in any way. We assumed the outcome would be basically the same as in our handled but nonshocked group, and that only the group given shock trauma would turn out to be different. What we actually found, much to our surprise, was that it was this group, the completely non-handled group, that showed a bizarre outcome.

Now you asked about the natural history of these animals. Because our laboratory is sound-proofed, light-cycled and air-conditioned the rats develop in an essentially static, barren environment. We are expecting them to grow up normally in an environment which does nothing. In nature, rats obviously do not exist in a static, barren environment: the temperature varies, there are predators, their mother's response is going to alter to a variety of natural stimuli and so on. What we have done with the laboratory animals is to insert into their barren environment some aspects of what they would normally get in the natural environment. We have introduced certain kinds of stimulus complexity and change early in development, which we think may have specific effects later on.

The Roles of Temperature Variation and Distress Calling

DENENBERG: To put the question in a different way: is this just an interesting laboratory phenomenon or does it have some generality to the nature of the beast in its natural setting? When a litter is packed together, whether it is in a laboratory cage or in a natural setting, some animals are on top and some are underneath. The animals on top will presumably be cooled more; some of them will escape and, if not found for a while, they will cool right off. We have some evidence that the cooled animal has a greater corticosteroid response than the noncooled animal. Sometimes, again, the mother bites them a little too hard and they squeal: they are getting stimulation from her that way. I believe we are uncovering here some of the causes of individual differences among animals that come from the same litter. I think our handling may be analogous to cooling and that electric shock may be analogous to being bitten. I hope that what we do in our laboratory bears some relationship to the natural environment of the animal.

PRECHTL: Can you come back to events in the natural environment by means of your experiments?

DENENBERG: This is just what we intend to do in our laboratory, using TV cameras. If we can get two classes of mother such that, while maintaining their young, one scatters the young and the other does not, the prediction would be that the scattered young should be much like handled animals. The scattered young would have more temperature loss than the nonscattered young, and it may be that handling has a major consequence in temperature reduction. It does not necessarily follow that temperature reduction is the only or principal factor at work. It may be that the young, when taken out of the nest, call more and this then causes the relationship between the mother and the young to change slightly. A few years ago it was found that young rodents call at between 30 and 50 kilocycles. This is ultrasonic, but you can pick these calls up with bat detectors. They occur particularly when the young are cold or when they are scattered outside the nest. This suggests that handling and various other kinds of stimulation may have the effect of disrupting the behaviour of the young pups. As a consequence they call, and this affects the relationship between mother and offspring. The prediction from this would be that all those stimuli which have long-term effects on the pups do so because they cause them to call more; consequently they receive more stimulation from the mother.

LEVINE: I think this is probably an oversimplification, but it should be mentioned that if you slow down tape-recordings of these rat calls until they are audible they sound like childrens' screams.

HAMBURG: Has anybody observed the effects of such calls on the mother?

LEVINE: Yes, the mother does respond and with some agitation. You can blind the mother and she will locate the offspring by these calls and transport them back to the nest. Also, it has been reported by Noirot that male and female young show different frequencies of calling, and that the mother has a preference for retrieving the females.

GINSBURG: This would be very adaptive for the species.

LEVINE: It also might account for a number of sex differences that have been found in various studies (R. F. Mullins and S. Levine. 1968. *Physical Behaviour*, **3**, 333 and 339). Unfortunately we only worked with one sex.

HAMBURG: To return to possible threads of continuity to species that have more complex brains, the few workers who have studied non-human primates have repeatedly emphasized the powerful effect of the infant's distress call upon the mother. It would be very interesting to have an experimental set-up in which various taped monkey sounds, including the distress call, were played to the mother. If you also had a bar-pressing arrangement whereby the mother could turn off these sounds, the prediction from the field studies would be, I think, that shutting off the distress call sound would show a very high priority. It is interesting that some clinicians have recently identified a sub-group of the battered child syndrome. They have enquired what was the final precipitating stimulus for the attack upon the child. This was found to be a period of persistent distress crying on the part of the infant which the mother just could not shut off. As the crying persisted it became unbearable for the mother. At that point she began to beat the infant to shut it up. What I am driving at is the extraordinarily powerful effect of the distress cry in primates.

The Reaction of Nonhandled Animals to Novelty

HAMBURG: Could you say more about nonhandled animals. For example, to what extent do you regard this treatment as some kind of partial stimulus deprivation?

LEVINE: It is difficult to put this into a stimulus deprivation framework since there is a mother in the environment which does perform adequately. There are certain behaviour characteristics which have been observed in mother-deprived organisms, whether primates or dogs, which are very similar to what we see in our nonhandled animals. The hyperactivity, the lack of adaptation to novelty, the arousal/fear response in the face of novel stimuli, all appear to be essentially the same. I think that the concept of novelty is very important here because this kind of organism seems to lack the capacity to generalize from one environment to another. Each set of circumstances is seen as unique. Habituation to one circumstance is not carried over to another that is only slightly different. In terms of the Sokolov model of habituation, such that in a mismatch of neural nets there is a learning or orienting response until matching is obtained, the process of handling gives the animal some basis for matching. Further experience gives it more of a basis for matching since there is not as much of the arousal, orienting or learning response that there is in the nonhandled animal. The nonhandled animal doesn't seem to have this capacity to generalize and match: in effect, it is continually thrown by novel environments.

BRUNER: You use the Sokolov model; in terms of the interpolation activity, you get a discrepancy. It is apparent that what the nonhandled animals are doing is giving first priority, according to their past history, to a defence reaction which swamps out the learning reaction. In effect, if you try to find out whether, for example over a whole battery of physiological parameters, there is the usual kind of desynchronization, you would find that there is a different pattern right from the start.

LEVINE: I think this could be done. Already it is certain that physiological as well as behavioural changes do occur at the time of stimulation. This is not a kind of quiescence in which the organism is just buffered. Because we observe changes in one system it doesn't mean that other things are not occurring concomitantly. The system that we are measuring must be linked to the other systems you mention.

Utility of the Concept of Critical Period

BATESON: Do you find that there are different critical periods for the effects of different kinds of stimulation?

LEVINE: It depends what functions you study in adulthood. It is likely that different functions are subject to modification at different critical periods. We tend to talk about a critical period instead of critical periods. There is no reason to assume either that any given function can be modified only at one critical period or that simulation applied at any given period is going to affect all functions uniformly. There is very clear evidence, for example, in the case of gonadal hormones. Administration of such hormones at one period will affect the morphogenesis of the urogenital tract. At another period, however, when this tract is already developed, such hormones appear to affect the central nervous system. So there are different critical periods which refer, not to the effects of different kinds of manipulation, although these may have different effects, but to the different kinds of function which may be affected in adulthood.

DENENBERG: I have become disenchanted with the critical period concept. If one uses the term in the original embryological sense, then certain consequences follow. Embryologically it does not really matter which of a number of insults you use on a developing embryo at any given time because each will have the same consequence. For example, a variety of insults applied at a certain time will result in a cleft palate. Yet any one insult, given a little earlier or later, will not affect the palate but will affect something else. This is the sense in which J. P. Scott has used the term "critical period", and I think there is very little data to suggest that the concept has much meaning after birth. From then on, however, there is no question that there are sensitive periods, that is, periods which are optimal as opposed to suboptimal for susceptibility to certain kinds of stimulation. The injection of hormones is certainly the clearest example of this: injection during the first 5 days produces one kind of effect, but injection after 5 days produces a different kind of effect.

KAGAN: Are you going to call the first 5 days a critical period for this intrusion? Isn't it unreasonable to assume that that is the only time it produces pathological effects?

LEVINE: I think it is highly unreasonable. What we want is a term which implies that the labile state of the developing organism is uniquely different at one time from what it is at any other time. Incidentally, in calling the injection of hormones an insult, you make the assumption that those things that we impose upon animals are indeed insults. In fact, in our own work, it may be that it is what we don't impose upon them in the usual laboratory environment which amounts to an insult.

BATESON: The trouble is that the critical period concept has acquired explanatory overtones which can be misleading.

KAGAN: The effect of a particular intrusion, be it hormonal or external, will be maximal when applied at one time and weaker when applied at others.

DENENBERG: The connotation of the critical period concept I object to is that of irreversibility. One can demonstrate long-term effects from one time to another only if one introduces no therapy between the two times. The notion of irreversibility, however, means that if any kind of therapy is applied it will be unsuccessful in changing the organism's behaviour. There are virtually no experiments on this. However, it is true that if a hormone is injected on day 2 or 3, and the organism then becomes a female, nothing can be done about reversing that pattern.

LEVINE: The fact that behavioural effects can be altered or reversed in one situation does not imply that such effects can be reversed over a wide spectrum of situations. For instance, if handled and nonhandled animals are exposed daily to an open field situation, in a matter of 5 or 6 days one cannot discriminate between these animals. In that situation they neither look different nor behave differently. If, however, a loud bell is then rung, the groups become clearly bifurcated. This is because a new set of conditions has been imposed: subjected to a new kind of novelty, the animals behave distinctly. Behaviour therapy can be used to reverse certain effects of early experience, but this doesn't mean that a permanent or chronic reversal will be obtained over the whole spectrum of behaviour that is affected by early experience.

DENENBERG: The consequences of behaviour therapy are exceptions to the concept of critical periods as used in embryology. If you use the term "critical period", then you have got to stick to the connotation used in embryology. I would prefer to use another term in respect of behaviour after birth. This is a matter of semantics.

GINSBURG: The important thing as regards the behavioural consequences of early stimulation is to identify what has happened to the organism with regard to such things as steroids, central neural mechanisms and other biological factors. We should leave the semantic discussion until after we have examined more experimental evidence and considered the mechanisms involved.

BATESON: Semantics are important at this stage. It is essential that we understand each other. If we mean by the term "critical period" that certain stimulation has a specific effect when applied at a particular stage in the life cycle but not when applied either before or after, then let's stick to that meaning. Denenberg is rightly objecting to the superfluous meaning of the term.

AINSWORTH: In implying irreversibility the critical period concept may be too rigid. Just as we now feel that the distinction between innate and learned is unclear since it is more convenient to think of a continuum between the relatively stable and the relatively labile, we should also regard irreversibility in the same way: something that is more or less easily reversed by more or less intensive treatments.

GINSBURG: Some people who took over the term "critical period" use it more rigidly than is warranted by indications from new data. The same thing has happened with the term "imprinting". The important thing is to focus on the real biological and psychological data instead of quibbling about terms at this stage.

LEVINE: I regard the critical period concept as having importance in pointing to certain urgent research problems. There are several areas which need to be elaborated. One is the generality of infantile stimulation effects among different organisms. Another concerns the range of behaviours over which these effects are manifested. The question of mechanisms is very important here. The critical period concept is helpful in focusing upon mechanisms in so far as important things seem to happen at one time or within a very limited space of time. We then begin to look for mechanisms that operate at that time. If, however, there is a diffuse time range over which things occur, then mechanisms become more obscure in terms of how one needs to specify what is acting at a given point in development.

Experimental Programming of Life Histories in the Rat[1]

VICTOR H. DENENBERG[2]

Purdue University

ONE OF THE most exciting things about doing research in the areas of infantile stimulation and early experience is that there are so many intriguing avenues to explore. Some in which I have been involved include the effects of physical stimulation on later behaviour, the search for physiological mechanisms underlying infantile stimulation, investigations of developmental processes, two effects of early social interactions upon later behaviour, inquiry into the critical period hypothesis, setting up model (or simulation) situations to test hypotheses derived from human clinical observations, and programming of life histories. This paper discusses the last of these research areas.

If we look at any mature organism and ask the question "Why does it behave in this manner?", a number of answers immediately come to mind. One of these answers would emphasize the relevance of the animal's past experiences. Now we know that all past experiences do not have equal impact. Some tend to cancel each other, others summate together, while others interact in a complex fashion. Some of the organism's experiences may affect it only during a relatively brief period in its life span and not leave any residue which has long-terms effects. Other combinations of experiences may cause behavioural and physiological modifications throughout the complete life of the animal and may, indeed, affect the length of its life span. In fact, some of these combinations of experiences may have such broad impact that the behaviour and physiology of subsequent generations are significantly modified.

Yet the manner in which different experiences, singly and in combination with other experiences, affect a particular adult behaviour

[1] The research described in this paper was supported, in part, by Research Grant No. HD 02068 from the National Institute of Child Health and Human Development.
[2] Now at University of Connecticut.

pattern is not well known. Research in the fields of infantile stimulation and early experience has isolated a number of procedures which have been shown to affect a wide variety of behavioural and physiological responses. However, most studies to date have not investigated the effects of combining different experiences. The usual procedure has been to vary the organism's experience during one phase of its developmental history (between birth and weaning for infantile stimulation, from weaning up to early adulthood for much of the early experience work), keeping everything else constant, and to test the animals in adulthood to determine the effects of the earlier stimulation.

We, too, started out in this same manner, varying one condition at a time during early development and studying its consequences in adulthood. However, we have recently begun to do research in which several early experience variables were put together or "programmed" in various combinations, thereby generating different schedules of experience for our animals. In this fashion we have been able to vary systematically the accumulated experiences which animals have received during their lifetime, and we have found marked behavioural differences among our experimental groups. Now when one talks about an organism's behaviour pattern varying as a function of its accumulated experiences one is talking about that organism's "personality". And, as indicated previously (Denenberg, 1967), one of the heuristic values of early experience research is that it allows us to create, by experimental manipulations, different types of personality.

Since most of the data which I shall discuss are from published papers, my purpose will be to try to give a review of our research strategy and of some of our general findings without going into methodological details. Information concerning these details can be obtained by reference to the cited articles.

PROGRAMMING LIFE HISTORIES

Independent and Dependent Variables

How does one determine which experiences to administer to rats during their development and which dependent variables to measure? In terms of an animal's early experiences, two classes of events appeared to us to be important: social interactions and stress experience. So we decided to manipulate independent variables which could be conceptualized as belonging to one or both of these classes.

In much of our prior research we had measured activity and defecation in the open field (Fig. 1) and used these scores as an indicator of the construct of "emotional reactivity". We had found open field performance to be a sensitive dependent variable for the kinds of early experience we were studying. Therefore we chose independent variables

FIG. 1. Adult rat under test in an open field situation.

which were known to affect open field performance. The independent variables which we selected, and their effects, were as follows.

Handling in infancy. Many studies from different laboratories have shown that rats which are handled daily between birth and weaning are much more active and defecate less in the open field than do non-handled controls (Denenberg, 1962 and 1964).

Handling of mothers of experimental subjects. Since handling acts to reduce emotional reactivity it was natural, in the case of females, to ask whether the handling experience which they had received in their infancy would have any effect upon their offspring. What we expected to find was that females which had been handled in infancy would have less emotional offspring because they would, somehow, communicate to their offspring nonemotional behaviour. (This is not a Lamarckian position.) In fact, we already had data showing that offspring emotionality was related to maternal emotionality through both genetic and nongenetic mechanisms (Denenberg *et al.*, 1962; Ottinger *et al.*, 1963). We did indeed get significant effects but they were opposite to those expected (Denenberg and Whimbey, 1963): we found that offspring of handled females were significantly more emotional as measured by open field performance than were offspring of nonhandled females.

Preweaning rearing habitat. It is customary to place pregnant laboratory rats in a maternity cage where they give birth to, and rear, their young. There is nothing sacrosanct about this environment, and there is certainly no evidence that this is the best setting in which to raise young rats; in fact, one can develop a good case for putting the pregnant mother into a larger and more complex environment. We therefore undertook a study in which pregnant rats were placed into Hebb-type free environments where they gave birth to, and reared, their young until weaning (Morton, 1962). We found that rats which had been reared in this habitat until weaning were significantly more active in the open field than were control animals raised in maternity cages.

Postweaning habitat. At the time of weaning, laboratory rats are usually placed in small cages where they remain until summoned by a researcher to engage in some behaviour which he finds interesting. To the human onlooker life in such a small cage appears to be exceedingly monotonous, and that raises the question whether such conditions may act to increase an animal's emotional reactivity by restricting its behavioural degrees of freedom. It would appear reasonable to assume that animals raised in a more complex environment after weaning would behave differently from cage-reared animals in an open field test situation. This assumption was tested in two experiments, and in each case the rats reared in free environments after weaning were found to be significantly more active in the open field than were cage-reared controls (Denenberg and Morton, 1962, 1964).

Each of these variables had been shown to affect open field behaviour when manipulated singly. What would happen to the animal's behaviour when these four variables were combined? We decided to vary each of them at two levels as follows:

Mother of experimental subjects:	handled or not handled in her infancy
Experience of experimental subjects:	handled or not handled in their infancy
Preweaning habitat:	maternity cage or free environment until weaning (21 days)
Postweaning habitat:	laboratory cage or free environment from weaning until 42 days of age

The complete combination of these variables gives us a 2^4 factorial design with 16 different programmes of experience for our animals. The experimental design is shown in the first 4 columns of Table I.

Factor Analysis Findings

We had conceived of these 16 schedules of experience as being experimental methods of creating different "personalities". This is another way of saying that significant individual differences would be created by experimental means. The purpose of our first study was to determine whether a meaningful set of behavioural dimensions would emerge from an analysis of these experimentally created individual differences. To do this we designed an experiment which would allow us to carry out a factor analysis to determine whether an interpretable set of factors would be found (Whimbey and Denenberg, 1966, 1967a).

All the animals in the experiment were given a large battery of tests, many of these being chosen because they were presumed to measure the construct of emotional reactivity. However, one of the measures of this construct is the animal's activity in an open field, and this is also used to measure the construct of exploratory behaviour. Therefore several tests which were presumed to measure the latter construct were included in the battery. Other tests included measures of avoidance learning, social preference, and body weight. In doing the factor analysis, each of the 16 groups of rats was treated as a single individual, and intercorrelations were obtained over all the tests for these 16 individuals. These data were then subjected to a factor analysis with orthogonal rotation, and three meaningful behavioural factors were extracted. These were identified as (a) emotional reactivity, (b) field exploration, and (c) consumption—elimination.

The tests defining the factor of emotional reactivity included ratings of emotionality, defecation in the open field, and defecation in an avoidance learning situation. All these had positive loadings, while food and water consumption during the day had negative loadings, as did the number of times the animal entered the stimulus half of a box which contained novel stimuli, and the total amount of time spent in the stimulus half of that box.

The field exploration factor was defined by activity scores on a variety of measures (including the open field), all of which were loaded positively, as well as by defecation in the open field which had a negative loading. Since open field activity has generally been assumed to be a measure of the construct of emotional reactivity, the absence of this variable in the emotionality factor was surprising. Actually, it is present in this factor as well as in the exploration factor, but the situation is complicated. The complication is brought about because the first day of open field activity loads positively on the emotionality factor (i.e. the more emotional rats are the more active), while the activity scores thereafter all have negative loadings, which is the usual finding. Thus, when activity was summed over all 4 days the positive and negative characteristics tended to cancel each other out. We have discussed this particular set of findings in detail elsewhere (Whimbey and Denenberg, 1967b).

The consumption—elimination factor was defined by food and water consumed during the night, and by urination and defecation scores.

We may conclude from this experiment that stable and relatively permanent complex individual differences, of the sort often assumed to be genetically determined, can be generated by the appropriate manipulation of experiences during early life.

Analysis of Variance Findings

The factor analysis described above had isolated a set of meaningful behavioural dimensions. The individual differences among the groups had been generated by the programmed life experiences of the animals and were independent of their genetic background.

Which characteristics of these programmed experiences were the causes of the animals' adult behaviour patterns? To answer that question we carried out a series of analyses of variance on those tests which had been found to have significant loadings on the behavioural dimensions of emotional reactivity and exploratory behaviour (Denenberg and Whimbey, 1968). Two interesting findings emerged from this analysis. First, the major variable affecting emotional reactivity was the handling experience of the pups in infancy. Regardless of the other characteristics of their programmed experience, animals handled in infancy were less emotionally reactive than were nonhandled controls. Furthermore, this variable interacted only once with any of the other independent variables, therefore demonstrating that this is a robust main effect with considerable invariance over the other experimental treatments used in this study. The second major finding was that the dimension of exploratory behaviour, unlike the dimension of emotional reactivity, was characterized primarily by the presence of interactions. In other words, an animal's exploratory behaviour is not determined by one or two events in its early life but is markedly affected by the complete pattern of its experiences.

The remainder of this paper will be devoted to an expansion of this last finding.

PATTERNS OF EXPERIENCE

The animals used in the factor analysis research were part of a much larger experiment involving the same four independent variables in early life. One group of these animals was used for the factor analysis study as described above, while the remaining littermates were used for another extensive investigation which is described in detail elsewhere (Denenberg et al., 1968). In the latter experiment we introduced two forms of stress experience in adulthood to see how these stress variables would interact with our early experience variables. Those particular findings are not relevant here. But in that same experiment we had animals which did not receive adult stress experience, and their data are relevant. One subgroup within this experiment was tested for the first time at 70 days of age, while a second subgroup was first tested at 190 days of age. In both instances the first test was in the open field. Tests were made on 3 successive days which is in contrast to the Whimbey and Denenberg (1967b) study in which animals were given 4 days of testing in the open field starting at 220 days of life.

We have, therefore, three semi-independent replications of the same experiment in which the animals were tested at three different ages and by different experimenters under somewhat different test conditions. In each of the replications open field activity was the first variable measured. Since activity in the open field had been shown, by the factor analysis, to be a measure of the dimension of exploratory behaviour, and since the analysis of variance findings had revealed that this test was involved in a number of significant interactions, we have the opportunity to use the activity data to examine in detail the 16 programmes of life experiences for each of the three replications. The purpose of doing this is to see whether certain patterns emerge which will give us some insight into the manner in which these early experiences combine to affect open field activity.

Table I presents the mean activity score for each of the 16 groups for each replication. If one goes through these data carefully, putting the 16 groups in rank order and looking for consistency of ordering, certain characteristics stand out. Of the 16 different programmes of life experiences listed in Table I there are 10 programmes which give uniform results within each replication. These programmes are listed in Table II together with the mean activity scores. These have been placed in rank order, from that programme of experiences which results in the least open field activity to that which results in the greatest amount of activity. Although there are some inversions among the three replications, these are of a relatively minor order.

Having chosen a set of programmes which give us consistent activity scores across the three replications, we must ask whether there are certain characteristics which distinguish those programmes which result in high open field activity from those which result in low activity. For one thing, it is more likely that a nonhandled mother and/or a handled pup will be associated with high open field activity than with low activity. If one takes as a reference point those animals which are born of a nonhandled mother, are themselves nonhandled in infancy, and spend their lives in maternity cages and laboratory cages (the sixth group in Table II), then it may be noted that the addition of handling experience to the pup increases open field behaviour (the eighth group in Table II), while the addition of handling experience to the mother reduces the activity score (the fourth group in Table II). These have been our usual findings in prior experiments. From other prior experiments, as I indicated earlier, one would predict that the addition of free environment experiences, both before and after weaning, should also result in an increase in open field activity. This prediction is found to hold true when one looks at the groups with the highest activity scores in Table II. However, that this is not a simple additive effect may be seen by looking at the fifth group, which differs from the tenth group only with respect to the nature of the mother. The second group brings out the same point: it has the same set of experiences as the tenth group, except that the animals are born and reared in a maternity cage until weaning. It is, of course, these peculiar combinations which make for the significant interactions in our data.

TABLE I. MEAN OPEN FIELD ACTIVITY SCORES FOR EACH OF THE THREE REPLICATIONS

Mother's experience	Offspring's experience	Preweaning housing	Postweaning housing	Denenberg et al. (1968) 70-day data	Denenberg et al. (1968) 190-day data	Denenberg and Whimbey (1968) 220-day data
NH	NH	MC	LC	79·2	54·9	40·3
NH	NH	MC	FE	48·8	59·8	111·3
NH	NH	FE	LC	80·4	56·1	102·3
NH	NH	FE	FE	63·8	91·7	23·0
NH	H	MC	LC	101·1	58·8	141·6
NH	H	MC	FE	56·4	25·2	29·0
NH	H	FE	LC	124·2	35·4	86·7
NH	H	FE	FE	182·0	82·1	253·7
H	NH	MC	LC	82·0	48·2	10·0
H	NH	MC	FE	85·5	23·2	57·0
H	NH	FE	LC	56·6	57·9	17·0
H	NH	FE	FE	45·0	48·0	8·0
H	H	MC	LC	119·4	58·9	155·3
H	H	MC	FE	145·0	49·0	39·3
H	H	FE	LC	31·8	19·2	120·3
H	H	FE	FE	81·2	57·3	34·7

FE = free environment
H = handled in infancy
LC = laboratory cage

MC = maternity cage
NH = nonhandled in infancy

TABLE II. MEAN OPEN FIELD ACTIVITY SCORES FOR THOSE PROGRAMMES OF EXPERIENCE[a] IN TABLE I WHICH GIVE CONSISTENT RESULTS FOR THE THREE REPLICATIONS

Mother's experience	H	NH	H	H	H	NH	NH	NH	H	NH
Offspring's experience	NH	H	NH	NH	H	NH	NH	H	H	H
Preweaning housing	FE	MC	FE	MC	FE	MC	FE	MC	MC	FE
Postweaning housing	FE	FE	LC	LC	FE	LC	LC	LC	LC	FE
Denenberg et al. (1968) 70-day data	45·0	56·4	56·6	82·0	81·2	79·2	80·4	101·1	119·4	182·0
Denenberg et al. (1968) 190-day data	48·0	25·2	57·9	48·2	57·3	54·9	56·1	58·8	58·9	82·1
Denenberg & Whimbey (1968) 220-day data	8·0	29·0	17·0	10·0	34·7	40·3	102·3	141·7	155·3	253·7

a   Programmes are listed in rank order

FE = free environment   MC = maternity cage
H = handled in infancy   NH = nonhandled in infancy
LC = laboratory cage

All I can say with certainty is that we have been able to isolate several different schedules of experience which result in consistent differences in adult open field behaviour, and that these differences appear to be some complex function of the nature of the mother and her interactions with her offspring, the handling stimulation given those offspring, and the nature of the rearing habitat both before and after weaning. However, now that we have succeeded in isolating procedures for giving us animals with different performance scores, the way is open to a more systematic analysis of the causes of these differences. One very important approach to understanding these causes will be by means of an ethological analysis of the social dynamics within each of the unique groupings.

SEPARATION OF PRENATAL AND POSTNATAL EFFECTS

One approach to a better understanding of these programmes of experience is through a descriptive analysis. Another attack is by further analysis and refinement of our experimental variables. For example, in the research described above the pups remained with their natural mothers from birth until weaning, and were thus exposed to the impact of handled or nonhandled mothers during both prenatal and postnatal life. In order to determine whether the nature of the mother's handling experience affects her young during prenatal life it is necessary to cross-foster animals at birth. We have conducted such an experiment (Denenberg and Whimbey, 1963) and have been able to show significant prenatal as well as postnatal effects.

In this experiment, adult female rats—some handled and some nonhandled during infancy—were bred to a random sample of colony males. At birth some litters were left with their natural mothers while other litters were fostered. Here I am concerned only with the fostered animals. The pups were reared in maternity cages until weaning and were kept in laboratory cages thereafter. From 50 days of age the animals were given 4 days of testing in the open field. The experimental design and results for open field activity are summarized in Table III. The analysis of these data showed a significant interaction between the prenatal and postnatal mother. Young born of nonhandled mothers and fostered to handled mothers were significantly more active than the young from the other three groups.

It is clear, therefore, that part of the behavioural differences we see among animals in adulthood is a function of the interaction between the pregnant mother and her developing embryo and fetus *in utero*.

To account for these data we assume that, in the females handled in infancy, the handling had affected and changed their physiology and biochemistry relative to the physiology and biochemistry of nonhandled controls. We assume also that the different physiological systems of the handled and nonhandled mothers had different kinds of interaction with the developing embryo and fetus.

TABLE III. MEAN OPEN FIELD ACTIVITY SCORES OF OFFSPRING AS A FUNCTION OF THE INFANTILE EXPERIENCES OF THEIR NATURAL MOTHER AND OF THEIR REARING MOTHER[a]

Infantile experience of prenatal mother	Not handled		Handled	
Infantile experience of postnatal mother	Not handled	Handled	Not handled	Handled
Mean activity	114·9	188·4	139·6	121·5

[a] From Denenberg and Whimbey (1963).

A GRANDMOTHER EFFECT

We showed above that the handling experience which a female had in infancy significantly affected her offspring's performance. A logical question here is: how far into the future can such effects be projected? We have recently demonstrated that the experience which female rats underwent during their infancy significantly affected the behaviour of

TABLE IV. MEAN OPEN FIELD ACTIVITY SCORES AS A FUNCTION OF GRANDMOTHER'S INFANTILE EXPERIENCE AND OF MOTHER'S REARING HABITATS[a]

Grandmother's experience	Mother's preweaning housing	Mother's postweaning housing	Mean activity
NH	MC	LC	32·0
NH	MC	FE	44·3
NH	FE	LC	22·4
NH	FE	FE	27·1
H	MC	LC	29·7
H	MC	FE	35·5
H	FE	LC	49·8
H	FE	FE	28·8

[a] From Denenberg and Rosenberg (1967).

their grandpups (Denenberg and Rosenberg, 1967). The experimental design as well as the results are given in Table IV. In this experiment some female rats were handled and some were nonhandled in infancy. They were reared in maternity cages and laboratory cages until adult, when they were mated. When pregnant, the animals were placed either in maternity cages or in free environment boxes. The animals which were born in these units were the mothers of our experimental subjects. At the time of weaning the pups were placed either in laboratory cages or in free environment boxes where they remained until 50 days of age, at which time all animals were placed in laboratory cages. When mature, these animals were mated and gave birth to offspring in maternity cages.

These offspring (the grandchildren of the original handled and nonhandled females of the study) were given 1 day of testing in an open field at 21 days of age, when they were weaned. Their activity scores are summarized in Table IV. The following interactions were found to be significant: Grandmother Handling × Mother Preweaning Housing, Grandmother Handling × Mother Postweaning Housing, and Preweaning Housing × Postweaning Housing. The data in Table IV show that the nature of the habitat in which the animals were reared is relevant. If we had only taken the female offspring of handled and nonhandled grandmothers, and only maintained them under standard laboratory caging conditions from birth until adulthood (this would be the first and fifth groups listed in Table IV), most of our significant findings would have disappeared. Thus, the occurrence of free environment experience at some time during the mother's early development is necessary for the effects of the grandmother handling experience to express itself in the grandpups.

These data are particularly fascinating because we have demonstrated, in these last two experiments, a nongenetic method of communication across generations. My frustration arises from the fact that I do not know for how many generations this effect will extend.

In summary, I have raised more questions than I have answered. The importance of this type of early experience research is that it opens up a way by which we can begin to study how experiences over time accumulate and interact to affect an organism's later behaviour. This is probably the most difficult type of early experience research to undertake, but it is exceedingly important. Perhaps after we have learned how personality is created by our programming of experiences in the rat, we shall have a better understanding of some of the principles involved in the development of personality in the human.

REFERENCES

DENENBERG, V. H. 1962. The effects of early experience. In E. S. E. Hafez (Ed.), *Behaviour of domestic animals*. Baillière, Tindall & Cox, London.

DENENBERG, V. H. 1964. Critical periods, stimulus input, and emotional reactivity: a theory of infantile stimulation. *Psychol. Rev.* **71**, 335–351.

DENENBERG, V. H. 1967. Stimulation in infancy, emotional reactivity, and exploratory behavior. In D. C. Glass (Ed.), *Biology and behavior: neurophysiology and emotion*. Rockefeller University Press and Russell Sage Foundation, New York.

DENENBERG, V. H. and MORTON, J. R. C. 1962. Effects of environmental complexity and social groupings upon modification of emotional behavior. *J. comp. physiol. Psychol.* **55**, 1096–1098.

DENENBERG, V. H. and MORTON, J. R. C. 1964. Infantile stimulation, prepubertal sexual-social interaction and emotionality. *Anim. Behav.* **12**, 11–13.

DENENBERG, V. H. and ROSENBERG, K. M. 1967. Nongenetic transmission of information across two generations. *Nature, Lond.* **216**, 549–550.

DENENBERG, V. H. and WHIMBEY, A. E. 1963. Behavior of adult rats is modified by the experiences their mothers had as infants. *Science, N.Y.* **142**, 1192–1193.

DENENBERG, V. H. and WHIMBEY, A. E. 1968. Experimental programming of life histories: toward an experimental science of individual differences. *Devl Psychobiol.* **1**, 55–59.

DENENBERG, V. H., OTTINGER, D. R., and STEPHENS, M. W. 1962. Effects of maternal factors upon growth and behavior of the rat. *Child Develop.* **33**, 65–71.

DENENBERG, V. H., KARAS, G. G., ROSENBERG, K. M., and SCHELL, S. F. 1968. Programming life histories: an experimental design and initial results. *Devl Psychobiol.* **1**, 3–9.

MORTON, J. R. C. 1962. The interactive effects of preweaning and postweaning environments upon adult behavior. Unpublished Ph.D. thesis, Purdue University, Lafayette, Indiana.

OTTINGER, D. R., DENENBERG, V. H., and STEPHENS, M. W. 1963. Maternal emotionality, multiple mothering, and emotionality in maturity. *J. comp. physiol. Psychol.* **56**, 313–317.

WHIMBEY, A. E. and DENENBERG, V. H. 1966. Programming life histories: creating individual differences by the experimental control of early experiences. *Multiv. behav. Res.* **1**, 279–286.

WHIMBEY, A. E. and DENENBERG, V. H. 1967a. Experimental programming of life histories: the factor structure underlying experimentally created individual differences. *Behaviour* **29**, 296–314.

WHIMBEY, A. E. and DENENBERG, V. H. 1967b. Two independent behavioral dimensions in open field performance. *J. comp. physiol. Psychol.* **63**, 500–504.

Discussion

Exploratory Behaviour and Emotionality as Dependent Variables

SCHAFFER: In explaining the effects of the various patterns of early experience which you have manipulated, it is important to take account not only of the content of the experiences but also of the number of discontinuities of experience encountered by the various groups. Translating this into human terms, I would expect both the number and also the degree of disruption experienced by the individual to affect outcome over and above the specific experiences themselves.

DENENBERG: That's a good point, because shift from a maternity cage to a free environment or vice versa has profoundly different effects from just staying in the same cage. Although a maternity cage is not the same as a laboratory cage, they are both small restricted types of world. To show up the differences you must introduce free environment experience somewhere during early development. Such experience is a necessary condition for the grandmother effect to appear.

LEVINE: You are talking here primarily about open field activity which is a very specialized and subtle kind of variable. But if you take another variable like emotionality, do you not get very different kinds of effect?

DENENBERG: Yes. When working with measures of emotionality we get big main effects. Interactions are not significant. When we choose a clear-cut index like defecation, we find that a handled animal is placed at the opposite end of the dimension from a nonhandled animal. This is a major variable. When looking at measures of exploratory behaviour, however, the situation is much more complicated. I chose to look at activity for two reasons: first, we already had a lot of data on activity; second, it is heavily weighted on the exploratory behaviour dimension. Our findings indicate that emotionality is relatively simple as compared to the subtlety and complexity of exploratory behaviour.

LEVINE: I agree that, in the determination of emotionality, handling is a major variable that outweighs everything else. In one of our experiments (Levine. 1967. *Science*, **156**, 258) where we took offspring of handled and nonhandled mothers, we found a very striking effect on the stress response in weanling pups as a function of maternal handling. We also found, however, that if we introduced handling of the offspring, this wiped out the maternal handling factor. Subsequent experiments (unpublished) of a rather different kind showed similar results. We took two genetic strains of mice which differed very strikingly in their behaviour, and when handling of the offspring was introduced, we obliterated the effects of the two different strains. Thus handling does superimpose itself. It may do so by essentially the same mechanism in the handled/nonhandled offspring as that which causes the difference arising from the handled/nonhandled mothers. If you consider that when you handle the offspring you are really altering the mother, then you may be making handled and nonhandled mothers essentially equivalent.

Denenberg talked, on the one hand about a set of major effects on behaviours related to emotionality, and on the other hand about the subtle kind of effect on open field exploration, but we do not yet know the significance of exploration in an open field.

KAGAN: It may help to consider an analogy from human behaviour. A cognitive variable like ease of learning a prose passage, an IQ, or a reading score always has a social class effect that swamps variance due to personality. Class is a major effect, like handling versus nonhandling. Remove it and you often find subtle differences—meaningful but complex.

DENENBERG: Had I talked about the determinants of emotionality, which is what most of my work has been about, I could have given you six different measures of emotionality and shown you clear-cut main effects there. I chose to give you another behaviour dimension, namely exploration, which is important and meaningful for human behaviour as well. We found that its interactions were relevant but I couldn't make much sense out of them. The problem of how exploratory behaviour is affected by early experiences is much more difficult for us to solve than that of how emotionality is affected, because it involves complex interactions and not just main effects.

HAMBURG: You call the measure of exploratory behaviour "open field activity". Have you distinguished between typical exploratory behaviour and the animal that goes darting frantically around the open field grid in a kind of Brownian movement?

DENENBERG: We have been able to distinguish between these two types of behaviours by means of our factor analysis (Whimbey and Denenberg. 1967a. *Behaviour*, **29**, 296). We took the activity scores and the defecation scores for each day separately and then intercorrelated these among each other as well as with the other tests in our battery. We found that activity on Day 1 was *positively* correlated with the defecation scores while activity scores for all subsequent days were *negatively* correlated with defecation scores. When we looked at the orthogonal factors which had been extracted from the analysis, we found that we had an emotional reactivity factor as well as an exploratory behaviour factor. Defecation scores were primarily loaded on the emotional reactivity factor. In addition, the Day 1 activity score was also loaded on the emotionality factor with the same sign as the defecation data, yet all activity scores were also loaded on the exploratory behaviour factors. What we find, then, is that exploratory behaviour is factorially complex, loading both on the emotionality and on the exploratory factors. The interpretation to give to this score changes from Day 1 to subsequent days. Thus what Hamburg calls Brownian movement is definitely present with our nonhandled animals on Day 1 and then it drops out. This is really a hyperactivity type of phenomenon; it's very different from typical exploratory behaviour.

Clarification by Observation of Mother–Young Interaction

FREEDMAN: Will you succeed in explicating these and other mysteries by looking at them in an ethological way. Are you seriously planning to do this?

DENENBERG: I have set up a closed-circuit TV system to take recordings, and with a videotape recorder and programming equipment I shall be able to time-sample an animal's behaviour over long periods and analyse the tape at my leisure. The camera has a tube which is sensitive to infra-red light so that I can record in the dark as well.

LEVINE: Does that make it ethological? When do you look at the animals and what are you looking at?

DENENBERG: We're looking at them for 24-hour periods, which is why I have the TV recording system. One of the things we shall do is to count the number of times the mother contacts the pups. This may be the equivalent of our handling, but there may be several things which the mothers do with their pups. We shall draw up a behavioural check-list on mother-young interactions; to do this I shall get many people involved as they are likely to see things differently from each other.

The Variable of Body Weight

BATESON: Do you take animals from different litters and, if so, have you got a possible bias here? What about body weight, for instance?

DENENBERG: We have independent groups in our experiments and we use the litter as the unit of analysis in our statistical evaluations. It's the differences between litters, not between animals, that count. Body weight differences show up between litters but these are related to differences between handled and nonhandled mothers.

BATESON: I think that any weight differences you find would be worth looking into carefully. There is a study (J. J. Cowley and R. D. Griesel. 1966. *Anim. Behav.*, **14**, 506) which showed a second generation effect of protein deficient diets.

The Grandmother Effect

LEVINE: How does the grandmother effect operate?

DENENBERG: I can only speculate about it at this stage. There are two major mechanisms: one operates through the uterine environment and involves physiological and biochemical effects; the other is through maternal behaviour. There certainly is clear evidence of a prenatal but nongenetic effect in our data as well as a postnatal effect.

AMBROSE: Have you looked at the grandmother effect in the light of Harlow's findings (B. Seay, B. K. Alexander, and H. F. Harlow. 1964. *J. abn. soc. Psychol.*, **69**, 345) about motherless mothers?

DENENBERG: No, but I would think there may be some superficial kinds of similarity here. The motherless mother, that is, one who was reared in isolation with no peer interaction with other monkeys, is an emotionally disturbed organism just as is our nonhandled animal.

HAMBURG: These isolation-reared mothers have difficulty in copulating and have to be specially impregnated. When they are with their infants it's a touching sight to see the infant's persistent attachment efforts in the face of the mother's neglect or abuse, that is, without any obvious reward. There are considerable individual differences in the mother's response. Some of them just ignore the infant's initiative in its efforts to get into a better position on her and, after many approaches, will swat the infant away. Others seem to have more potential for an aggressive reaction and will hurt the infant. This kind of thing will go on right through infancy. It is certainly plausible that the infant who has been so badly neglected or abused by the isolation-reared mother would become a peculiar mother herself. It is not difficult to conceive a third generation effect in this way.

FREEDMAN: Pertinent to this is a study (J. K. Kovach and E. H. Hess. 1963. *J. comp. physiol. psychol.*, **56**, 461) in which chicks were shocked on the imprinting table with the result that the chick followed even closer. There was an optimum amount of shock: too much shock destroyed following, too little shock made them follow less closely. The same kind of thing was found (H. Fisher, personal communication) in geese in a natural situation: after a predatory attack the little ones followed the mother much more closely.

The Significance of Applying Stimulation to the Young Laboratory Rat

PRECHTL: What would the expectation be if you were to handle animals which had been kept in rather natural conditions instead of in the very abnormal laboratory conditions? Are you taking already highly abnormal animals and curing them by your handling treatment? Isn't it wrong to try to show the effects of handling in laboratory conditions which are very abnormal and which inevitably produce abnormal animals?

HAMBURG: Against the impoverished background of the laboratory the handling is a big event. Against the background of a wild rat it might be less significant. The life of the wild rat is presumably full of various forms of intense stimulation.

LEVINE: Animals have been studied under numerous conditions that diverge from those of the natural environment: they have been reared on terry-cloth mother-surrogates, castrated, or given a hole in the head and a brain lesion. Yet none of these conditions are regarded as in any way detracting from the value of the information obtained under them.

HAMBURG: True, but it's important to try to analyse the relation between your experimental manipulation and what usually occurs under natural conditions.

DENENBERG: The rodent is an extraordinarily immature beast at birth and I would be doubtful if there is much intercourse with its environment at that time, whether it is in a natural environment or in a laboratory cage with a nest of shavings.

LEVINE: That may be true; nevertheless the mother has a great deal of interaction with the environment in a natural situation.

HAMBURG: In designing experiments on the effects of various kinds of stimulation on developmental processes, these are likely to be more revealing if you start with a knowledge of the stimulation that occurs in the natural environment. You will then choose forms of stimulation that are likely to be most effective. I am reminded of a study by Henry (1967. *Psychosom. Med.* **29**, 408) in which, after a long history of no success in creating experimental hypertension in mice, he achieved it by exposing them to cats in a bell jar. The mouse apparently does not know that the cats cannot get at it from the jar and it develops sustained hypertension. Whereas all kinds of conditioning techniques failed to do that, he found that the most experimentally effective form of stimulation was one that was adaptively relevant.

PRECHTL: Also, although handling of young rats in a deprived laboratory environment may do them good, this does not necessarily imply that handling of young in the natural environment will do them good. I would like to ascertain what really happens when young rats are handled.

DENENBERG: There are some anthropological data with respect to stress in human infants and subsequent height which link with our findings (Landauer and Whiting. 1964. *American Anthropologist,* **66**, 1007). We found that animals which have been handled or shocked in infancy weigh more in adulthood. Landauer and Whiting found that, in those cultures where stress was imposed in infancy by circumcision or binding, the males in adulthood were more than 2 inches taller than the average height in tribes where the infants were not stressed. This finding was replicated in an independent sample. This type of evidence suggests that what we do with rats may have some generality to the human. Prechtl says handling isn't good; how do we know this?

PRECHTL: I'm not saying that handling is not good, but it is obviously unnecessary under optimal natural conditions.

LEVINE: This is absolutely not true. I recall that, after I had read a paper a number of years ago, someone got up and accused me of not loving my rats. Then Escalona got up and asked the questioner "What is the nature of love?" She pointed out that, in the love interaction, one of the critical things that happens is provision of stimulation. Now, when we look at the host of data on maternal deprivation and the way it has been interpreted, there has always been this belief that there was something terribly unique about "Mama". Undoubtedly there is in certain respects, but some deprivation effects may not have been due to absence of "Mama" *per se*, but to loss of one particular function that she serves in being a source of stimulation. I think that the kinds of experiment we are talking about point to a phenomenon that is related to this function, namely the stimulation that occurs in the interaction between mother and young. We have shown that stimulation is important. As a result of this one begins to look with a different perspective on different kinds of relationship to see to what extent stimulation may play a role in them; one also has a different focus in considering what kinds of mechanism may be operating in certain kinds of interaction.

DENENBERG: A good example of how we humans deprive our young of stimulation is the incubator. In this stimulus-constant environment variability is minimized in all dimensions. The rationalization for this is that one is relating the infant to the intra-uterine environment. Why do we not consider an incubator in which one has stimulus variation, not in respect to oxygen or temperature, but to auditory, visual, kinaesthetic and proprioceptive stimulation?

KAGAN: It is not accurate to call the nonhandling condition one in which there is no stimulation. The nonhandled rat is not in complete stimulus isolation; it is with its mother. Similarly, it is not correct to call the handling condition "stimulation"; it is something more than stimulation.

LEVINE: There seems to be some indication that what we are doing in stimulating the young is affecting the mother-young interaction. But you must still face the fact that we are doing something to the young itself which causes different interactions with the mother to occur.

A Nonexpectancy Model

KAGAN: The reason I do not like the word "stimulation" in your context is because it implies that the more stimulation, the better the organism's development.

LEVINE: In an early paper (S. Levine. 1962. In A. J. Bachrach (Ed.), *Experimental Foundations of Clinical Psychology*, p. 139. Basic Books, New York) I made the statement that the critical dimension here may be change in stimulation. Lord Adrian has commented that it may have to do with what the animal does not expect.

AMBROSE: One of the striking things about your handling experiments is the brevity of the handling which you apply: something like 3 minutes every 24 hours. A possible test of whether this brief stimulation is so effective because of its being unexpected would be to try applying different durations of stimulation. Presumably the longer or the more frequent the stimulus periods are, the more familiar will they become, and so, proportionately, the less will be the effect.

DENENBERG: We have done several studies similar to that which you suggest. In one set of studies we have varied the number of days of handling, using 3-day, 5-day, 10-day, and 20-day periods during infancy. When we do this we get a "dose-response" type of relationship which is monotonic with respect to our measures of emotionality, but is curvilinear with respect to other measures. We have also studied the effects of spaced versus massed handling and have found that spaced handling has more impact than massed. In that study (Karas and Denenberg. 1961. *J. comp. physiol. Psychol.*, **54**, 170) the amount of time away from the nest and from the mother was kept constant, as was the number of times that the experimenter touched the animal. The only difference was that the massed groups had handling experience in one 3-minute time interval whereas the spaced groups had three 1-minute sessions spread over at least 6 hours. The spaced groups were found to be less emotionally reactive than the massed groups.

GINSBURG: Jumonville (J. Jumonville. 1968. Ph.D. thesis, Dept. of Psychology, University of Chicago) has done a similar study. She compared the effects of 2 minutes' versus 3 minutes' early handling stimulation, testing at two different times in adulthood. She found, at one of those times, very different results from 2 versus 3 minutes' stimulation.

HAMBURG: This is extremely helpful. We were discussing the question of what relation the rat-handling experiments have to the natural situation. "Handling" is used by you as a descriptively operational term. In fact what you are doing in your handling experiments may well be to provide the animals with some unexpected development, perhaps some abrupt movement. If you ask whether abrupt or unexpected developments take place in the natural environment, the answer is that they certainly do and very much more often than in the laboratory situation. In the wild, one more abrupt unexpected movement would, I suppose, be like a bucket of water in the ocean as compared with in the relatively monotonous laboratory background against which you introduce your experimental handling. If we move up to this level of abstraction we can at least begin to make some comparisons between the laboratory and natural environments.

Stimulation within the Nest and Size of Litter

DENENBERG: This all assumes that the laboratory rat in the maternity cage is sensorially deprived. But in a group of eight squirmy, squiggly animals, there is much stimulus input. They are all packed closely together, and if, due to its squirming, one moves slightly away from the others it is yanked back by its mother. To do this, she must get off the nest and the others then scatter around: it's a very complicated set of events. I am not at all happy with the notion that the young, neurologically immature, laboratory rat is living in a stimulus deprived world.
LEVINE: I am not convinced that mother-young interaction in the laboratory nest is so critical for our experiments. There was a very interesting study done by Evelyn Thoman (unpublished) in our laboratory. Having developed a technique for hand-rearing rats, she first compared rats that were individually isolated from birth with animals that were reared in groups, and then compared these hand-reared animals with mother-reared animals. Whereas the effects of group-rearing as opposed to individual rearing were minimal, the effects of hand-rearing as opposed to mother-rearing were profound, and this was irrespective of whether the mother-reared animals were reared as singletons or reared as a group.
DENENBERG: On the single versus the group-reared animals, I must cite a study (E. F. Adolf (Ed.), 1961. *The Development of Homeostasis.* Czechoslovak Academy of Sciences, Prague) on the nutritional competence of these animals, and on their longevity and their ability to learn. There are profound differences between the isolation-reared and group-reared animals in these respects. Furthermore, raising a rat in isolation produces a massive animal because it has a good milk supply, but raising it in a large litter produces an under-weight animal. In fact

litter sizes of 4, 8, or 16 result in great differences in animal weight. In addition there are also differences in mating behaviour, activity, and hoarding of food pellets.

LEVINE: Do animals reared in smaller groups, as compared with large groups, tend to be more like handled animals?

DENENBERG: Within the limits of 4 to 12 pups, the smaller the size of the litter, the more active is the animal.

Equivalence of Different Forms of Stimulation

HAMBURG: Is it true that you get similar effects from handling, rocking the cage, and three or four other kinds of stimulation having some sort of rough-and-tumble characteristics?

DENENBERG: You can shock or handle the rats and these have the same consequences on both open field activity and on defecation.

LEVINE: They also have the same consequences on the corticoid, on avoidance conditioning and on consummatory activity.

An Endocrine Theory of Infantile Stimulation[1]

SEYMOUR LEVINE[2]:

Stanford University

INTRODUCTION

THIS PAPER PRESENTS a theory accounting for the effects of infantile stimulation. The theory is based on the following assumptions: firstly, that the central nervous system is organized and that this organization accounts for the individual patterns of neurophysiological, neuroendocrine, and behavioural responses; secondly, that hormones acting directly upon the central nervous system during development participate in the organization of the central nervous system; thirdly, that the effects of infantile stimulation may be due to changes in circulating corticosteroids as a function of stimulation during sensitive periods in development.

CENTRAL NERVOUS SYSTEM ORGANIZATION

The concept of central nervous system organization, as used within the context of this paper, refers primarily to the organization of neuroendocrine function. This is not to imply that it is only the hypothalamus that is concerned in such organization, since there is ample evidence that there are many neural systems (Ganong, 1963) involved in modulating neuroendocrine activity. As far as gonadal function is concerned, at least two major differences have been shown to exist between the central nervous system of male and female mammals. To quote Harris (1964): "In most female species the brain regulates the

[1] The work on which this paper is based was supported by Research Grant No. 02881 from the National Institute of Child Health and Human Development and a Research Grant from The Leslie Fund, Chicago.

[2] During his work the author was maintained by Research Career Development Award K3-MH-19,936 from the National Institute of Mental Health.

secretion of gonadotrophic hormone in a cyclic fashion, which results in the rhythm of ovulation and corpora lutea formation in the ovary and in the estrous or menstrual cycle. In males, on the other hand, the secretion of gonadotrophic hormone is maintained at a more steady and constant level, and rhythms or cycles corresponding to those in the female are not apparent.

"The second sexual characteristic of the brain concerns the predominant behaviour pattern (male or female) mediated under different hormonal conditions. Although some homosexual activity is of normal occurrence in many species, and may be exaggerated under appropriate conditions of hormonal administration and trigger stimulus, there is an obvious quantitative difference between this and the ease with which heterosexual behaviour may be evoked in the normal animal. This difference reflects, in all probability, some anatomical or biochemical difference in the central nervous system of the two sexes."

The case that these different male and female patterns of gonadotropic regulation and behaviour are a function of differences in central nervous system organization, although based largely on circumstantial evidence, is indeed conclusive. The now classic experiments by Harris and Jacobsohn (1952) demonstrated that the pituitary is indeed an indifferent organ which will produce whatever pattern of gonadotropin secretion is characteristic of the host in which the pituitary may be found or transplanted. Thus, the pituitary taken from a normal adult male rate, when transplanted into the sella turcica of a female rat, will exhibit cyclic, gonadotropic secretion; conversely, the pituitary derived from a female, when transplanted into the same anatomical region in the male, shows the tonic secretion of gonadotropin characteristic of the male.

The evidence regarding normal patterns of sexual behaviour and their dependence upon circulating hormones is consistent with the hypothesis that there are differences between the male and female central nervous systems in the regulation of behaviour. Firstly, whereas the female is cyclic in her sexual activity, the male tends to be acyclic. Secondly, whereas in the female the pattern of sexual receptivity is easily elicited by the appropriate regime of estrogen and progesterone replacement following castration, in the male these patterns appear to be suppressed and are difficult to elicit with doses of estrogen and progesterone that are many times higher than those required for the female. Thus it appears that one of the differences in central nervous system organization between male and female is the differential sensitivity of the target organ, the brain, to similar levels of circulating hormones (Levine, 1967a).

There are sufficient data to suggest that the central nervous system is organized for the neuroendocrine regulation of corticotropin (ACTH), which results in different patterns of secretion of adrenal steroids following stressful stimuli. It has been reported that there are marked differences in ACTH secretion between male and female rats (Kitay, 1961; Barrett, 1960). Although these differences can be attributed in part to differences in estrogen secretion acting directly at the level of the adrenal, there is sufficient evidence to indicate that this is only one aspect of these differences and that, in the absence of ovaries or gonads, the differences in ACTH secretion are still apparent between male and female organisms (Levine and Mullins, 1967).

In a recent series of experiments (Davidson et al., 1965), repeated measurements of plasma steroids were taken on the same animal, either over days, or at different times within a given day. It was observed that, although there were marked individual differences between animals, the values obtained following either anaesthesia or electric shock were remarkably consistent over time for any given animal. Thus, if stress in one animal caused elevation to approximately 50 μg % corticosterone, this animal showed very little variation around this value over repeated measures. Another animal, in contrast, elevated to 70 μg %. Again, this value was constant for that particular animal. One explanation of these individual differences is that, for a given individual organism, there is established a hormonostat which monitors and regulates the output of corticotropin from the pituitary. This aspect of the present theory is derived from the position taken by Yates and Urquhart (1962) who have postulated that there exists a homeostatic feedback mechanism, presumably in the central nervous system, by which the concentration of corticosteroids in the blood is monitored and compared with the controlling setpoint. If the concentration of circulating steroids is higher than the setpoint, ACTH secretion is diminished. If the concentration is below the setpoint, then ACTH is released and more steroids are produced. We can add that this setpoint is not identical for all organisms and that differences in the setpoint may be a function of those events which occur during ontogeny.

It has been demonstrated that stimulation in infancy modifies the adult patterns of ACTH secretion and steroidogenesis to stress. Animals stimulated in infancy show more rapid and enhanced steroid response to a brief but intense electric shock in adulthood than is shown by animals not handled (Levine, 1962b). The nonhandled animals respond more slowly to the stress, and in these animals the response tends to persist over much longer periods (Haltmeyer *et al.*, 1967). Furthermore, the handled animal shows a lower steroid response when exposed to novel stimuli as compared with its nonstimulated counterparts (Levine *et al.*, 1967).

In addition to infantile stimulation as one of the parameters influencing adult patterns of neuroendocrine activity regulating ACTH secretion, a number of other factors have also been shown to influence neuroendocrine activity in the adult organism. Levine and Treiman (1964) have shown that there is a significant genetic determinant of neuroendocrine function in the adult organism. More recently in a series of experiments in our laboratory, results have been obtained which demonstrate maternal influences on the adult response to stress. Nonstimulated offspring of females which themselves had been stimulated in infancy showed a significant reduction in the steroid response after exposure to novelty, as compared to offspring of non-stimulated females (Levine, 1967b). As was indicated in my introductory paper, removing the mother from the nest during the first 7 days also markedly affects the subsequent adrenocortical response to stress in the offspring (Levine and Thoman, 1967). Thus there seems to be little question that the organization of neuroendocrine activity in the adult organism is some function of the interaction between environmental and genetic factors that occurs during sensitive periods in the development of the organism.

Although it has been conclusively demonstrated that steroid hormones, emanating from the gonads, have an important role in the activation and maintenance of sexual behaviour, the evidence that the hormones involved in the stress response are related to behaviour is much more recent. There now exists a body of evidence which indicates that ACTH and adrenal steroids are also involved in behaviour. Lissak and Endroczi (1961) and Levine and Jones (1965) reported that animals which had significantly greater adrenocortical activity showed an increased resistance to extinction in a passive avoidance situation.

A relationship between neuroendocrine activity and behaviour is suggested again by the recent discovery of a significant positive correlation both between endogenous steroid activity and avoidance conditioning (Bohus *et al.*, 1963) and also between free-operant avoidance performance proficiency and endogenous steroid activity (Wertheim *et al.*, 1967). In addition to these studies and others (Mason *et al.*, 1966), which have all indicated correlations between behaviour and endogenous steroid level, there are numerous studies which demonstrate that the injection of hormones normally released from the pituitary and the adrenal cortex is implicated in the control and regulation of various kinds of aversive behaviour (De Wied, 1966; Levine and Brush, 1967; Wertheim et al., 1967).

In my introductory paper it was repeatedly emphasized that one of the major effects of infantile stimulation is a change in the emotional reactivity of the stimulated organism. This change cannot be described simply as a reduction in the physiological and behavioural response associated with emotional reactivity, because it has been demonstrated that under certain conditions the animal stimulated in infancy shows a more vigorous response to stress. In view of these findings it was hypothesized that infantile stimulation endows the organism with the capacity to make finer discriminations of the relevant aspects of the environment, enabling it to respond more appropriately to the demands of the environment, including making appropriate responses to stress. These gradations of response are not usually seen in nonstimulated animals, which appear to respond in an all-or-none fashion.

Since differences in behaviour between stimulated and nonstimulated organisms occur mainly in situations in which increased activity of the CNS-pituitary-adrenal system has also been observed, the question is raised as to whether these behavioural differences may be related to differences in patterns of ACTH and corticosteroid secretion. The evidence that elevated steroids are correlated with superior avoidance conditioning might lead to the conclusion that these are indeed meaningful correlations. However, increased or decreased neuro-endocrine activity may be only one aspect of a more generalized difference in arousal levels, which could also account for other behavioural differences attributed to infantile stimulation. We have now identified behavioural systems which enable us to evaluate the degree to which the pituitary-adrenal hormones involved in the stress response are also involved in the modulation of behaviour. Thus, it is now possible to examine more closely the relationship between the difference in the behaviour of stimulated and nonstimulated animals and the difference in ACTH and corticosteroid secretion also observed in these animals.

HORMONAL INFLUENCES ON CENTRAL NERVOUS SYSTEM ORGANIZATION

It has been proposed (Harris, 1964; Young, 1961) that hormones exert a direct action on the central nervous system of the developing organism, and that such action produces profound and permanent changes in the subsequent psychophysiological processes of the organism. Thus, the organization of the central nervous system is in part a function of the action of hormones on the developing brain. Support for this hypothesis comes primarily from the now abundant literature on the effects both of neonatally administered gonadal hormones and of removal of the hormone-producing organ during early postnatal development in the rat. Thus, sex hormones appear to organize the sexually undifferentiated brain with regard to patterns of gonadotropin secretion and behaviour. Specifically, this hypothesis states that androgens acting on the central nervous system during sensitive periods in development are responsible for the programming of male patterns of gonadotropin secretion and sex behaviour in much the same way as the development of anatomical sexual characteristics. In as much as the major purpose of this paper is to attempt to account for the effects of infantile stimulation in terms of hormone action occurring at the time of stimulation, the information on the action of gonadal hormones does not require our further attention— it is only illustrative and, by analogy, provides a clue as to a possible mechanism.

As early as 1956 it was hypothesized (Levine *et al.*) that the effects of infantile stimulation could be due to the possibly stressful aspects of the stimulation procedure. However, this position was subsequently rejected (Levine, 1962a) on the ground that notions of stressful or traumatic stimuli all convey the idea that there is some way of knowing the meaning of the stimulus to the stimulated organism. It was difficult to justify the interpretation that the effects of infantile stimulation were due primarily to the stress of stimulation. First there was little or no information as to the effects of the usual stimulation. Second, all the evidence indicated that the period of time during which the animal appeared most sensitive to the effects of infantile stimulation corresponded almost exactly to that period which was postulated as being a stress nonresponsive period. The literature on the response of the neonatal rat to stress indicated that stressful stimuli could not activate the pituitary-adrenal axis. Jailer (1950) suggested that a postnatal period was necessary for the maturation of the pituitary-adrenal system, and Schapiro *et al.* (1962) concluded that the first 8 days of life are a stage in an animal's life when pituitary-adrenal activation is not evoked by stressor agents. However, the conclusion that the newborn rat is unable to respond to any stressful stimuli is no longer valid. Haltmeyer *et al.* (1966) stressed rats by exposing them to heat or electric shock on days 1 to 5 inclusive. The animals were sacrificed

15 minutes after the termination of the stress. At each age, in these nonhandled neonatal rats, the stress was sufficient to increase both plasma and adrenal corticosterone levels.

The results of two series of experiments lead directly to the hypothesis that the effects of infantile stimulation could be attributed to alterations in adrenal steroids during sensitive periods in development. In one series (Levine and Mullins, 1966; Levine 1968), newborn rats were handled to determine whether infantile stimulation had an effect on the maturation of the adrenal response. It was found that control animals, nonhandled, showed little or no increase in plasma corticosterone concentration in response to either electric shock or ether and surgical trauma until about 18 days of life. In contrast, handled newborn rats exhibited a significant elevation in plasma corticosterone concentrations following stress at 3 days of age. The response to ACTH was equivalent in both groups. Plasma steroid levels were elevated following ACTH injection at 3 days of age, after which there ensued a period during which a marked suppression of the response to stress and ACTH was observed in both groups. This period lasted until about 15 to 18 days of age. The cogent result in these studies was that the effects of stimulation were seen during the period in which central nervous system organization is presumed to be occurring.

More recently it has been shown (Denenberg et al., 1967) that handling per se results in a significant elevation in circulating corticosterone levels in the infant rat. These data indicate, therefore, that very early in development the animal which has been subjected to extra stimulation in the form of handling is indeed different in respect of the variations in circulating corticoids during the immediate postnatal period.

In as much as all the empirical evidence indicates that there is a difference between animals handled in infancy and their nonhandled counterparts in respect of the neuroendocrine mechanisms regulating ACTH secretion and possibly synthesis in the adult, we propose that this difference is a function of some action of the adrenal steroids during sensitive periods which permanently modifies the organization of the central nervous system and results in different patterns of ACTH secretion. Further, we argue (Levine and Mullins, 1966) that the setpoint of the hypothetical hormonostat is differentially organized as a consequence of the action of adrenal steroids during infancy. "In this hormonostat, moreover, the setpoint is not fixed at a given level; it can vary to some extent, depending upon the demands of the environment and the inner states of the organism. The sensitivity in the hormonostat is determined by the number of values this setpoint can have between its minimum value, which corresponds to the concentration of steroids when the animal is resting, and its maximum value, which corresponds to the concentration under conditions of extreme stress. Thus it may be that handling, by causing variation in the concentration of adrenal steroids in the infant animal, modifies the setpoint during a critical time in development so it can vary in a graded manner in the adult, with several values between the minimum and the maximum. This could explain why handled rats are able to respond to novel but not physically threatening stimuli, such as the open field, with a moderate increase in adrenal steroids, and to shock with a large and rapid release. In the nonhandled newborn rat there is less variation in adrenal steroid concentration during the critical period, and the setpoint develops fewer possible values. In these animals the hormonostat tends to operate either at 'resting' level, if there is no change in the environment, or at levels close to maximum if there is any change at all, whether or not the change is physiologically threatening."

Thus in slightly more than a decade since the publication of our first study on the effects of infantile stimulation, it appears that we have made the complete circle. We are again attributing the effects of infantile stimulation to the fact that the stimulation procedures employed are intrinsically stressful to the newborn organism. As a consequence of the effects of altering adrenal steroids by stimulating the newborn organism, we conclude that the central nervous system of such an organism is organized in a different manner from that in one which has not been exposed to the stimulation procedures.

We have developed this theory principally on inferential evidence. One cannot point to any specific structure or structures and observe an anatomical or biochemical difference which can be empirically specified "central nervous system organization". The hypothesis that adrenal steroids are implicated in early handling is also based on circumstantial evidence and, even if confirmed, presents only the beginnings of an attempt to understand the mechanisms of action. To date there is no evidence which indicates the mechanisms of hormone action on the central nervous system. Beyond the statement that this is obviously a biochemical action there is a complete gap in our knowledge.

Although our principal concern so far has been with the effects of infantile stimulation on the neuroendocrine regulation of ACTH, it must be emphasized that infantile stimulation has been shown to affect other neuroendocrine processes. Injecting female rats with saline immediately after birth reduces the amount of mounting observed when they are given testosterone following castration in adulthood. Handling in infancy advances the onset of puberty in rats (Morton *et al.*, 1963), an event which is partially controlled by the sex and thyroid hormones. These results are only an indication of the complexity of neuroendocrine organization and neuroendocrine function.

In spite of its enormous complexities, one of the more exciting and promising areas of research in developmental psychobiology lies in the investigation of the effects of hormones on the developing nervous system. Although we can find no reasons to contradict the assumption that the mechanism of hormonal action during development is primarily biochemical, there is no evidence as yet to support this assumption and little expectation that information of this kind will become available in the near future. Furthermore, even at the present descriptive level, many aspects of the relationship between hormones in infancy and adult behaviour have yet to be determined.

REFERENCES

BARRETT, A. M. 1960. Some factors affecting blood ACTH levels. In F. Fuchs (Ed.), *Acta endocrinologica, supplement*. Periodica, Copenhagen. Pp. 119–120.

BOHUS, B., ENDRÖCZI, E., and LISSAK, K. 1963. Correlations between avoiding conditional reflex activity and pituitary-adrenocortical function in the rat. *Acta physiol. scand.* **24**, 79–83.

DAVIDSON, J. M., JONES, L. E., and LEVINE, S. 1965. Effects of hypothalamic implantation of steroids on plasma corticosterone. *Fedn Proc. Fedn. Am. Socs exp. Biol.* **24**, 191.

DENENBERG, V. H., BRUMAGHIM, J. T., HALTMEYER, G. C., and ZARROW, M. X. 1967. Increased adrenocortical activity in the neonatal rat following handling. *Endocrinology* **81**, 1047–1052.

DE WIED, D. 1966. Opposite effects of ACTH and glucocorticosteroids on extinction of conditioned avoidance behaviour. In L. Martini, F. Fraschini and M. Motta (Eds.), *Proceedings of the Second International Congress on hormonal steroids*. Milan. Pp. 945–951.

GANONG, W. F. 1963. The central nervous system and the synthesis and release of adrenocorticotropic hormone. In A. V. Nalbandov (Ed.), *Advances in neuroendocrinology*. University of Illinois Press, Urbana. Pp. 92–157.

HALTMEYER, G. C., DENENBERG, V. H., THATCHER, J., and ZARROW, M. X. 1966. Response of the adrenal cortex of the neonatal rat after subjection to stress. *Nature, Lond.* **212**, 1371–1373.

HALTMEYER, G. C., DENENBERG, V. H., and ZARROW, M. X. 1967. Modification of the plasma corticosterone response as a function of infantile stimulation and electric shock parameters. *Physiol. Behav.* **2**, 61–63.

HARRIS, G. W. 1964. Sex hormones, brain development and brain function. *Endocrinology* **75**, 627–648.

HARRIS, G. W. and JACOBSOHN, D. 1952. Functional grafts of the anterior pituitary gland. *Proc. R. Soc. B.* **139**, 263–276.

JAILER, J. W. 1950. The maturation of the pituitary-adrenal axis in the newborn rat. *Endocrinology* **46**, 420–425.

KITAY, J. I. 1961. Sex differences in adrenal cortical secretion in the rat. *Endocrinology* **68**, 818–824.

LEVINE, S. 1962a. The effects of infantile experience on adult behaviour. In A. J. Bachrach (Ed.), *Experimental foundations of clinical psychology*. Basic Books, New York. Pp. 139–169.

LEVINE, S. 1962b. Plasma-free corticosteroid response to electric shock in rats stimulated in infancy. *Science, N.Y.* **135**, 795–796.

LEVINE, S. 1967a. Influence of gonadal hormones in infancy on adult behaviour. In K. Lissak (Ed.), *Symposium on Reproduction*. Congress of the Hungarian Society for Endocrinology and Metabolism. Akademiai Kiado, Budapest. Pp. 229–241.

LEVINE, S. 1967b. Maternal and environmental influences on the adrenocortical response to stress in weanling rats. *Science, N.Y.* **156**, 258–260.

LEVINE, S. 1968. Influence of infantile stimulation on the response to stress during development. *Devl. Psychobiol.* **1**, 67–70.

LEVINE, S. and BRUSH, F. R. 1967. Adrenocortical activity and avoidance learning as a function of time after avoidance training. *Physiology Behav.* **2**, 385–388.

LEVINE, S. and JONES, L. E. 1965. Adrenocorticotropic hormone (ACTH) and passive avoidance learning. *J. comp. physiol. Psychol.* **59**, 357–360.

LEVINE, S. and MULLINS, R. F., JR. 1966. Hormonal influences on brain organization in infant rats. *Science, N.Y.* **152**, 1585–1592.

LEVINE, S. and MULLINS, R. F., JR. 1967. Neonatal androgen or estrogen treatment and the adrenal cortical response to stress in adult rats. *Endocrinology* **80**, 1177–1179.

LEVINE, S. and THOMAN, E. B. Maternal factors influencing subsequent adrenocortical activity in the offspring. Presented at Symposium on Postnatal Development of Phenotype. Liblice, Sept. 1967.

LEVINE, S. and TREIMAN, D. M. 1964. Differential plasma corticosterone response to stress in four inbred strains of mice. *Endocrinology* **75**, 142–144.

LEVINE, S., CHEVALIER, J. A., and KORCHIN, S. J. 1956. The effects of early shock and handling on later avoidance learning. *J. Personality* **24**, 475–493.

LEVINE, S., HALTMEYER, G. C., KARAS, G. G., and DENENBERG, V. H. 1967. Physiological and behavioral effects of infantile stimulation. *Physiology Behav.* **2**, 55–59.

LISSAK, K. and ENDRÖCZI, E. 1961. Neurohumoral factors in the control of animal behavior. In United Nations Educational, Scientific and Cultural Organization Symposium, *Brain mechanisms and learning*. Blackwell, Oxford. Pp. 293–308.

MASON, J. W., BRADY, J. V., and TOLSON, W. W. 1966. Behavioral adaptations and endocrine activity. Psychoendocrine activity. Psychoendocrine differentiation of emotional states. In R. Levine (Ed.), *Endocrines and the central nervous system*. William & Wilkins, Baltimore. Pp. 227–250.

MORTON, J. R. C., DENENBERG, V. H., and ZARROW, M. X. 1963. Modification of sexual development through stimulation in infancy. *Endocrinology* **72**, 439–442.

SHAPIRO, S., GELLER, E., and EIDUSON, S. 1962. Corticoid response to stress in the steroid-inhibited rat. *Proc. Soc. exp. Biol. Med.* **109**, 935–937.

WERTHEIM, G. A., CONNER, R. L., and LEVINE, S. 1967. Adrenocortical influences on free-operant avoidance behavior. *J. exp. Analysis Behav.* **10,** 555–563.

YATES, F. E. and URQUHART, J. 1962. Control of plasma concentrations of adreno-cortical hormones. *Physiol. Rev.* **42,** 389–443.

YOUNG, W. C. 1961. The hormones and mating behavior. In W. C. Young (Ed.), *Sex and internal secretions.* Williams & Wilkins, Baltimore. Pp. 1173–1239.

Discussion

Role of the Mother in Subserving Infant Stimulation Effects

LEVINE: Following the application of stimulation to the offspring, the major process by which the adrenal steroids are affected occurs as a function of what happens to the mother. We have shown by a number of experiments that stimulation of the offspring in infancy alters the behavioural or hormonal characteristics of the mother which then transmit effects back to the offspring.

We have also shown that merely inducing changes in the mother alone alters the characteristics of the offspring. Let me give you some examples (S. Levine and E. B. Thoman. 1969. *Physiol. Behav.* **4,** 139). If we stress the mother by giving a single exposure to ether or electric shock at 3 days postpartum, the offspring of the whole litter are markedly different in adulthood with regard to both avoidance conditioning and adrenal steroids. Again, if we briefly remove the mother from the nest, as opposed to removing the young from the nest, we get essentially the same effects. If we give hormones to mothers in two different strains of animal we find that the effects on the mothers are markedly different in the two strains. We then do the appropriate experiment with all the cross-fostering and we find that the predominant effect is a maternal one: the mother with high steroids has newborns that are different from those of the mother with low steroids. Although this appears to be a postnatal effect, we can also get prenatal effects. For example, if we maternally adrenalectomize the mother, the offspring even though fostered on to normal intact females, will have markedly different patterns of stress response in adulthood. Therefore, although there is much evidence that stimulation of offspring has direct effects on it, there is also clear evidence which indicates a fairly complex inter-active process via the mother. Something undoubtedly happens to the organism as a function of what happens to the mother.

GINSBURG: Strain, litter and individual handling effects occur in a number of handling paradigms, in different strains and different cross-fostering experiments. Add to that Denenberg's grandmother effect and my ova transplant effects which persist over several generations, and you have all the complexities you want in the biological situation.

Nevertheless, I think the importance of these very early handling effects, in the period which was previously presumed to be a "silent period", is extremely critical. We were badly burned by our ignorance of these effects during our earlier experiments on the effects of neonatal gonadectomy and on the differences between male and female behaviour immediately after weaning. Although we found significant sex differences, we had not used a control group until after some of these experiments had been done. We had been anaesthetizing the animals as neonates between days 1 and 3 by freezing them and then doing the gonadectomy. The control experiment, however, showed that most of the effects observed at weaning age were attributable to the freezing rather than to the gonadectomy.

Experimenting with ACTH

BATESON: Are there any ACTH inhibitors?

LEVINE: There are no chemical methods of inhibiting ACTH but steroids will inhibit it.

BATESON: If you could raise the ACTH level artificially in one group and lower it in another, would the effects be the same as in handled and nonhandled animals?

LEVINE: We intend to try this. A difficulty is that, in raising the level artificially by injecting corticosterone, even the minimum dosage causes an enormous amount of gross abnormality in the newborn: they become stunted and show gross growth retardation. I have now obtained some synthetic ACTH which can be put in a zinc phosphate base: this will be long-acting and maintain adrenal steroids for about 72 hours. We shall inject this into the newborns and see if it produces effects similar to those of handling. The difficulty is that we don't know for how long the elevated steroid level is maintained. Furthermore, elevation itself may not be the main factor: changes in elevation may be the important thing. We don't yet know whether we need a constant setpoint or a variable one.

KAGAN: What do we know about the chemical composition of the rat mother's milk in terms of ACTH?

LEVINE: There is much evidence that steroids come through the milk.

KAGAN: Is the steroid output of the rat mother's milk different from that of cow's milk?

LEVINE: The composition of cow's milk given to rats is very different from that of rats' milk in terms of sodium and carbohydrates. These dietary differences may have important effects.

Magnitude and Timing of Hormonal Effects

GINSBURG: Do I understand you correctly that the effects of stimulation, through the steroid mechanism, are to enhance growth development, eye opening and so on?

LEVINE: Yes. But the problem with hormone dosage is that it does not have a linear action. Too much steroid is almost as bad as too little. It is because dosage is so important that we have striven to get the organism to produce its own steroids rather than resort to hormone injections. The other problem is that the composition of the steroid alters as a function of development. By giving, say, corticosteroid or hydrocortisone we may not be using the most effective steroid. The adrenal gland has a variety of outputs and not just corticosterone. We must not assume that only one particular steroid compound is operative. It is interesting that, when carrying out experiments on the genesis of sexual differences, the most effective treatment is not to inject testosterone into the female but to remove the gonads in the male. You then see an unblemished picture of feminization. While androgen given to the female produces certain characteristics that are masculine, others are not changed at all.

GINSBURG: We found marked behavioural differences in castrated dogs depending upon whether they were gonadectomized at birth or after sexual maturity.

HAMBURG: Not all the effects of hormones, or for that matter of brain lesions, are greater earlier. Some effects are greater later. For example, we know from studies of the effects of cortisone on growth that the stunting effect is considerably greater in the 5-week rat than in the 3-week rat, although the direction of change is the same. There is, in fact, a very confusing picture concerning the relation of cortical steroids to overall body growth. In humans it is well documented clinically that the exogenous administration of large doses of cortical steroids can have a gross stunting effect in children. This of course was a by-product of administration for other purposes. From this you would expect that children with growth retardation coming from very disturbed families would, because of their continual stress, show high cortical steroids and that the cortical steroid probably plays some role in the growth stunting. However, a recent study at Johns Hopkins showed that in this type of child there were low cortical steroids. There was also a perfectly adequate adrenal response to ACTH. Although the syndrome is generally reversible, about half to two-thirds of the children still show some tendency towards low circulating cortical steroids after effective treatment of the growth retardation.

The Adrenal Steroid Model contrasted with a Neural Threshold Model

GINSBURG: Another problem concerns the organization of the neural mechanisms involved. Certainly there are different kinds of steroids which, at different times during development, when changed quantitively can have different effects on neural organization. Nevertheless there might also be a differential conditioning of the target organs. It may be that early stimulation, by elevating steroids of short temporal duration, results in long-term changes in target organ thresholds. These could have prolonged effects on what happens later, even if steroid levels fluctuate. But we don't have the techniques with which to investigate this adequately at present. There is undoubtedly genetic variation in it. Anything that varies genetically ought to be variable in other ways as well. In terms of the present data I do not see any way of distinguishing between the steroid model and the neural threshold model.

LEVINE: This is true for the present, but the adrenal steroid model is a new line of thinking and the data are not yet complete. The model is based largely on circumstantial evidence, and our evidence mainly concerns the organization of the central nervous system with respect to the gonads. I am trying to account for the different organisms responding markedly differently to a given set of stimuli. For example, if I expose different strains of rat to standard electric shock, I find large inter-strain differences but very small intra-strain differences. Yet if I give ACTH to all of the same animals, I find the same adrenal responses in all. Now one can argue that the strain differences found are a function of differences in their neuroendocrine regulation in respect of ACTH production. Since it is an ACTH effect and not a steroid effect I don't see how one explains this with a neural threshold model.

HAMBURG: In analysing this issue, would it not be helpful to take inbred strains that are controlled for age and to use a variety of techniques for varying the exposure of the brain to hormone over a very broad range? The range could be in terms of absolute concentration of hormones, rates of change in them, or duration of a given level, whatever you regard as important. There are various techniques for doing this whether by adrenalectomy, by chemically blocking synthesis of the hormone in the adrenal, or by implanting minute pellets of steroids that will block the feedback in the brain. These would all diminish the circulating steroids.

GINSBURG: I don't think you can do this because there may be other things that influence the activity of the ovary: you can't assume that your interfering and blocking techniques are doing everything. Since there are probably other unknown factors at work you would have to add a detailed monitoring device and this would amount to a complete fractionation.

HAMBURG: You can analyse the metabolic transformations of steroids in the brain; you can also localize by radiographic techniques where these transformations are occurring in the brain and find out what the hormone is doing, say to protein synthesis, at a particular site.

GINSBURG: We should learn a lot more from such techniques if we knew how to interpret the results unambiguously.

LEVINE: Granted all this I am still not clear how your neural threshold model is different from the adrenal steroid model that I am proposing.

BATESON: The question is whether the treatment affects the bias on the homeostat or the target organ. I am not sure that you can distinguish between these possibilities.

LEVINE: I think you can distinguish them very clearly. If you either remove the receptor or block the endogenous ACTH and then do a dose-response curve on ACTH in the target organ, the target will be different between stimulated and nonstimulated animals. The adrenal is capable of putting out the same amount of hormone. In this instance I don't think you can argue a target organ difference.

BATESON: Could it not be that the sensitivity of neural structures to adrenal steroids is affected?

LEVINE: No. I can argue against that in two ways. Firstly, if adrenal steroids are administered exogenously so that one can assume the same level of adrenal steroids, some of the behavioural effects will be obliterated: it is simply a differential sensitivity here. Secondly, there is now a lot of evidence that these behavioural effects are not adrenal steroid *per se* but actually ACTH *per se*. This has been shown in a sophisticated manner by David de Wied at Utrecht (1964. *J. Endocrinol.* **29**, 29). If extinction of the conditioned avoidance response is studied in an adrenalectomized animal, that is where ACTH is markedly increased by elimination of the feedback loop, the animal does not extinguish. By contrast, in an animal given corticoids there is marked extinction. In this way it is possible to see whether or not there is an ACTH effect. The ACTH molecule has a sequence of amino acids; in order to increase the output of adrenal steroids it is necessary to use the sequence of amino acids 1 to 24. If this molecule is fractionated to give the 4 to 10 amino acid sequence, which has no adrenal steroid properties and does not increase adrenal steroidogenesis, this has the same effect on behaviour.

KAGAN: How does this relate to the differences between handled and nonhandled rats? If I take two equivalent groups of adult rats and give one group cortical steroids and the other ACTH, which group will behave more like rats handled in infancy?

LEVINE: It depends partly on the behaviour studied. If you take behaviour upon which we know ACTH is markedly effective, increased ACTH gives effects which look like nonhandled animals. We did this with mice, giving handled and nonhandled animals a passive avoidance situation: we found that the nonhandled animals showed a much greater passive avoidance in adulthood. If we then gave ACTH to both groups we obliterated the differences.

KAGAN: What is the primary factor here, tolerance for ACTH?

LEVINE: No, it's release of ACTH: there are different patterns of release of ACTH. The handled animal will show a more momentarily modulated release of ACTH.

GINSBURG: If, having genetically fractionated the population, and also having fractionated the kinds of behaviour, one then does a multiplicity of behavioural tests on the effects of early handling, effects will appear on different behaviours that are of different magnitude and direction. The result has to do with the setting of the neurostat.

LEVINE: I agree that we are talking about a neurostat, a neural mechanism. If handling and nonhandling experiments are done on two different strains, very striking differences appear as a function of the strain. The strains that are most affected by handling are those which seem to have the greatest lability in their steroid response, that is, in their whole neuroendocrine organization. Strains which are not affected seem to be those which have the least lability. This is, however, only part of the picture; we are attempting to get a working model on which to base experiments.

GINSBURG: Shouldn't the model be opened up at this point to allow for the possibility of the differences, to which you refer, being related to the setting of neural sensitivities, of neural thresholds? I shall elaborate on this in my paper.

DENENBERG: Let us get back to behaviour. The mother has two major functions: one as a source of stimulation, the other as a source of behaviour. I doubt if her only function is to modify the hormonal picture. This is shown by certain inconsistencies in our data.

If, at the behavioural level, one increases emotionality in the mother, the offspring show increased emotionality when adult. We used two procedures to show this, one by increasing maternal emotionality post-natally, the other by increasing it prenatally. In the former case we shocked the mother each day outside the cage and put her back with her pups. This is a sure way of getting corticosterone into them. Now one would expect that this would produce a "handled", less emotional, type of animal. In fact we got the opposite, a highly emotional beast which behaved as if it had not been handled. The other procedure was based on individual differences. We tested a bunch of females for emotionality in the open field and selected the highs and the lows. At birth we cross-fostered the young between those two groups. We found that the females which were more emotional would raise more emotional offspring. We then experimentally generated high and low emotional mothers, by means of handling. The result was the opposite of what one would expect; the nonhandled female which was more emotional had offspring that were less emotional. To explain this apparent inconsistency we must suppose that, in addition to chemical factors, behavioural factors are also operating. This is why we are now about to employ a TV system: we want to find out how these mothers interact with their pups.

BRUNER: I should like to question you on three points. Firstly, you talk about emotionality as if avoidance behaviour is just a unitary thing. We know from all of R. F. Solomon's work that it consists of a whole series of related acts. It may very well be that the avoidance behaviour you see in an organism that has been shocked without any instrumental means open to escape would be quite different from the kind where an animal can get away.

Secondly, there seem to be three kinds of effect which could be interacting, and it might require an ambitious factorial design to study these. One is the possibility of ACTH operating directly on behaviour in the way that you described in the case of extinction of the avoidance reaction. A second possibility is that it operates to change the setting of the hormonostat. Whether this changes the mean response, or whether it changes the limits of the distribution of responses to high stresses compared with in the resting state, is uncertain. In any case it is cutting down the repertory of responses available to the organism. A third intriguing possibility, is that there may be a change in the way the mother responds to her offspring when subjected to your procedures.

Thirdly, there are a whole series of things which have to do with the "vicariousness of function". It is a question of whether the behaviours that you are getting are in effect the result of behavioural pressures on the organism that change the response pattern, which in turn works its way back into the steroid chemistry, or whether they are the result of some kind of a diffuse response that changes the steroid chemistry which then works its way back into behaviour.

LEVINE: I indicated in my paper that an increase or decrease in the steroids is one aspect of a more generalized difference in arousal levels which could account for many of the differences. In my laboratory over the past 5 years we have been able to show some very specific behavioural effects of hormones that are not dependent upon generalized arousal levels. There are systems which seem to be exquisitely sensitive to hormones with regard to behaviour. In some aspects of behaviour we're dealing with differences between handled and non-handled animals which are very much like the same differences that we see when experimenting with hormones.

As regards your first point, this is a very important one. I tend to be rather more cautious and talk about "emotional reactivity".

BATESON: Do you think that, in the nonhandled rats, the bias of the hormonostat is in a sense more wobbly, so that the variability of ACTH levels would be greater than the mean levels?

LEVINE: No, just the opposite. My argument is that in the nonhandled rat there is very little movement for bias: what happens is that input leads essentially to the same response regardless of the nature of the stimulus. In the handled animal by contrast, the bias is much more variable as a function of exposure to the gradations.

HAMBURG: What you're saying is that you recognize that there is a great deal going on in the neonatal rat, not to speak about the human infant. There are many processes of great importance for later behaviour and physiology and, what's worse, they almost all interact with each other. But you're selecting out one aspect which you think has, in its own right, considerable importance for later development. The chief model you are relying on is the role that testosterone plays in facilitating the organization of circuits in the brain that will later mediate the control of gonadotropin, sex behaviour and some aspects of aggressive behaviour. You are saying that in some way changes in adrenocortical hormones induced by infantile stimulation are participating in and facilitating the organization of some circuits in the brain later destined to mediate certain behavioural and physiological functions. One implication of this is that you are talking about the organization of circuits which will have some kind of regulatory function. Specific predictions about the direction of change then become less salient. A regulatory system will be able to turn on or off; it will both elevate and decrease levels of compounds or activities. Many factors may be relevant to direction and magnitude of change, but you are saying that a regulatory system is influenced in its organization by the presence of hormone in the brain during a critical time.

This raises the interesting question "What circuits are being organized"? I refer not only to anatomical circuits, but also to the kinds of behavioural and endocrine functions which will ultimately be regulated by these circuits. You have emphasized mainly what would be the counterpart of gonadotropin regulation in the testosterone story, i.e. the ACTH regulation. It is as though you were saying that some cells in the hypothalamus have to see a good deal of corticosteroid early in order to recognize it later and to deal with it effectively in a feedback system. A slightly more accurate version might be that they would have to see a considerable range of variability in order to respond efficiently to variation later as environmental conditions vary.

Early Stimulation Effects, Learning Theory, and Early Social Isolation Effects

Different Effects of Pre- and Post-weaning Stimulation in Rats

DENENBERG: A major research area in early experience not so far covered in our discussions is the work that Donald Hebb initiated at McGill University (D. O. Hebb. 1949. *The organization of behaviour.* Wiley, New York) The procedure was to place a weanling rat into a complex enriched environment, called a "free environment", for 3 to 6 weeks. This experience led to tremendous advances in problem solving and in perceptual and cognitive behaviours. These results are in marked contrast to our findings in which we manipulate the rat between birth and weaning by means of handling. When we test these handled animals for problem solving, we get no evidence of any effects whatsoever (Denenberg and Morton. 1962. *J. comp. physiol. Psychol.* **55**, 1906). The fact that Hebb gets a major effect from giving rats enriched experience after weaning suggests that the type of thing that we are doing in handling an animal between birth and weaning must affect the animal at very different levels and influence different biological systems. Whereas those who use the postweaning rat work at a cortical level, affecting perceptual and cognitive processes, we work at the level of physiological and biochemical processes with our very early stimulation.

We can demark as one major period in ontogeny the time between birth and weaning. We do not do our handling experiments in this period just because mother-young separation normally occurs at weaning. We chose this period primarily because of the fact that the animal at the time of weaning has all senses functioning, is able to learn and retain information, and can interact and cope with its environment relatively effectively.

Much of the stimulation received by the young between birth and weaning may be termed "unpatterned physical stimulation". Types of unpatterned physical stimulation used by us include heat, cold, handling and electric shock. If, with the rat, one applies one of these types of stimulation somewhere in the time-interval between birth and weaning one subsequently finds, in the adult, differences in two major classes of event. There are behavioural differences in what I call emotional reactivity or emotionality, and there are differences at a physiological or biochemical level. If, on the other hand, one asks what is the most powerful type of stimulation that can be introduced after weaning to affect subsequent behaviour, one finds that it is not handling or gentling but an enriched free environment experience. I call this kind of stimulation "patterned physical stimulation". It affects such events as perception, problem solving, and neural activities. These relationships are summarized in Table I.

TABLE I. RELATIONSHIPS, IN RATS, BETWEEN TWO TYPES OF EARLY EXPERIMENTAL STIMULATION AND TYPES OF EFFECT IN ADULTHOOD.

Period of experimental stimulation	Effective property of early stimulation	Types of effect in adulthood
Birth to weaning	Unpatterned physical stimulation	Emotionality Physiology Biochemistry
After weaning	Patterned physical stimulation	Perception Problem solving Cognition Neural activity

Now in making weaning the transition point I do not mean to imply either that patterned physical stimulation has absolutely no effect between birth and weaning or that unpatterned stimulation has no effects after weaning. What I am saying is that, in terms of the relative impact of these events, the preweaning period is where one gets massive effects by use of heat, shock, handling, or cold, while environmental enrichment has greatest effect after weaning. We have in fact shown that enriched experience between birth and weaning does facilitate problem solving in adulthood (Denenberg *et al.* 1968. *J. comp. physiol. Psychol.*, **66**, 533), but the preweaning experience is less effective in modifying problem solving than is enriched experience after weaning. We have done other studies as well which demonstrate that free environment enrichment after weaning reduces emotional upset in the rat (Denenberg and Morton. 1962. *J. comp. physiol. Psychol.*, **55**, 242; Denenberg and Morton. 1964. *Anim. Behav.*, **12**, 11), but again we find less of a reduction in emotional upset by postweaning enrichment than we do by preweaning handling. This is all consistent with the findings of other investigators such as Lindholm (1962. *J. comp. physiol. Psychol.*, **55**, 597), who has demonstrated that preweaning shock has qualitatively different effects from postweaning shock.

The mother, whether the rat mother or the human mother, through her social interactions with the young, serves two major functions. The first is to supply the infant with unpatterned physical stimulation, the second is to supply patterned physical stimulation. I realize that there is a slight paradox here, because I stated earlier that patterned stimulation is most effective after weaning and yet I claim that the mother supplies patterned stimulation before weaning. This paradox is due, in large part, to our experimental procedures whereby patterned stimulation is not introduced until we wean the animals. However, the baby rat can hear, see, and locomote quite effectively by 15 days and I suspect that it is around this time that the role of the mother shifts from being a supplier of unpatterned stimulation to being a supplier of patterned stimulation. I think it important, however, to keep these two roles of the mother conceptually separate and distinct, even though they may overlap to some extent.

The social interactions between mother and young, as well as between peers, are extremely complicated. Although we can override some of the effects of these interactions by our handling manipulation, such effects can influence our results. For example, we have placed animals of different emotional backgrounds into an enriched environment and have then examined subsequent emotional behaviour (Denenberg and Morton. 1952. *J. comp. physiol. Psychol.*, **55**, 242; Denenberg *et al.* 1964. *Anim. Behav.*, **12**, 205). The findings were extraordinarily complex and were obviously a function of the social interactions among the animals in our groups.

BRUNER: I am puzzled by the fact that unpatterned physical stimulation didn't make much of a difference to the postweaning cognitive activity, that is, to exploration and problem solving. I would have thought that, in order for a young organism to be capable of exploratory behaviour and hypothesis testing, there would have to be a certain amount of stabilization of the earliest responses to novelty. Maybe the organism is sufficiently well buffered so that it timidly works its way into the environment and gradually manages to explore it. It would be interesting to try to compound the effects so that one had a kind of 4-pole design. An organism that was not handled, that received none of this early physical stimulation, that lived in a deprived environment, and that didn't have an opportunity for gradual entry into the world of patterned stimulation, might produce some syndromes that would be extremely sharply demarcated. Although this organism would have a readiness to explore novelty, it would be lacking in an adequate model of the environment: in this sense it would be a very sick cognitive beast indeed. From the point of view of trying to understand developmental patterns, what we really must ask about is the interaction between the environmental supply of stimulation and the organism's willingness to go out and explore it. This is the critical factor.

KAGAN: I do not like Denenberg's idea of patterned physical stimulation, because it suggests that stimulation effects operate on a continuum If you deprive a cat of all light, it goes blind, but if it has only a little light it does not. Children in the natural environment get enough patterned stimulation, but that is not the dimension that matters. What is critical is the distinctiveness of the stimulation. A one-room ghetto with television and many adults contains more physical stimulation than a suburban second floor bedroom. But the child in the latter context is exposed to more distinctive cues.

DENENBERG: We needed an adjective that would make a distinction between such things as heat, cold and shock as one type of stimulus input, and things in the free environment which exert an influence, such as interactions occurring in the mother-young association. What would you call heat, cold, and shock?

KAGAN: Heat and shock are different: one is continuous stimulation, the other is an abrupt change.

PRECHTL: Perhaps what they have in common is that they are both very stressful stimuli.

DENENBERG: I like the terms "stressful" instead of "unpatterned" and "distinctive" instead of "patterned" for the different types of stimulation. I am only concerned to make a distinction between the types of stimulation we apply in our experiments. We are studying two major stimulus dimensions which I think are relevant for the rat, at least in early life. One is the mean level of stimulus input, the other is the variation of the stimulus. In working with these dimensions it doesn't really matter whether the stimulation comes from the mother or whether it comes from physical input.

Early Stimulation Effects and Learning Theory

LEVINE: It is clear that in a wide variety of species early stimulation has effects on later performance: on the ability of the organism either to learn or to perform adaptively under a number of circumstances. It is interesting to consider, therefore, whether the mechanisms of the early stimulation effects cannot be brought into a learning framework.

A fact that still surprises most people is that a newborn organism *can* learn. The real issue, however, is *"What* does it learn?" In our laboratory, for example, we have been able to demonstrate that learning can occur in the feeding response system of the newborn rat, which has a very underdeveloped nervous system. Over the first 2 days of life, within a matter of 8 feedings, you see markedly different feeding behaviour to the tube during hand-feeding from that in the non-hand-fed animal. Furthermore, you can also train aversive reactions in feeding by putting quinine on the tip of the tube instead of using milk. In the newborn, however, the response system of feeding is highly organized because the animal is dependent on it for survival. Just because you can demonstrate that the newborn organism can learn in relation to its feeding response does not imply that there is a learning mechanism operating in all its responses. For evidence that learning can occur in other responses you have to be able to elicit a classically conditioned response. When you apply the massive sensory input involved in handling, what you get is a massive undifferentiated response. Unless you believe that these massive undifferentiated responses can be conditioned, the question of whether learning is implicated as a function of such early stimulation effects becomes a very dicey one.

I believe that the effects which we see as a result of early stimulation are indeed learning phenomena: the massive input which we apply modifies the central nervous system. I'm not necessarily basing this on the adrenal notion, because there is a variety of mechanisms by which this modification could occur. But whatever the mechanism, there is in effect an alteration of the programming, or of the basic wiring diagram, so that all other inputs become modified according to the alterations brought about in this early base-line environment.

DENENBERG: How does one use a learning mechanism to account for the following effects that one gets from early stimulation: firstly, earlier maturation on half a dozen different systems; secondly, a massive difference in body weight in adulthood; thirdly, greater ability to survive various forms of stress; fourthly, the offspring of the animals are affected; fifthly, the grandchildren are affected as well? I don't see how a learning mechanism can in any way account for these effects.

KAGAN: Levine is creating a straw man. Whoever said that all changes or effects in an organism are a function of learning? The difficulty comes from your choosing the word "stimulation" to describe your experiments. You have imposed events; events change organisms, sometimes through learning, sometimes not involving learning. I don't think one would defend the notion that all changes in an organism at some future date are a function of learning.

LEVINE: I haven't created a straw man. This issue is continually brought up in discussions on maturation. You must conceive of something going on in the newborn which is different from a process of learning. There is a whole area of physiological psychology that does this, which says that physiological events affect behaviour. It's so much easier for me to conceptualize what we are doing as altering physiological processes, which then subsequently interact with the nature of the behaviour that these organisms emit.

BRUNER: Isn't that true of most skilled learning?

LEVINE: Yes, in the sense that the organism needs motor responses for such learning, and underlying circuits are built up in the central nervous system. What I'm talking about are prior events which programme the physiological events which, in turn, will affect the nature of the emitted behaviour.

KAGAN: You think of learning in terms of motor responses, but learning can be much more than that. Learning is a relational concept, a bond between units. One can list at least four kinds of bond: between an external event and a public response, between an external event and an internal response, between an internal response and a public response and between two internal responses. Obviously the profile of these classes of bonds will be different at different points in development. In using the word "learning", therefore, we should not think only in terms of one kind of bond.

BATESON: One's approach to learning depends upon the kind of thing one is looking at. In your (Kagan) work you are mainly looking at learning skills; the differentiation there is on the response side. In the imprinting situation many of the response mechanisms are already established by the time that learning begins; it is in what is responded to that changes occur. Both of these are important aspects of the development of the young organism and one shouldn't overemphasize either of them.

Effects of Early Social Isolation in Primates

LEVINE: The discussion so far has been focusing on what stimulation does. I think we ought to be focusing on what nonstimulation does. In our work, what creates the neurological damage and the failure of the adaptive programming is the artefact of the laboratory environment, which is a very unnatural situation. It's the lack of stimulation that is the critical point.

HAMBURG: Although we are speaking about stimulation very broadly, there has been a notion of a continuum embodied in much of our thinking. This consists of three ranges: a minimum of stimulation which we associate with grossly maladaptive effects, an upper end of the range which could also be damaging, and a mid-range which is optimal and which produces an organism that is highly adaptable over a range of environmental conditions.

Following up Levine's point about the critical significance of lack of stimulation, I should like to draw your attention to a study (R. K. Davenport and E. W. Menzel. 1963. *Arch. Gen. Psychiat.*, 8, 99) carried out at the Yerkes primate centre in Atlanta. Chimps were reared for 2 years in what Harlow would call the "total isolation condition": this was a box which permitted some visual or auditory input, but no clear vision or clear hearing of other chimps. They found that 2 years in this box, out of a 10-year span to maturity, was sufficient to produce profound effects: severe withdrawal, avoidance of contact with other animals, and stereotypies. These stereotypies developed within the isolation chamber but they became exacerbated on emergence from it and particularly when the chimp was confronted with any kind of novel or noxious stimulation.

Levine and Denenberg were referring to this kind of total isolation condition as being related to their minimal stimulation, or nonhandled, condition. It seems most unlikely that any human environment is so devoid of stimulation that it would be comparable with this condition of total isolation. Nevertheless, there is no question that the paediatric services do see cases of very severe neglect. It may be that the *partial* social isolation condition of Harlow is more relevant to our understanding of human disturbances.

The monkeys which Harlow used to call his normal controls were in fact reared in bare wire cages. Since becoming familiar with the field observations on primates, however, he has called this rearing condition "partial social isolation". The monkeys can see and hear other monkeys, and also people, but they have no intimate interaction with them during the first 6 or 12 months of development, depending upon the study being carried out. Eighty-four of these monkeys have now been followed up for several years. The main effects found (H. Cross and H. Harlow. 1965. *J. expt. res. Pers.*, **1**, 39) may be summarized as follows.

There were severe deficiencies in copulatory behaviour, so that the females had to be raped in order to get them pregnant. There were severe deficiencies in their maternal behaviour: they neglected and abused their babies. There was progressively increasing and lasting emotional disturbance, the severity of which depended upon the duration of partial isolation; particularly prominent was self-directed aggression. There was a sex difference in fear and aggression, the fear-type response being more prominent in the female and the aggressive-type response being more prominent in the male, which showed occasional outbursts of violence. Fearful avoidance was, however, prominent in both sexes. There were all kinds of serious deficiencies in social behaviour. There was, however, adequate discrimination learning if the animal was tested in its own cage, although not if tested in a different situation. By permitting some peer play, considerable but not complete compensation has been obtained; this peer play was, however, a good deal less than has been observed in the same species in the wild. Nevertheless, it does call attention to the developmental potentialities of early peer relations. This kind of partial social isolation does seem to me broadly to be the first or second cousin to the minimal stimulation condition which Levine and Denenberg have been employing in their work.

Genotypic Variables Affecting Responses to Postnatal Stimulation[1]

BENSON E. GINSBURG[2]

University of Chicago

INTRODUCTION

It is both a paradox and a challenge that, in this decade of technological and scientific achievement in which we are able to put men on the moon and to unravel the skein of the DNA helix, we are still working with a black box where behaviour is concerned.

Two generations ago a psychiatrist shook it, listened to its retrospective noises, and distinguished three moving parts: a primordial id, an epigenetic ego, and a hobnailed superego, all interconnected with one another and related to the events impinging upon the box through a psychohydraulic servo-mechanism. For the system to remain behaviourally intact, a proper balance was thought to be necessary among these forces, which would enable them to assimilate external and internal pressures and subordinate these to those of the ego and the superego, the latter acquiring their strength as a result of the developmental history of the individual. The id forces were conceptualized as stemming from the phylogenetic endowment of the species. The representations of the resultant of these pressures in the consciousness provided the topography of the behavioural landscape and the colouring of its emotional tone. This relationship was thought of as commutative, and the forces could thus be identified and restructured through their

[1] These researches were supported by Grant No. MH-03361 from the National Institute of Mental Health and by the State of Illinois Department of Mental Health, Project No. 17-302.
[2] Now at University of Connecticut.

topographical representations in the mental-emotional landscape of conscious thought and feeling. This conception, connecting the mental ordinate with the emotional abscissa, becomes three dimensional by the addition of a time axis, in which a variety of different progressions of psychosexual events produces predictably different topographies. This schema has been applied to therapy, art, anthropology, and sociology. With each succeeding application it has taken on a more extreme environmentalist orientation, until the black box representing the organism—you or I—becomes almost infinitely malleable as it is progressively shaped by the events which set the psychohydraulic balance between the trinity of essences that provide the motive power for behavioural development and modification. They are somehow, on this view, the "real" biological elements, out of which behaviour and feelings are built. But what are they, and where are they, if indeed, they are? Freud claimed to be providing a science of mental events which, according to his expressed hope, could eventually be related to physiological phenomena and morphological entities. How have we progressed?

Since any answer to this question involves animal experimentation with vertebrates, as well as observation and manipulation of human material, one must arrive at an examined position regarding the relationship between the universe of human and nonhuman behavioural data. Is the Freudian analysis, on the basis of which so much human behavioural has been "explained", applicable to animals that cannot verbalize? Is there a partial overlap between aspects of animal behaviour and those human behaviours that have been analysed in the terms of dynamic psychology? To what degree and in what ways can animal data serve as models for the exploration of human behavioural variations?

RELEVANCE OF ANIMAL DATA FOR THE STUDY OF HUMAN BEHAVIOURAL MECHANISMS

The first analogies that come to mind are naturalistic case history type studies of captive and free animals, and those dealing with the development of animal behaviour under natural, as compared to laboratory, conditions. While many of these are purely descriptive, others are analytic and come to grips with the motive forces underlying the ontogeny of behaviour in a variety of ways. Comparative studies have emphasized phylogenetic continuities and behavioural homologies, thus giving the biological determinants of behaviour their due. If the epitomizing example of dynamic psychology is a shapeless bundle of biological potential moulded by environmental events, then the counterpart in many animal behaviour studies is that of a biologically pre-programmed individual with genetically determined drives, instincts, orienting movements, innate releasing mechanisms, or, in sum, built-in behavioural tendencies that are determining and adaptive over the normal range of environmental variation. Lorenz (1965), in stating the classical position of the ethologist, considers that much of what appears to be learning involves simply the maturation of response mechanisms, and that flexibility of behaviour in vertebrates is achieved in a phylogenetic sense by the intercalation of learned components and biologically determined components in chained sequences. This position has been disputed (Lehrman, 1953) on the grounds that the possibility of learning in the egg or *in utero* has not been excluded in those experiments purporting to identify innate components of behaviour. Nature-nurture interactions in early development therefore constitute a particularly important investigational focus for the clarification and resolution of many of these problems.

As conceptualized by the ethologists, the innate components of vertebrate behaviour involve many built-in automatisms in the perceptual field (releasers) as well as central mechanisms relating these to particular behavioural outcomes (innate releasing mechanisms), especially in the realms of sexual behaviour and aggression. It has been pointed out (Ginsburg, 1949) that these innate components may constitute the phylogenetic unconscious of the Freudian scheme. This congruence between the concepts of ethology and dynamic psychology in no way constitutes evidence for the scientific validity of either scheme, but it indicates that students of both human and animal behaviour have been independently impressed by the stereotypy of mental and behavioural events forming the motives for sexual behaviour and aggression, and by the relevance of these for other forms of social behaviour. For the generic Freudian, this phylogenetic substratum has such relevances as providing a formal explanation for those aspects of the unconscious expressed in symbols that cannot be elucidated by free association, and as providing a place in the general scheme to which phylogenetic factors can be relegated. Nevertheless, according to this view, development of the behavioural potential of an indiviudal is still (except for cases of severe biological limitation) dependent on his psychosexual history, especially during the early formative years.

Animal behaviour studies in no way deny this. The phenomenon of imprinting, as it occurs in some birds, is characterized both by having an early and definable critical period and by resulting in an altered behavioural outcome, the basis for which is still being argued. Such sensitive periods for other aspects of social behaviour have also been described for mammals (Scott, 1962). However, in all these instances, the biological determinants remain a prominent feature of the explanation. Not all species of birds have the biological property of being imprintable, and among those that do, this varies in degree, in kind, and in the nature of the substitutable object, as well as in the timing and duration of the critical period during which the phenomenon can occur. When it is brought about in an experimental situation, it is seen as the transfer (learned or otherwise) of a social bond from the usual object to another. The bird is genetically programmed to form an adaptive social bond in its normal environment. Only the object to which the bond attaches is changed. On this view, the variability referred to above is considered to have a genetic basis.

The more labile behaviour of mammals is no less biologically based for being less stereotyped. The narrowness or broadness of the behavioural repertoire, or indeed its lability with respect to environmental circumstances, is no measure of the degree of biological determination. The "nature-nurture" question is not meaningful as it has usually been formulated. Genes can pre-programme the possibilities for labile interaction with the environment as well as restrict the degree of freedom of behavioural capacities. Meaningful researches bearing on the question are directed to particular aspects of behaviour in organisms that are biologically defined—from species to precise genotype—and under conditions that are sufficiently well described to be repeatable.

The problems of cross-species comparison and of the relevance of animal data to man are not solved by comparative, descriptive approaches. Let us compare, for example, dogs and wolves. Dogs are easily socialized to human handling if this occurs during the appropriate period in their development (Scott, 1962). Prior to this period, during earliest postnatal development, the organization of the canine nervous system is not sufficiently advanced to permit experiential input to produce any meaningful results with respect to social behaviour. The end of the period is at approximately 12 weeks of age, as shown by the fact that, in dogs deprived of appropriate social experiences until then, it is much more difficult to establish the desired social behaviour patterns by either standard or compensatory means. Dogs that are permitted to run wild from puppyhood become extremely difficult to socialize as adults. When reared wild in their own social groupings, strong individual bonds are formed, including dominance relationships and mating preferences. However, there is no obvious or systematic relationship between any of these aspects of their social history and the particular dyadic relationships formed (F. A. Beach, personal communication).

In wolves, on the other hand, early socialization to human handling does not produce such lasting results as does delayed socialization, or socialization persisting well into adulthood (Ginsburg, 1968). Evidence from a 10-year study of a captured wolf pack suggests that, within their own social groupings, females form social preferences—which extend to mating—for the male who was dominant during a given female's second season, regardless of his status in the pack later on (Woolpy and Ginsburg, 1967). There are thus some major differences between the effects of early experience on dogs and wolves, let alone between those on dogs and monkeys, or on monkeys and man, and these could not have been predicted from a study of any species alone.

Moreover, there are profound differences between breeds of dogs, such that predictions made on the basis of manipulating the early experience of one breed do not necessarily hold for another (Fisher, 1955; Freedman, 1958). This is true with respect both to learning variables and to emotional aspects of behaviour such as aggressiveness. In the latter instance breed differences have been shown to be profound, and manipulating the early experience of a particular breed and pedigree can produce remarkable results that will not necessarily occur in another genetic sample (Fisher, 1955; Ginsburg, 1966).

McClearn (1967) has emphasized the importance of genetic control in the evaluation of data concerned with behaviour. The use of isogenic stocks where practicable (including human monozygotic twins) provides for such control, but it limits the spectrum of the biological sample being explored. Hirsch (1962) has dealt with the same problem in terms of individual differences, and so has Ginsburg (1966) from the point of view of the population. Such approaches using controlled genetic samples standardize the biology of the subjects but they do not, of themselves, ensure the relevance of the conclusions reached to other genotypes, strains, breeds, races, or species. In comparisons across taxonomic groups, biological affinity and similarity of results are still the prevailing criteria for playing the cross-matching game. In part, this is based on sound biological reasoning, since mammalian nervous systems and endocrine systems have basic similarities, and researches have revealed a parsimony of biochemical and electrophysiological mechanisms. Yet, despite some similarities between deprived children and stimulus-deprived monkeys, what other analogies from the results of experiments with the latter can apply to the former? At the very best, they suggest hypotheses which, to be useful, must be testable.

As one who is working in the field of behavioural genetics, I should like to suggest that the criterion that will ultimately be most useful in comparative behaviour studies is that of homology of mechanism. The elucidation of mechanisms is at once troublesome and seminal. It is the findings of research of that kind that promise understanding and control of behaviour.

In an area that is subject to as many complexities and confusions as behavioural research, it is extremely important to maintain a high degree of precision and control in all aspects of the work, and especially as regards the biological substratum of any investigation. Similar behaviours can arise from a variety of causes, and definitions of behavioural entities are not necessarily isomorphic with the biological organization of the individual. Both biological and environmental control, including a characterization of developmental factors, are necessary for producing meaningful research conclusions. Two illustrations from our laboratory should illustrate what is meant and required here. The first is an instance involving work on convulsive seizures in mice.

A GENETIC APPROACH TO BEHAVIOURAL MECHANISMS EXEMPLIFIED IN THE STUDY OF SEIZURES IN MICE

Convulsive seizure, in mice, is a behavioural entity that is clear and unequivocal. Some genotypes within a mouse population show spontaneous seizures. Others have low thresholds for the induction of seizures by sound and other means. Still others are resistant. Of those that are susceptible to seizures, in the same way and from the same causal agent, there are variations in degree of susceptibility, latency, type of seizure, and age of greatest vulnerability. If we use these differences as the basis for differentiating among various seizure syndromes, we find that there are still other sub-categories not distinguished on the basis of these criteria. Thus, changes in the sources of fat in a presumably normal diet exacerbate the seizures in some individuals and not in others. Lesions in the hippocampal area have similar selective effects (Maxson, 1966). Selection experiments have demonstrated a genetic basis for certain types of seizure proneness (Ginsburg, 1967a). However, in some instances affected individuals do not belong to a genetic phenotype with appreciable convulsive risk: they have become phenocopies as a result of accident or disease. Genetic studies have shown that there are several genetic paths to a seizure-prone phenotype (Ginsburg and Miller, 1963; Ginsburg, 1967a; Ginsburg et al., 1969; Ginsburg, 1958).

By means of genetic analyses, it has been possible to control and distinguish among the genotypes within the seizure-prone phenotypes. In mice these represent essentially two clusters of biological situations. One involves a genetic effect on the nucleoside triphosphatase activity of the granular cell layer within the dentate fascia of the hippocampus (Cowen, 1966). The level of activity in this area is controlled by an identifiable series of alleles in which the heterozygote is intermediate. The relationship between this metabolic anomaly and the actual phenotypic expression of convulsive seizures is dependent on the genetic background. Each allelic combination is linearly expressed as an actuarial probability of seizure risk on one genetic background in which it has been tested, but not in another, where the presence of a second genetic defect is necessary for the expression of the first (Ginsburg and Miller, 1963). The second series of alleles involves an aspect of glutamic acid metabolism (most probably glutamic acid decarboxylase), which also contributes towards seizure susceptibility. This second anomaly is genetically and functionally independent of the nucleoside triphosphatase aberration. A third genetic situation under active investigation is associated with an intermediate level nucleoside triphosphatase activity in the granular cell layer in question, and with a morphological increase in the number of cells in that layer. Preliminary results suggest that the time at which the nucleoside triphosphatase activity reaches its maximum is controlled by a separate series of genes, possibly associated with the brown pigment locus through linkage, and that these timing genes determine whether the activity level made possible by the previously mentioned aspect of the genotype will be reached by the third week postpartum, or deferred up to about 45 days after birth. Similar timing effects of independent genes occur with respect to the glutamic acid decarboxylase activity. These latter are closely associated with the period of onset of susceptibility to seizures (Ginsburg et al., 1969).

I have chosen seizures as an example of the use of biological control in the study of mechanisms because many of the complexities that attach to studies of other behaviours are avoided here. Furthermore, as explained later on, the mechanisms underlying this behaviour are very likely to be involved in aspects of learning and memory. As seizures can occur spontaneously in mice and men the question of whether seizure is a naturally occurring entity is avoided. The effects are severe and have well known physiological concomitants. They can be induced in normal animals by a variety of means, thus permitting further study of both the behaviour and the mechanisms which underlie it. Even so, biological control and analysis is absolutely essential for an understanding of what is wrong with a high-convulsive risk organism, how it differs from the normal, and how the convulsions can be best controlled. The characteristic itself defies simple genetic analysis as an entity because several different genetic aberrations each produce the same behavioural end result. Earlier studies, which came to the conclusion that seizures in mice had an inherited basis, and that this was polygenic and complex, were a natural reflection of this situation. Screening experiments, involving attempts to affect the seizures by chemical means, demonstrated that when the syndrome was dissected genetically, some agents could be found that were highly protective for some genotypes, and others for other genotypes. With the newer knowledge of the mechanisms involved, these diverse effects on what appears to be a single behavioural entity become easier to interpret. Convulsive seizures seem to constitute a clear and well defined syndrome. Even so, they depend on a number of different underlying biological situations, some of which are amenable to control by different chemical agents which may not have similar effects; some of which have one genetic basis, while others are due to quite different genetic abnormalities; and still others of which are phenocopies, depending on accidents of development, injury, or disease. How much more difficult it will be, therefore, to deal in a similar manner with the underlying causes of less well defined entities such as schizophrenia or intelligence (Ginsburg, 1954). The intellectual and scientific problems are no different in kind or in magnitude, but rather in accessibility and amenability of the materials for appropriate investigation.

The identification of some of the mechanisms discussed involves another refinement of methodology. The initial approaches to genetic control relied upon the use of inbred strains, each representing a series of individuals of virtually identical genotype and differing genetically from other strains. However, strains differ from one another by many genes, and genes that happen to be associated together in a given strain will, of course, produce correlated effects, especially if they happen to be on the same chromosome. If tail length and seizures are correlated for such fortuitous reasons, there is probably not much danger that such a relationship might become the focus of irrelevant research. If, however, such correlations should occur with respect to important metabolic systems, or to neural transmitters, they become the basis for hypotheses that have only an accidental chance of being correct. For this reason many of the studies in our laboratory depend on the identification of particular genes which affect the behaviour in question, each of which is studied as a component of an allelic series or in combination with other known genes on one or more identifiable and constant genetic backgrounds. In this way the biological variability is reduced to a minimum, and correlations with known genetic differences have direct causal implications. Such correlations as have been reported in the literature have involved the oxidative phosphorylating mechanisms, the biogenic amines, the acetylcholine system, carbonic anhydrase, GABA, and many others (Abood and Gerard, 1955; Schlesinger *et al.*, 1965; Roberts, 1967). The particular controlled genetic situations under study in our laboratory have revealed two groups of genetic anomalies that are causally associated with seizures. These do not preclude the possibility that there are also others. Genetic researches have also demonstrated that some previously reported correlations between convulsive seizures and other factors were based on the fortuitous association of genes separately determining each, in at least one instance through linkage (Cowen, 1966; Ginsburg, 1967a).

The question of the relevance of animal to human studies can now be re-evaluated in the light of these and similar researches involving behavioural entities that correspond to each other in humans and other animals. This relevance depends upon the homology, or even identity, of mechanisms in such instances. Mouse seizures associated with deviations in glutamic acid decarboxylase activity are ameliorated by the administration of monosodium glutamate. Those due to the hippocampal defects described, are not. Thus, a simple screening technique differentiates one mechanism from others. Assuming parallelism of mechanism between mouse and man in this respect, such screening procedures could have direct carry-over in diagnosis. Once a number of biological deviations from normal, associated with a given behavioural entity, have been identified in other animals, it becomes possible to determine whether or not these same mechanisms obtain in clinical cases.

The relevance of the example I have been using for other behavioural entities depends not only on the methodological considerations that have been discussed; it has much broader interests, and implications that are substantive as well as methodological. The hippocampus has been associated with short-term memory. Seizures are known to produce characteristic amnesias. The identification of gene-controlled mechanisms involving (a) a particular area of the hippocampus, (b) a range of metabolic and morphological anomalies in that area of the brain, and (c) genetic differences in the timing of the development of these enzymatic capacities, has implications not only for convulsive behaviour but also for those aspects of memory and learning that have been identified with hippocampal function and that are affected by seizures.

The findings related to genetic anomalies which affect glutamic acid metabolism and seizures have similar broad implications. The identifiable genes involved affect the level of glutamic acid decarboxylase activity, as well as the time course of development of this activity in early postnatal life (Ginsburg et al., 1969). Since the result of this metabolic activity is the production of GABA, an inhibitory neural transmitter, the implications for other forms of behaviour are manifold (Roberts, 1967). Two sets of experiments (Ginsburg and Ross, in preparation; Hughes and Zubek, 1956, 1957; Hughes et al., 1957) have demonstrated that in both rats and mice some types of maze learning are improved by the administration of monosodium glutamate—but only in particular genotypes. In mice these are the same genotypes whose seizure risk is diminished by the administration of this substrate. Other seizure-prone genotypes not affected by glutamic acid do not improve in the maze learning situation when on this substrate. It is possible that the effects on seizures and the effects on learning may be mediated through overlapping mechanisms acting in different parts of the brain. It must be pointed out that the so-called learning effects in question here may not depend on what might usually be thought of as an augmentation of mental function, since the behaviour in the case of the treated mice is characterized by less aimless running, jumping, squeaking, and other erratic manifestations. There could, therefore, be a rather different interpretation of the effect of glutamic acid. The treated animals are not in any way lethargic, nor do they show reduced activity in an open field.

The methodology of identifying a naturally occurring behavioural entity, and bringing it under precise biological control, amounting to one-gene differences between control and experimental groups has, as pointed out, resulted in the identification of several neural mechanisms associated with the behaviour in question. Because of the nature of these mechanisms, implications for other behaviours are clear, and these implications are bolstered by actual experimental results as indicated. What is of primary interest here is the fact that genetic variation extends not only to the level of a given metabolic activity in a portion of the hippocampus, or to the capacity of the whole brain to manufacture a given neural transmitter, but also to the timing of these effects in early postnatal development.

This suggests that there are central mechanisms which cannot be activated before these developmental events have occurred, and that a population of a given species is genetically variable with respect to the timing of the rate of maturation of these mechanisms. Several aspects of the genetic effects on the development of glutamic acid decarboxylase activity are noteworthy (Fig. 1). In the first place, the strain

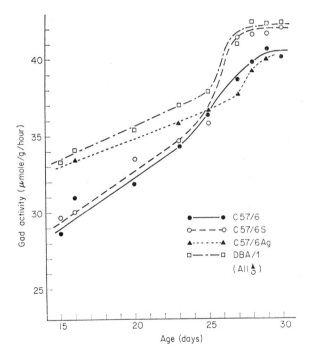

FIG. 1. Mutant genes affecting the development of glutamic acid decarboxylase activity.

differences indicated in the parallel curves appear to represent normative levels at any given developmental period. The mutants are not intermediate, but follow one curve for a given period of development and then follow another. As may be seen from the data, the switch-over can go either way. A second important point is that, when a change from one level to another occurs, it happens abruptly, within a period of less than 2 days during the developmental history of the animals. The relationship between these changes and convulsive risk is that the onset of seizure susceptibility in the mutants occurs in association with the time of rapid change of enzyme activity (and therefore presumably of other behavioural characteristics as well). It may also be seen that, in addition to the direction of the effect, the time at which it is produced is characteristically different for each mutant. Screening experiments are now in progress to identify other mutants affecting this same system, and to determine whether intermediate levels are possible and what the range of timing effects might be in a mouse population. Another line of investigation is being pursued to discover whether the time at which rapid increase in enzyme activity normally occurs in a given genotype can be altered by experiential input. It may be that some genotypes are more labile than others in this respect, if such flexibility is indeed possible. These investigations must, therefore, be carried out on the basis of controlled genetic substitutions on a variety of inbred strain backgrounds, since the lability of the reaction may be affected not only by the gene in question but by the interaction between it and the total genome.

GENOTYPIC VARIABLES AFFECTING RESPONSES TO POSTNATAL STIMULATION IN MICE

The foregoing constitutes one illustration of a genetic approach to behavioural mechanisms that may occur on a cross-species basis and which include differences among members of a given population with respect to postnatal and preweaning events associated with behaviour. The second illustration has not been as well worked out as far as mechanisms are concerned, but it is perhaps of greater interest because it concerns genotype-environment interactions in relation to early experience variables, and especially to so-called "early handling" effects.

A detailed account of the findings in our laboratory in relation to genetic variability with respect to so-called "early handling" effects has been provided elsewhere (Ginsburg, 1966, 1967a, 1967b). The salient points for purposes of this presentation are as follows.

The effects of early handling on later development and behaviour in mice are strain-specific. Some inbred strains do not differ significantly as between experimentals and controls on a variety of early handling paradigms as measured by later behavioural outcomes. Others vary in their lability, depending upon the type of early manipulation used, the time in the postnatal development of the animal when it occurs, and the kind of behavioural outcomes that are measured later—and how much later. When the handling procedures are the same (for example, removal to a small container for a specified period followed by replacement in the nest) and the behavioural outcomes are measured at a time and in a way designed to reveal the greatest possible effect, the sensitive periods during which the greatest effects may be achieved are also functions of strain, and therefore of genotype. In some strains, cumulative experience during the entire preweaning period produces a maximal effect. In others, the major effects occur early in postnatal life; and in still others, they are most effectively produced during the second half of the preweaning period. The magnitude and direction of the effect is also strain-specific. A handling paradigm that will increase the later aggressiveness of male mice in one strain, will significantly decrease it in another. The central tendency of a genetically mixed population must therefore be viewed as an expression of the statistically prevailing genetic potential. Individuals drawn from such a population would be expected to vary in all the respects mentioned.

In one experiment (Ginsburg, 1967a) continued manipulation of C57BL/10 male mice enhanced their aggressiveness over the nonhandled controls. This same strain can be made more or less aggressive during the preweaning period, depending on whether it is raised by a mouse or by a rat mother (Denenberg et al., 1964). The interpretation given to these latter results is not a nutritional one, but rather depends on the amount of stimulation the individual pup receives because of differences in the retrieving behaviour as between rat and mouse mothers. Variations in the time and mode of handling produce different results with respect to later aggressive behaviour in the same strain (Jumonville, 1968).

In the search for mechanisms through which these effects are mediated there has been a concentration on adrenal steroid responses. Hamburg (1967) has summarized the known mechanisms relating to these responses, indicating the points at which genetic variability is theoretically probable, as well as those at which it is known to occur. Levine and Treiman (1964) have demonstrated that there are in fact strain differences which affect the timing, magnitude, and duration of these responses; they have also compared strains of laboratory mice with wild mice in this respect. Early stimulation may activate the pituitary-adrenal axis sooner than would otherwise occur, and thereby produce changes in neural organization which in turn affects later behaviour. Our evidence indicates that there is a supplemental problem, since the genotype can determine when these sensitive periods occur. The most obvious hypothesis is that central mechanisms mediating between the external stimulation and the hypothalamic-pituitary-adrenal axis probably mature at different rates in different genotypes, and that this is one limiting factor which affects the time parameter during which early stress or other stimulation can become effective. The particular central mechanisms that we have studied and that have been shown to be under the influence of genes so far as their rate of development is concerned, can be correlated with variations in sensitive periods occurring beyond the second week of postpartum life in the mouse. Since some differences (for example, glutamic acid decarboxylase activity levels) manifest themselves much earlier, these same mechanisms could play a role then.

While it is tempting to speculate that mechanisms shown to be genetically variable on the appropriate time scale might be those involved in setting thresholds that must be reached before mediation between external events and activation of the steroid responses can occur, there are other transmitter systems—not yet well studied in this regard—that may be equally important. Further researches are obviously necessary to explore the relevance of the mechanisms that can be biologically controlled in connection with this problem, as well as to investigate other possibilities such as the role of the development of the catechol and indole amines. One must also learn when, in these same genotypes, the steroid responses can first be elicited; how their characteristics change during early development; what the relationship is between these developmental data and the behavioural results obtained from early stimulation experiments; when the specialized secretory cells in the median eminence of the hypothalamus become capable of synthesizing and releasing the factors that stimulate the pituitary; whether this is genotypically variable; whether, if it is, different genotypes are differentially labile with respect to the ability of early stimulation to accelerate some of these processes; and how, in turn, this relates to the time of maturation of the particular processes that can be displaced by genetic substitution. So far as the latter are concerned, attempts are being made not only to identify these in whole brain and in particular gross structures, but also at the ultra-structure level and at particular sites. From a theoretical point of view we know where some of the interesting sites are. However, the techniques for doing detailed biochemical *cum* ultra-structure studies need further refinement for application to such problems.

I will now summarize some of the data dealing with the timing of early handling effects in various strains of mice. DBA/1 males were most profoundly affected if handled daily during the duration of the entire preweaning period, in respect of both latency to fighting and the percentage of fights initiated after sexual maturity. Latency to fighting decreased significantly as a result of this procedure (involving the removal of the mouse to a small dish for 2 minutes once daily). In the related DBA/2 strain similar results were produced, with the greatest effect occurring as a result of handling during the last 2 weeks before weaning. In C57BL/6 mice the sensitive period was similar to that in DBA/2, but the direction of the effect was opposite, that is, latency to fighting was markedly increased. Similar results obtain for C57BL/10 mice; however, the sensitive period for greatest effect was in the first 2 weeks following birth. Jumonville (1968) has extended these results to other handling paradigms, testing schedules, and behavioural measures, and has been able to determine which interactions in relation to which behaviours are most effective for the strains under study.

It is not the object of this paper to fully summarize these extensive and detailed data, which provide yet more illustrations of genotypic differences in response to various types of early stimulation. These strain-difference studies are now being augmented by more controlled studies using single-gene mutations on inbred strain backgrounds. Mutations affecting the processes so far identified in our laboratory are under investigation in the hope that these may provide an explanation for some of the phenomena mentioned. Another extremely important question has to do not simply with genetic variability in the timing of the sensitive period, nor with the threshold of sensitivity that may be correlated with the magnitude of the later effect, but rather with the underlying reasons determining the differences in the direction of the effect. Why, for example, should the same type of early stimulation during the most sensitive period in the preweaning history of one genotype produce a *less* aggressive male after sexual maturity, whereas in another genotype a *more* aggressive animal will be produced as a result of the same experience, and in still another, no differences at all will occur between experimentals and controls? If the central mechanisms determine the time at which external stimulation can become effective via neuroendocrine variables, and if these variables actually organize the neural circuitry with respect to later capacity for behaviour, then the detailed characteristics of the steroid responses become extremely important. It is possible that quantitative differences in steroid levels, or slight differences in timing that interact with the neural circuitry at slightly different developmental stages, could account for the qualitative differences in behaviour. There is also the possibility that the target tissues have some interacting property; these include the possibly genetically mediated selectivity of portions of the brain as receptor sites for steroid hormones.

Both the behavioural and neurophysiological complexities of the situation are such that I believe it is absolutely essential to use controlled biological materials in order to reduce the problem to an analysable basis. In the further elucidation and resolution of these problems I foresee a continuing convergence and mutuality between studies of the psychology of early experience, neurophysiology, neuroendocrinology, neurochemistry, ultra-structure studies, and genetics. It is in these biological areas that I look for the key to the riddle of the black box.

REFERENCES

ABOOD, L. G. and GERARD, R. W. 1955. Metabolic lesions and enzymatic inhibitors. A phosphorylation defect in the brains of mice susceptible to audiogenic seizure. In H. Waelsch (Ed.), *Biochemistry and the developing nervous system. Proceedings of the 1st international symposium, held at Magdalan College, Oxford; July 13–17, 1954.* Academic Press, New York. Pp. 467–472.

COWEN, J. S. 1966. A metabolic hippocampal anomaly associated with audiogenic seizures. Unpublished Ph.D. thesis, Dept. of Psychology, University of Chicago.

DENENBERG, V. H., HUDGENS, G. A., and ZARROW, M. X. 1964. Mice reared with rats: modification of behavior by early experience with another species. *Science, N.Y.* **143**, 380–381.

FISHER, A. E. 1955. The effects of differential early treatment on the social and exploratory behavior of puppies. Unpublished Ph.D. thesis, Dept. of Psychology, Pennsylvania State University.

FREEDMAN, D. G. 1958. Constitutional and environmental interactions in rearing of four breeds of dogs. *Science, N.Y.* **127**, 585–586.

GINSBURG, B. E. 1949. Genetics and social behavior: a theoretical synthesis. *Lectures on genetics, cancer, growth and social behavior.* Roscoe B. Jackson Memorial Laboratory Twentieth Anniversary Commemoration Lectures. Bar Harbor, Maine. Pp. 101–124.

GINSBURG, B. E. 1954. Genetics and the physiology of the nervous system. In D. Hooker and C. C. Hare (Eds.), Genetics and the inheritance of integrated neurological and psychiatric patterns. *Proc. Ass. Res. nerv. ment. Dis.* **33**, 39–54. Williams & Wilkins, Baltimore.

GINSBURG, B. E. 1958. Genetics as a tool in the study of behavior. In D. J. Ingle and S. O. Waife (Eds.), *Perspectives in Biology and Medicine.* Vol. 1. University of Chicago Press. Pp. 397–424.

GINSBURG, B. E. 1963. Causal mechanisms in audiogenic seizures. *Colloques internationaux du C.N.R.S.* **112**, 227–240.

GINSBURG, B. E. 1966. All mice are not created equal—recent findings on genes and behavior. *Soc. Serv. Rev.* **40,** 121–134.

GINSBURG, B. E. 1967a. Genetic parameters in behavioral research. In J. Hirsch (Ed.), *Behaviour-genetic analysis.* McGraw-Hill, New York. Pp. 135–153.

GINSBURG, B. E. 1967b. Social behavior and social hierarchy in the formation of personality profiles in animals. In J. Zubin and H. F. Hunt (Eds.), *Comparative psychopathology, animal and human.* Grune & Stratton, New York and London.

GINSBURG, B. E. 1968. Breeding structure and social behavior of mammals: a servo-mechanism for the avoidance of panmixia. In D. C. Glass (Ed.), *Genetics.* Rockefeller University Press and Russell Sage Foundation, New York. Pp. 117–128.

GINSBURG, B. E. and MILLER, D. S. 1963. Genetic factors in audiogenic seizures. *Colloques internationaux du C.N.R.S.* **112,** 217–225.

GINSBURG, B. E., COWEN, J. S., MAXSON, S. C., and SZE, P. Y. L. 1969. Neuro-chemical effects of gene imitations associated with audiogenic seizures. *Proc. 2nd Int. Cong. Neuro-genetics and Neuro-opthalmology.*

HAMBURG, D. A. 1967. Genetics of adrenocortical hormone metabolism in relation to psychological stress. In J. Hirsch (Ed.), *Behavior-genetic analysis.* McGraw-Hill, New York. Pp. 154–175.

HIRSCH, J. 1962. Individual differences in behavior and their genetic basis. In E. L. Bliss (Ed.), *Roots of behavior: genetics, instinct, and socialization in animal behavior.* Hoeber, New York. Pp. 3–23.

HUGHES, K. R. and ZUBEK, J. P. 1956. Effect of glutamic acid on the learning ability of bright and dull rats. 1. Administration during infancy. *Can. J. Psychol.* **10,** 132–138.

HUGHES, K. R. and ZUBEK, J. P. 1957. Effect of glutamic acid on the learning ability of bright and dull rats. 3. Effect of varying dosages. *Can. J. Psychol.* **11,** 253–255.

HUGHES, K. R., COOPER, R. M., and ZUBEK, J. P. 1957. Effect of glutamic acid on the learning ability of bright and dull rats. 2. Duration of the effect. *Can. J. Psychol.* **11,** 182–184.

JUMONVILLE, J. E. 1968. Influence of genotype-treatment interactions in studies of "emotionality" in mice. Unpublished Ph.D. thesis, Dept. of Psychology, University of Chicago.

LEHRMAN, D. S. 1953. A critique of Konrad Lorenz's theory of instinctive behaviour. *Q. Rev. Biol.* **28,** 337–363.

LEVINE, S. and TREIMAN, D. M. 1964. Differential plasma and corticosterone response to stress in four inbred strains of mice. *Endocrinology* **75,** 142–144.

LORENZ, K. 1965. *Evolution and modification of behavior.* University of Chicago Press, Chicago and London.

MAXSON, S. C. 1966. The effect of genotype on brain mechanisms involved in audiogenic seizure susceptibility. Unpublished Ph.D. thesis, Dept. of Psychology, University of Chicago.

McCLEARN, G. E. 1967. Genes, generality and behavioural research. In J. Hirsch (Ed.) *Behavior-genetic analysis.* McGraw-Hill, New York. Pp. 307–321.

ROBERTS, E. 1967. Synaptic neurochemistry: a projection. In J. Hirsch (Ed.) *Behavior-genetic analysis.* McGraw-Hill, New York. Pp. 194–210.

SCHLESINGER, K., BOGGAN, W., and FREEDMAN, D. X. 1965. Genetics of audiogenic seizures. *Life Sci.* **4,** 2345–2351.

SCOTT, J. P. 1962. Critical periods in behavioural development. *Science, N.Y.* **138,** 949–958.
WOOLPY, J. H. and GINSBURG, B. E. 1967. Wolf socialization: a study of temperament in a wild social species. *Am. Zool.* **7,** 357–363.

Discussion

Genetic and Timing Influences on the Directional Effects of Handling on Aggression

LEVINE: The notion of differential timing of sensitive periods for early experience could conceivably be related to differential timing of the appearance of the underlying systems. But the question of different genotypes going in different directions is extremely puzzling.

GINSBURG: There is so far nothing about the levels of adrenal response, as reflected by plasma steroid levels, that would account for the difference in direction.

HAMBURG: Can you say what is different in direction?

GINSBURG: The most clear-cut data have to do with aggression experiments (B. E. Ginsburg. 1967a. In J. Hirsch (Ed.), *Behaviour-Genetic Analysis*. McGraw-Hill, New York). In some of the strains, early handling, during the most effective sensitive period as defined empirically for that genotype, will produce a much decreased latency to aggression and an increased number of fights initiated by handled males as compared with nonhandled controls. In an analogous situation using another genotype, the same handling paradigm, during the sensitive period for that genotype, produces the opposite effect. In still other genotypes handling has no effect on later aggression.

LEVINE: In the two genotypes where there is a difference in the direction, is the sensitive period different?

GINSBURG: The sensitive period is the same.

KAGAN: This perplexity concerning the opposite effects on aggression might be resolved if we consider two links: one is between the external intrusion of handling and biochemistry; the other is between biochemistry and behaviour. It is possible that the same biochemical effects occur internally, but whereas genotype A reacts with minimal aggression to a given increase in ACTH, genotype B reacts with intense aggression.

GINSBURG: I don't have enough evidence about that sort of possibility. There are instances where a genetically male organism produces male hormone which is interpreted by all the tissues in the body as female hormone. The genetic male then differentiates into a morphologic female. This also occurs in the Sebright bantam with respect to plumage.

DENENBERG: At what age do you wean your animals?

GINSBURG: In these experiments we weaned them at 28 days.

DENENBERG: I wean my rats at 21 days. The black mouse is also weaned at 21 days and, when raised with the rat mother, it is a very pacific animal. The white mouse is a very aggressive animal, in fact we cannot reduce aggression in this animal, though we seem to increase its latency. I am just wondering whether, if I kept the animal for an additional week with the rat mother, this might completely reverse the effects. It may well be that the time when a particular system or sub-system comes in makes quite a lot of difference.

GINSBURG: We haven't done the experiment, but it would be interesting to do. Joanne Jumonville (1968) finds differences both from my results and from yours, according to whether she uses 2- or 3-minute handling periods and according to when, in the phase of post-sexual maturity, she tests for aggression.

BATESON: In your theoretical approach do you suppose that the effects of handling are selective rather than informative? The analogy would be with the hypothesis about antibody formation: that the foreign protein selects the right mechanism from a pool of protein-synthesis mechanisms rather than actually informing the system about which one should be synthesized.

GINSBURG: We thought about that and had some hope that it would be informative rather than selective. Our phenocopy experiments suggest that this may be so. If I interpret the Levine and Denenberg experiments correctly, they may also have circumstantial evidence to that effect.

LEVINE: Discussing aggressive behaviour reminds me of an early experiment of mine (S. Levine. 1959. *J. genet. Psychol.*, **94**, 77) on emotionality and aggressive behaviour in the mouse as a function of infantile experience. The interpretation of the results had very little to do with aggressive behaviour. Instead it had to do with the process of exploration. In order to initiate aggressive behaviour we had to ensure that the organism engaged in exploration. To what extent are you dealing with exploratory behaviour?

GINSBURG: We have activity measures in the open field. In the particular tests we used, aggression was something involving specific behaviours.

DENENBERG: We have also been doing this. The mouse reared by the rat is less active in the open field and it does not fight. But I'm not sure what the links are between these two sets of observations. If you place this mouse with another mouse that has been reared by a mouse mother, this mouse-reared mother will attack the other animal. Then, although the first response of the rat-reared mouse is to run away, it will eventually turn around and fight.

Inbred Strains as a Biological Freak

LEVINE: You have pointed out to me very often that when you study inbred strains of mice you are really dealing with a biological freak. If one examined a random population of outbred animals, would one expect to see a distribution of the different effects, some positive and some negative, across the random population?

GINSBURG: I would expect that, in the statistical tests for a random population, these differences would be homogenized: there would be a central tendency. I would also expect that, with a random-bred population, if one attempted to set up selection experiments to identify individuals that were aberrant with respect to the normative distribution by selectively breeding from these for differences in sensitive period and differences in response, the result would be the same as with different inbred strains. We are testing this assumption. If there are particular genes that make unequal contributions to a behavioural parameter, the key consideration is how they are distributed in a population. The central tendency of the population will be determined by the distribution of the relevant genes in that population.

HAMBURG: What we need to clarify this problem is further analysis of the underlying mechanisms. It is possible to construct models of the underlying biochemical processes that could account for such differences in response to stimulation. But the necessary experiments have not yet been done.

GINSBURG: One thing in favour of the choice of the C57BL/10 mouse as a genetic model is that it is the most labile strain we have, and as such provides an excellent detector for the effects of environmental influences. It is, at the same time, highly atypical because it is so sensitive. Grüneberg (1947. *Animal Genetics and Medicine.* Hoeber, New York) describes it as poised on a series of thresholds such that slight changes during development produce morphological variability, even though, as demonstrated by selection experiments, the genetic background remains constant. We have found (B. E. Ginsburg. 1967a. In J. Hirsch.) it to be equally labile with respect to behaviour, and we have confirmed the genetic constancy by means of selection experiments. The C 57 BL/10 mouse is a convenient but atypical research tool.

Phenotypic Buffering Systems

LEVINE: In this study group we have often used phrases which are related to evolution, adaptiveness, and so on. Presumably one of the buffering systems in terms of evolution is that of heterozygosity: it is presumably the heterozygotic animal that has been more adaptive, more vigorous.

GINSBURG: That's not necessarily true (B. E. Ginsburg. 1968. In D. C. Glass (Ed.), *Genetics*. Rockefeller University Press and Russell Sage Foundation). For example, Denenberg's C57 black strain of mice reared on mouse mothers are aggressive; mice of the same strain fostered on rat mothers are pacific.

LEVINE: There is another buffering system which I can illustrate. I take two inbred strains of mice which have different temporal patterns of steroids. I do the appropriate reciprocal crosses: the B by C and the C by B, where there is the C mother, and the B father and vice versa. The result, as shown in Fig. 2, is that the animals, which are genetically identical, show a pattern which is related to the gene-pattern of the mother. In fact, we have complex series of experiments which indicate that the buffering system is a maternal one.

GINSBURG: Most populations are buffered, and their latent genetic variability is assimilated to a common phenotypic norm by means of two mechanisms. One is that the homozygous freaks, of the kinds that are produced by continued intense inbreeding in the laboratory, don't occur very often in nature. Therefore genes that could have extreme effects are distributed in all sorts of combinations. They are just potentials in the population and the population as a whole is selected to a normative phenotype. Should the systems of mating and the forces of selection change, the population does have these other genetic potentials which can move it to different normative phenotypes. The second buffering mechanism is related to a host of applied environmental situations, including the effect of the mother and the effect of the grandmother. In a population that is at a particular adaptive norm, these environmental factors tend to pull the expression of the behaviour towards the mean. On this view, the genetic and the environmental factors reinforce each other in buffering the phenotypic variability of the population. The genetic freaks we use as biological models must be either specially produced, or harvested as natural rarities. The same considerations apply to environmentally induced variations. Both must break through the normal buffer, and both furnish valuable biological models for study purposes.

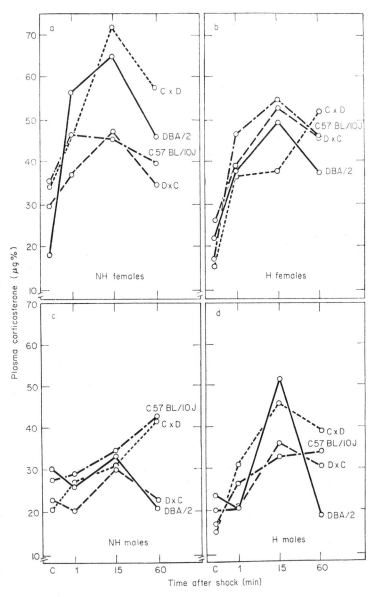

FIG. 2. Temporal patterns of steroids following electric shock in genetically identical mice related to the genepattern of the genetically differing mothers.

Genic Determination of Hormonal Effects on Behaviour

KAGAN: Can you say more about GABA and what it is supposed to do?

GINSBURG: GABA is the result of the decarboxylation of glutamic acid, a reaction which is catalyzed by the enzyme (glutamic acid decarboxylase) whose activity levels during preweaning development are regulated by one of the series of mutants I described. GABA is also used in energy metabolism as a shunt to the tri-carboxylic acid cycle. We are doing a study to see whether it is the energy metabolism or the neural inhibition that is involved in the phenomena we are studying. We're also doing regional studies of this system in the mouse brain, so that we shall have some idea whether there are particular sites that are more affected than others in particular genotypes. We presume that, at some synaptic sites, GABA selectively inhibits transmission from one cell to the next.

KAGAN: I would like to speculate that, in the first year of life, there is an interesting set of reflexes each of which is gradually inhibited, but at different ages in different children. Do you think that GABA might mediate these differences?

GINSBURG: Yes.

HAMBURG: Following on Kagan's very nice suggestion about the types of human study that might be stimulated by this animal work, I would like to comment briefly on another kind of human study that is stimulated by the steroid approach. It is very difficult as yet to study how the development of certain infant behaviours could be influenced by a particular genetic situation. There are now, however, one or two situations that are interesting to look at developmentally in infants which have scarcely been studied at all. There are some single-gene defects that have been reasonably well shown to hinder the biosynthesis of two hormones. One is cortisol, which is fundamentally the same hormone that Kagan and Denenberg were discussing. The other is thyroxine. Now it is possible to identify the children who have a single-gene defect that impairs the ability of synthesizing the hormone: there are certain biochemical and clinical correlates, and, to a limited extent, behaviour correlates also. The clearest case is in that subgroup of cretins who are cretins because of a genetically determined thyroid hormonal deficiency. This case is very interesting because there is obviously a major behaviour defect caused by a hormone deficiency which, in turn, is caused by a single-gene defect. The study of those situations is complicated, however, by the fact that they are grossly ill or defective in some way and the disability affects the way in which the parents handle the infant.

There is also the question of the siblings: some of these are going to be heterozygous for the gene involved in the defect of thyroxine or cortisol. In the thyroxine case, there is already some evidence that one can identify the heterozygote in at least one of the four well established defects. Very little work has been done in attempting to identify heterozygotes in the cortisol defect situation. But the time has come when it would be worthwhile to study the development of behaviour in such situations in relation to what might be called behaviour-relevant hormones. Even dependable negative results would be of biological interest.

GINSBURG: One of the things we'll all have to do is to look at many different mechanisms. The hypothesis has been advanced that there are correlations between particular steroid hormones and some aspects of behaviour. These may also be correlated with neural transmitter activity, and both may be correlated with genotypes that can be manipulated and investigated. These, however, are not necessarily the only pathways that are important for the behaviour, and I think the approach that you have suggested is absolutely necessary in order to fill in the total picture. I'm sure there is much more to the handling effect and to the ontogeny of the behaviours that we have been discussing than the particular systems that we have so far investigated.

HAMBURG: Although the diseases where you have the homozygous conditions are rare, the gene frequencies are fairly high. For example, one of the abnormal genes affecting cortisol synthesis is present in about one American in every hundred.

GINSBURG: The gene frequency and distribution studies are extremely important. They represent individual differences and are the source of future variability.

Applying the Infantile Stimulation Model to Research on Human Infants

GENERAL DISCUSSION

The Human Neonate as a Subject for Research on Early Stimulation Effects

HAMBURG: I hesitate to think of the first week of life in the human neonate as being closely comparable to the first week in the rat when you (Levine and Denenberg) do your handling experiments. The first week of life is certainly a much smaller proportion in the life span of the human than in that of the rat.

BATESON: I too feel a little uncomfortable about erecting a great theoretical edifice on the handling data when one doesn't really know how the handling affects the animals. One has some hypothesis about it but doesn't really know the form of the causal nexus. One knows the final points but not *how* they are connected to treatments in infancy. Until more is known about this, generalizations from the animal data may be wildly misleading.

BRUNER: The animal infantile stimulation model has to do with taking the young organism up to the verge of stress so that it can learn to deal with the surge of affect, fear, or whatever you want to call it. This seems to be a very different kind of process from what we do in our laboratory when we provide stimulation that gives a child an opportunity to shift its eyes from one fixation point to the other, or to grab hold of something and pull down on either side of the mid-line. Here the child is building up expectancies as to what things would be worthwhile in the environment. These two kinds of stimulation effect do not seem linked, although they may be related in some way.

SCHAFFER: Does the provision of unpatterned physical stimulation, which Denenberg described as the earliest of two kinds of maternal social function, essentially have arousal effects?

DENENBERG: Yes, I view this as arousal. In the human I would guess that, for the first month of life, the role of the mother is primarily that of being an arouser. With regard to this it would be interesting to know when the smiling response to the face comes, because I think of this response as an indicator of cognition. Let me explain what I mean. In the rat, as far as we know, until weaning there is no evidence of long-term memory or retention. There is an important paper by Campbell and Campbell (1962. *J. comp. physiol. Psychol.*, **55**, 1) which shows there is no evidence of retention of a learned fear response in the rat until 18 to 23 days of age. That is part of my argument that what we are not doing by our form of stimulation in very early life is having any direct effect upon cortical levels involving memory functions. I suggest that there is a similar situation in the human and that, from the first week to the first month of life, the baby does not have a sufficiently mature neurological system to retain information. I have interpreted the smiling response as an indication that the baby "recognizes" its mother, at least in a crude fashion.

AMBROSE: Smiling to the face doesn't usually start before 4 weeks of age. Before that age the infant's visual perceptual capacities have not developed sufficiently for the necessary eliciting stimulus within the face, namely the eyes, to be effective. Nevertheless, there is now a lot of research which clearly demonstrates that learning begins to occur as early as the newborn stage. For example, Lipsitt and I showed that you can even get temporal conditioning in the newborn (L. P. Lipsitt and J. A. Ambrose. 1967. Unpublished paper presented at Society for Research in Child Development). In this sense we could regard cognitive functioning as beginning with the newborn.

LEVINE: Yes, and the issue with which we are concerned is whether this very early conditioning shows any long-term retention.

PRECHTL: It is very important to emphasize that human newborns are capable of doing much more than we traditionally thought they could do. I am impressed by the great repertoire of newborns, but you must give them the chance to show it. If you put a newborn baby in a supine position in its cot and cover it with a blanket up to its neck, of course it gives the impression of being a kind of vegetable which just cries and sucks from time to time and that's all. But if, for example, you watch a baby on the skin of its mother, without clothes but at a warm temperature, it shows a lot of things: rooting, crawling, grasping, and numerous anti-gravity postural responses.

BRUNER: I would emphasize the same thing on the perceptual side. In the past, many of the studies done on the perceptual capacity of infants have employed static stimuli. But the most compelling stimulus for a very young infant is a moving one. Through using cinematography and methods of moving parallax-producing real objects, we have begun to realize what a fantastic response capacity they have in the perceptual system. For example, we find that 4-week-old infants will suck in order to bring a moving picture into focus.

AINSWORTH: There is no doubt that one can bring about changes in the behaviour of very young infants by varying their sensory inputs. For example, Louis Sander (1966. *Psychosom. Med.*, **28,** 822) has done this in connection with rhythms of activities. He took babies that had been put up for adoption or fostering and, by monitoring their behaviour continuously over 24-hour periods, he found differences between those that were kept in the hospital nursery and those that were kept under rooming-in conditions. The whole periodicity of activity level and crying in the two groups was different owing to the factor of the interventions provided by the foster mother allowed by rooming-in. The trouble is that one cannot possibly answer how long-term this effect is, because one can never test that independently of what happens afterwards. Also, the kind of extra stimulation that the rooming-in babies receive is not the same thing as that provided in the animal experiments of Levine and Denenberg, such as handling, electric shock, or cold.

LEVINE: But the fact remains that the newborn is in many ways very different from the older infant in terms of its neurological activity. These differences are reflected by such various factors as patterns of REM sleep, thermo-regulatory mechanisms, patterns of ACTH regulation and the metabolism of steroids.

PRECHTL: The things you have mentioned all undergo rapid changes in the first few days after birth. At about the third day, however, a stabilization of blood pressure, respiration, heart rate and also of numerous biochemical measures is reached: this is called "postnatal adaptation". From then onwards, the behavioural equipment of the newborn is highly adaptive to the ecological situation; and the natural ecological situation is neither the crib nor the incubator.

Studies of the Immediate Effects of Stimulation on the Human Neonate

HAMBURG: Supposing we could experiment with human subjects in any way we wanted, and we wanted to test out your (Levine and Denenberg) kind of findings in Homo sapiens, what kind of stimulation would you set up that would be the closest parallel to your infantile handling stimulation with rats?

DENENBERG: I made a recommendation about this for a study being done at the medical school in Oklahoma. There we are working with premature infants, but the same thing would also apply for normal term babies. The idea is to introduce more stimulus variability into the environment than is usual. Variation in visual stimulation is provided by using such things as striped sheets and pillowcases instead of the usual white ones, mobiles over the baby's head and other types of visual pattern. Variation in auditory stimulation is provided by having the mother or nurses talk to the baby, or by means of a radio. Proprioceptive and tactile stimulation is varied by rocking the incubator of the premature baby or the crib of the normal term baby, or by picking the baby up and handling him.

BRUNER: One of the things that troubles me is that there is no place in our current learning theory for reafference and the role of action in connection with stimulation. An extremely lively environment is no good unless you get some responses from the organism in order for it to build some kind of a postural schema or model, in terms of which a great deal of the environment can be structured. If the construction, say, of a postural-tonic pattern is not included within learning theory, then we must do something about learning theories.

KAGAN: Perhaps the closest parallel to the animal stimulation experiments would be a comparison of infants born with mild anoxia or mechanical trauma with those who have had the easiest possible birth. Unpublished data from the collaborative study show that the differences between these are minimal as long as brain tissue is not massively destroyed. When social class is controlled there are no gross differences in later learning ability or in I.Q.

PRECHTL: I don't think we need try to simulate the animal stimulation experiments in the human because this experiment happens daily in birth traumas. I wonder whether they do not all damage the nervous system to some extent. They do something, but I wouldn't call it a change in the programming of the nervous system. In our experience, if you look at the polygraphic records of mildly brain-damaged babies over the first few days of life you see dramatic things happening: dissociations of respiratory rate, heart rate and E.E.G. pattern. When following up these children at the age of 4 years we find that many of them show a pattern of instability in their behaviour: they fixate briefly, they show instability when they hold out their hands, and they often cannot maintain a stable posture. They also have difficulties in continuous performance tests: they usually solve the problem but it takes them a long time to do so because they oscillate so much.

FREEDMAN: I have talked to people working on various premature wards and there are some interesting stories about the care of prematures. One of the best premature wards in Chicago is at the Michael

Reese Hospital. Years ago, before they used an isolating incubator, they had an excellent record of never losing any of their prematures. They used to swaddle the babies; they also handled them a lot because they had more staff per baby than any other premature ward in Chicago. With the introduction of the incubator, however, Michael Reese's record of survival went down. The incubator resulted in prolonged periods of relative inactivity and absence of external stimulation until up to 3 months of age. This example is as close as I've been able to come to what indeed might be a parallel between the data on the non-handling of animals and sensory deprivation in human infants.

AMBROSE: Healthy mothers in pregnancy, especially those in primitive societies, are very active right up to the time of labour. Prechtl, is there any evidence about the offspring of mothers who, due to special confinement over the last weeks of pregnancy, are not very active and who do not therefore provide the fetus with much stimulation from loco-motory movements? Are these babies in any way different from those where the pregnancy has been entirely normal?

PRECHTL: There are mothers who have to rest for the last month or so, but then there is always an indication that there are other troubles such as toxaemia. Very often the offspring are in trouble, but probably because of the obstetric complication.

HAMBURG: Would you regard circumcision as having anything in common with your handling procedures?

DENENBERG: This is one of the criteria used by Landauer and Whiting (1964. *Am. Anthropol.* **66,** 1007) to define stressful care practices during infancy. In tribes where infants were stressed by scarification or binding, the height of the adult males was more than 2 inches greater than in primitive cultures where there was no stress during the first 2 years of life. In addition, Whiting (1965. In F. A. Beach (Ed.), *Sex and Behaviour*, p. 221. Wiley, New York) found that the age of onset of menarche was earlier in tribes which stressed their infants. The reason that I cite these data as being similar to our handling procedure is that we have recently shown that handling the infant rat is sufficient to release a significant adrenocorticosterone response within half an hour (Denenberg *et al.* 1967. *Endocrinology*, **81,** 1047). Also, we have previously shown in a number of papers that animals which are handled in infancy, and which are therefore stressed, weigh more in adulthood.

LEVINE: Mason, at the Delta Primate Center, Covington, has been studying some of the early parameters of the primate mother's behaviour which affect infants (W. A. Mason. 1968. In D. C. Glass

(Ed.), *Environmental Influences*, p. 70. Rockefeller University Press, New York). He has built a very ingenious device constituting a moving surrogate mother, and he is getting some very interesting results on socialization effects. For example, the primate infant raised on a moving surrogate, to which it attaches itself, shows very different social behaviour later on as compared with controls.

FREEDMAN: As soon as you look at these animals you can tell immediately which ones have been raised on a swinging bar and which have been raised on a bar fixed to the ground. Those raised on the swinging bar come forward, reach out a hand, or else circulate all around the cage, whereas the others usually stay in one corner, just like Harlow's contact-deprived monkeys.

With regard to the application of extra stimulation to premature infants, we also have been studying what effects may result from this. I was impressed by the fact that infants in the premature wards, because they are kept in incubators, are rarely roused enough to respond even though there is a great deal of movement by the fetus of the same gestational age. I also had in mind some of the literature (e.g. G. Gottleib and F. Y. Kuo. 1965. *J. comp. physiol. Psychol.*, **58**, 183), which indicates that movement in the developing duck embryo is necessary for the proper development of the embryo. So, on the basis of data such as these we decided to apply some sort of movement to the incubator in order to approach the natural situation for the 8-month fetus. It so happened that the Isolette Company had produced a rocker for quite another purpose, namely, for aiding newborns with respiratory problems. Apparently it has not succeeded in that respect, but it seemed a useful piece of apparatus for our purposes.

The Isolette rocker runs on oxygen pressure and there is a slight click at each excursion. Largely on an intuitive basis we decided to use 12 excursions per minute at the rocker's most shallow displacement which was 12°. We applied this motion for a half-hour in the morning and a half-hour in the afternoon, starting 7 to 10 days after an upward trend in weight had been established. We used babies between 900 and 1700 grams, 13 singletons with matched controls, and 9 pairs of identical twins with one as experimental and the other as control. Among the twins, the smaller and larger were equally divided between groups.

Adaptation to the rocker usually involved quite a bit of fussing, but thereafter most infants tended to be hyper-relaxed as shown by relaxed musculature and immediate drowsiness. Of particular interest was the finding that babies who did considerable spontaneous smiling on the premature ward smiled even more when on the rocker. On the other hand the rocker did not make smilers out of nonsmilers, so that when a baby was off the rocker he went back to his previous rate of spontaneous smiling. Regarding long-term effects we found that, although the rocked babies showed higher rates of weight-gain in comparison with controls (p > .05, Mann-Whitney), these differences disappeared once rocking stopped. We hope next to do some metabolism studies to ascertain what went into the differential weight gains. In general it is our distinct impression, on the basis of several follow-up cases, that our rocking had very little lasting effect in any meaningful domain.

It is quite possible, of course, that meaningful results were completely clouded by complex genetic and environmental interactions. Certainly the work of Jumonville on the influence of genotype-treatment interactions in studies of emotionality in mice (1968, Ph.D. thesis, University of Chicago) indicates how complicated the picture can get. She compared handled and nonhandled animals in 6 mouse strains, and found kaleidoscopic variation in resulting weight-gain, aggression, and susceptibility to audiogenic seizures. There were differences in direction of effect between strains, and sex differences within strains.

Could we hear about Ambrose's studies on the effects of rocking young infants?

AMBROSE: Our studies are incomplete as yet. I became interested in rocking when I began to study the kinds of stimuli which terminate crying in babies, particularly newborns. From observation in the natural setting, I had for long been struck by the fact that when a mother receives distress signals from her baby she very commonly picks him up and may feed him as well. Sometimes the crying stops just in response to the picking up and prior to the feeding. I have often seen crying stop soon after the baby is held in the mother's arms, and especially when she rocks him, pats him on the back, perhaps with the addition of cooing as well. I became particularly interested in what appeared to be the property of vestibular stimulation inherent in the rocking movement. Furthermore, at about the same time, an experiment was published by Gordon and Foss (1965. *Qu. J. Expl. Psychol.*, p. 79) which clearly indicated that stimulation of a noncrying baby by rocking has the effect of reducing the incidence of crying subsequently. I eventually had a machine made which enabled me to apply rhythmic vertical up-and-down movement to a baby at amplitudes and rates of oscillation which could be systematically varied. In effect, the machine applies vertical movement to a stabilimeter on which the baby lies supine. I called the machine a "vestibulator".

In the crying termination study I have been employing an amplitude of $2\frac{3}{4}$ inches and varying the oscillation rate from 30 per minute up to 90 per minute, going up by 10 per minute every half-minute. I have studied the effects of this stimulation on full-term normal babies of 5 days of age, taken 15 to 30 minutes after the midday feed, and connected to a polygraphic recorder. The babies were being studied for other purposes as well, but if any baby started to cry spontaneously and engaged in high intensity crying for as long as 2 minutes, then the vestibulator was switched on at a rate of 30 per minute and, step by step, taken up to the maximum rate. The principal finding has been that, without exception, babies always stop crying as soon as the middle part of the range is reached, usually at a rate of 60 per minute, occasionally at 70. Crying usually stops within 15 seconds of the oscillation rate reaching this level. Further increases in rate beyond that level do not result in resumption of crying. On switching off the machine after a minute or two's movement at the mid-level rate, babies almost invariably remain quiet.

LEVINE: Can you induce crying with this apparatus?

AMBROSE: No, this has never happened yet. Indeed, as an adjunct to polygraphic studies of other kinds the vestibulator provides an excellent means of stopping any unwanted crying and so of controlling the baby's state. We are now going on to study the effects of this procedure on noncrying babies in a variety of states. It is clear already that the effect of the changing oscillation rates on heart rate and on respiration rate and regularity is very dependent upon the initial state of the baby. I am, of course, particularly interested in what happens at around 60 to 70 oscillations per minute and, at this early stage of the work, I would just make two points about this. One is that even babies in deep sleep show changes in heart rate and respiration rate at this level of oscillation. The other is that the heart rate and respiration rate changes in awake babies appear to show a U-shaped curve in response to changes in oscillation rate from 30 to 90 per minute, and the bottom of the U occurs around the 60 to 70 per minute level.

PAPOUŠEK: Do you have any data on the incidence of overall crying after a baby has received the vestibular stimulation?

AMBROSE: Not yet. What I am beginning to study are the immediate and subsequent effects of applying vestibular stimulation at a rate of 60 oscillations per minute for a period of a quarter of an hour. The baby remains on the stabilimeter for a second quarter of an hour but without any applied movement. A group of such babies will be compared with a control group of babies that are put on the stabilimeter under similar conditions for half an hour but without any movement at all.

BRUNER: It would be very interesting to know what the periodicity of movement is when infants begin to engage in self-initiated rhythmic movements at around 3 months of age. When we tried to measure head and eye movements at that age we had the problem of keeping the babies stable in the experimental situation. We dealt with this by giving them a place for their feet to rest on. From time to time, when concentrating on a visual stimulus, they would move on their own in a rhythmic way but it never occurred to me to measure what the periodicity was. It would be very easy to do this with a view to seeing if it is anywhere around 60 per minute. It may be worth noting too that sucking usually occurs at about that rate as well.

DENENBERG: On the same point there may be evidence on the modal periodicity of the typical back-and-forth rocking patterns shown by autistic children.

Mother-Infant Interaction: Effects and
Biological Functions

Imprinting and the Development of Preferences

P. P. G. BATESON

University of Cambridge

IMPRINTING AND LEARNING

IN MANY ANIMALS preferences which are initially broad become restricted to stimuli experienced by them early in their life cycles. The ways in which such early preferences are acquired are often likened to "imprinting". Classically, this term is used for the process by which young birds come to respond socially to a specific class of objects, usually their own species. Generalizations are always tempting, but it is as well to realize that lumping together processes by which all sorts of different preferences and habits are acquired is potentially misleading. It is all too easy to slip into thinking that the underlying mechanisms resemble one another, whereas all that has been done has been to group together processes with similar outcomes or which are seemingly restricted to a single period in the life cycle. Such a classification also seduces one into thinking that all the processes termed "imprinting" differ from other types of learning. While that is certainly what some people intend, there is a world of difference between hope and reality, between inference and information. Make no mistake, the evidence for the peculiarity of classical imprinting is open to a variety of interpretations.

It is possible to take each one of the supposedly unique features of classical imprinting and show that it is also a characteristic of learning which occurs in some other situation (Bateson, 1966). This exercise on its own is not conclusive since the combination of characters could be unique and, as Lorenz (1966) rightly points out, biological classifications are nearly always based on clusters of variables. Certainly, imprinting seems to have a special flavour of its own which cannot be dismissed as readily as has sometimes been done in the past. The impression that, with imprinting, we are dealing with a special phenomenon stems from a combination of factors: the learning begins at a particular stage in the life cycle, is specific to a particular collection of responses, occurs rapidly, and can have stable long-term effects. When, however, we consider the context in which imprinting occurs and those in which learning is conventionally studied we ought, perhaps, to be more surprised by the similarities than by the differences. After all, imprinting occurs early in development whereas learning is usually studied in adult animals. Therefore, when considering the context of imprinting we should ask what effect previous experience has on the rapidity with which preferences are established and on the stability of those preferences.

Other aspects of the imprinting situation that also warrant close analysis are the mechanisms which ensure that young birds respond to specific types of stimuli at a particular stage in development. These mechanisms need have nothing to do with the process of acquisition even though their effects on its outcome are obviously enormous. I find it more plausible, more parsimonious, and generally more helpful to attribute the characteristics of imprinting, inasmuch as they are collectively peculiar, to the situation in which they are found rather than to some special kind of learning. But whatever view one takes, it should be clear that the concept of imprinting, with its vivid mechanical connotations, may not be the useful explanatory device it is sometimes made out to be.

When we seek to generalize about the ways in which bonds between mother and offspring are formed, we must obviously be alert to the possibility of convergent evolution. Thus Salzen (1967) was right to consider the very different phylogenetic backgrounds of birds and primates before comparing imprinting in domestic chicks (*Gallus gallus*) with the development of affectional bonds in rhesus monkeys (*Macaca mulatta*). However, having found several features in common, he left the impression that the underlying processes are fundamentally similar. The conclusion does not follow from the evidence, of course, because the similarities may well reflect a common biological function.

MEANING OF BIOLOGICAL FUNCTION

At this point it is perhaps necessary to digress in order to clarify what is meant by "biological function". The term has caused some confusion, partly because the meaning of function in its mathematical sense is completely different, but mainly because its biological usage is not wholly consistent. Thus a question about the function of behaviour might be concerned with why the activity evolved, with its survival value at the present time, or with the end to which it is directed. The answers to these questions are not necessarily the same. The approach to the historical evolutionary question is necessarily indirect, since a behavioural fossil record obviously does not exist. Nevertheless some progress has been made by comparing the behaviour of species which, on other grounds, are regarded as being closely related (e.g. Tinbergen, 1959). Thus the derivation of a courtship display may become apparent when a closely related species is observed to perform in the same situation a recognizable movement, such as preening a particular feather. By employing this approach and by relating an animal's behaviour to its natural habitat it is often possible to suggest why the behaviour evolved in the way it did.

At one time the uncertainties of the evolutionary argument also surrounded hypotheses about survival value. However, in recent years an increasing number of studies, notably by Tinbergen and his co-workers, have shown that the problem is susceptible to experimental analysis. For example, Tinbergen *et al.* (1962) analysed the survival value of the tendency in the Black-headed gull (*Larus ridibundus*) to remove egg shell from its nest a few hours after a chick has hatched. There were a number of possibilities. The sharp edges of the shell might injure the chicks; the shell might slip over an unhatched egg thus trapping the chick in a double shell; it might interfere in some way with brooding; it might provide a breeding ground for bacteria or moulds; finally it might attract the attention of predators and so endanger the brood. Since species such as the Kittiwake (*Rissa tridactyla*), which nest on steep cliffs and are safe from predation, do not carry away their egg shells from the nest the last possibility seemed most likely. Tinbergen and his co-workers therefore examined the effects on predation of leaving egg shells alongside intact eggs; they found that the level of predation was much higher than when no shells were left in the nest. They concluded that the adults' tendency to remove shells functions to decrease predation and thus increases the chances of the brood's surviving.

It must be emphasized that a demonstration of the way in which a given behaviour pattern increases the chances of survival does not necessarily furnish the explanation for its evolution. If the habitat and pattern of predation have changed, the selection pressure may also have altered; in other words the consequences of a behaviour pattern that increase the chances of survival now may not be the same as in the past.

A statement about an animal's goal, or the end towards which its behaviour is directed, is sometimes regarded as a loose way of saying that the outcome increases the chances of survival, presumably because evolutionary arguments are frequently couched in teleological terms. However, the way in which the behaviour pattern has evolved has no bearing on any statement, teleological or otherwise, about the way in which the system operates in the present. Moreover, the way in which the behaviour pattern increases the chances of survival may be quite different from the consequence which brings the behaviour pattern to an end.

Twenty or thirty years ago the concept of goal-directed behaviour was tainted with vitalism. However, with the building of increasingly elaborate servo-mechanisms and the rise of cybernetics it has become clear that the statement that an animal's behaviour is goal-directed can be public and testable. To be sure, as Hinde and Stevenson (1969) point out, the concept has its dangers and, when the temporal relations between events are straightforward it adds virtually nothing to our knowledge. However, it can be very helpful if we wish to relate a variety of independent events that can precede a common outcome. In the nineteenth century Sir William Hamilton recognized the value of this procedure in the physical sciences (Hamilton, 1940) and, of course, the concept of appetitive behaviour is plainly teleological. Thus, rather than refer separately to all the ways in which a predator can catch its prey, it is convenient, at least in the initial stages of an enquiry, to group them together as "hunting". Another illustration is provided by activities relating to the mother in young precocial birds such as domestic chicks. If they have wandered away from her in the course of doing something else, they approach her; if she moves off, they follow; they avoid unfamiliar objects and situations; and they search for their mother in her absence. All these activities can be regarded as leading to the common goal of keeping close to the mother.

Whether we talk about the adaptiveness of behaviour in the past, its survival value in the present, or the event which brings it to an end, we are referring to outcomes. Logically there are many ways in which these can be reached and therefore we are in no position to infer anything about mechanism from a classification based on function. If we want to base generalizations, whether about the ways in which mother-offspring relations are established or about the ways in which preferences are established, upon classical imprinting, we must examine the constellation of factors that affect its outcome. These will not be described exhaustively here. There are, however, some aspects of imprinting which raise general issues as far as the development of behaviour is concerned, and these will be discussed later.

SENSITIVE PERIOD FOR IMPRINTING

One of the most striking features of imprinting is its apparent restriction to a sensitive period early in the life cycle. As Thorpe (1963) has pointed out, nearly all animals show a greater propensity to learn at certain stages of the life cycle than at others. What is more, the effects of most reinforcing stimuli are confined to limited periods which occur as the result of short-term fluctuations in the physiological state of the animal. Nevertheless, it is reasonable to distinguish, as Thorpe (1961) has done, between periods of sensitivity occurring at many stages throughout the life cycle and periods that occur only once. Of the learning processes that are seemingly confined to a single period, imprinting provides a particularly clear-cut and well studied example. I must make it clear that I intend to use the term "sensitive period" descriptively here. Attempts have been made to imbue it with explanatory properties by linking it with maturational processes. This was the fate of the alternative term "critical period", which was abandoned partly for this reason and partly because it wrongly implies an all-or-nothing effect. The terminological shuffling continues, of course, and matters have not been helped by those who wish to retain both terms for different types of evidence (e.g. Fabricius, 1964; Fox, 1966). However, all that matters for my present purposes is that a distinction be drawn between the *evidence* for the period of sensitivity and the *causes* of its existence.

Procedure and Findings

To consider the evidence it is necessary to be clear about procedure in imprinting experiments. Most investigators have used domestic chicks or Mallard ducklings (*Anas platyrhynchos*). These birds are capable of actively closing the distance between themselves and their mother when separated from her and will usually follow when she moves away. The experiments, while differing greatly in detail, generally comprise two stages: a period of training during which the bird is exposed to a single source of stimulation, and a subsequent test period when the preference for this stimulus is measured. While notions of what constitutes an adequate test for such a preference have varied considerably, the extent to which the birds direct their filial responses towards the training stimulus during testing is usually taken as a measure of imprinting. In order to control for the possibility that the birds prefer the training object from the outset, some birds should be trained with A only, others with B only, and each group then given a choice between A *and* B.

The sensitive period for imprinting is measured by exposing birds to an object at different ages and subsequently measuring their preference for it. Since the birds cannot be returned to a naive state, each age group consists of birds with no previous experience of the training object. One of the first quantitative demonstrations was by Ramsay and Hess (1954) whose results have been widely quoted. They found a peak in the proportion of birds that were imprinted in the group trained 13–16 hours after hatching. Subsequent workers have not been able to get quite such clear-cut results as this, but the basic picture has nevertheless been repeatedly confirmed (See Bateson, 1966). Since many sources of variability have been identified, exact values cannot be given for the length of the sensitive period and the age at which most

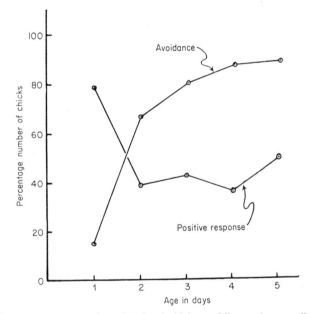

FIG. 1. The percentage number of isolated chicks avoiding and responding positively (socially) to a strange moving box on successive days after hatching.

birds of any one species can be imprinted without first specifying the conditions of rearing, training and testing, as well as the methods of measuring behaviour.

The decline with age in the readiness of birds to learn the characteristics of, and to develop a preference for, the experimenter's training object can be linked to a change in their behaviour in the training situation. As shown in Fig. 1, the proportion of birds directing filial responses towards the object declines with age, and the proportion avoiding it increases (Bateson, 1966). It is as well to realize that many of the birds begin by avoiding the object and end up by following it. In natural conditions avoidance will usually take the animal away from a strange source of stimulation but in the experimental situation, where the object is repeatedly presented, as shown in Fig. 2, the time

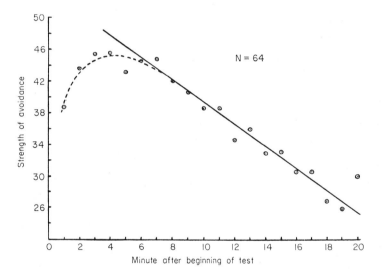

FIG. 2. The mean strength of avoidance of 3-day-old chicks in each minute of a 20-minute test with a novel moving object. Only the scores of chicks which avoided for the whole test have been used. The strength of avoidance is expressed as the percentage of each minute spent avoiding (from Bateson, 1964b).

spent avoiding it wanes in almost linear fashion (Bateson, 1964b). To clarify the point, if we present a moving object to a typical 3-day-old chick which has been reared in social isolation we find that initially it spends a large part of each minute in avoidance (Fig. 3). By degrees, avoidance declines until eventually it stops altogether and the chick

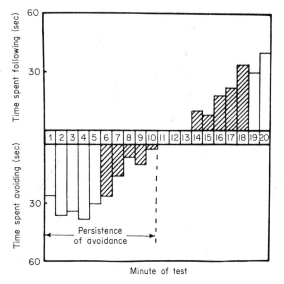

FIG. 3. The behaviour of a typical 3-day-old domestic chick during a 20-minute period of exposure to a novel moving object.

suddenly starts to respond socially to the object. The lapse of time from the first presentation of the strange object to the moment avoidance ceases increases as the birds get older.

Ending of the Sensitive Period

The first explanations for the end of the sensitive period were based on these changes in behaviour in the training situation. There were two related hypotheses. The first, which was widely supported, postulated an endogenous increase in "fear" (e.g. Hess, 1959a). The second, which received little attention, suggested that in addition to an increase in "fear" there is also an endogenous decrease in the "internal motivation of the following reaction" (Fabricius, 1951). Three types of argument have been advanced in favour of the view that maturational changes are responsible for the end of the sensitive period. First, it was suggested that since birds reared in the dark eventually avoid illuminated objects, the development of avoidance must be independent of sensory experience (e.g. Schaller and Emlen, 1962). This inference is based, however, on the implausible assumption that darkness does not constitute an environment and that birds do not learn to detect the difference between it and illuminated objects. Secondly, having found that the injection of adrenergic stimulants into chicks facilitates the following response and imprinting up to 18 hours but thereafter interferes with them, Kovach (1964) implicated the autonomic nervous system in the termination of the sensitive period. His results, however, do not allow any inference about what causes the physiological and behavioural changes. Finally, avoidance conditioning studies have led to the suggestion that, whereas young chicks do not escape from or learn to avoid aversive stimuli, older birds do (James and Binks, 1963; Peters and Isaacson, 1963; Fischer and Campbell, 1964). Although this seems to supply independent evidence for the maturation of a system which controls avoidance, the relations between the processes involved in learning to avoid specific noxious stimuli and those involved in escape from unfamiliar stimuli are, at best, hypothetical. In any event, as I hope to show, the development of an avoidance system cannot provide a sufficient explanation for the evidence.

In accounting for the end of the sensitive period the postulation of maturational changes that are independent of experience might have become necessary if the point when the period ends had been unaffected by the conditions of rearing. But that is very far from being the case. Guiton (1959) and Sluckin and Salzen (1961) among others, have found that social experience shortened the length of the sensitive period in domestic chicks, and Moltz and Stettner (1961) found that in Peking ducklings (*Anas platyrhynchos*) it is extended when they are denied patterned vision. These results suggested that the sensitive period is brought to an end by some consequence of visual experience. Since imprinted birds avoid objects that are unfamiliar but do not avoid their companions, we may ask whether all avoidance is a consequence of lack of familiarity. The notion of animals, including man, avoiding the unfamiliar is not, of course, a new one (e.g. Hebb, 1946). To test whether this is the case in isolated birds, I reared chicks in two different kinds of pen and then, after 3 days, exposed them to two kinds of moving box, one with the same pattern as that of the home pen and the other with a different one (Bateson, 1964a). The results were clear-cut (Fig. 4). The chicks avoided the boxes with the unfamiliar pattern far longer than they avoided those with the familiar one. Moreover, a much greater proportion of chicks responded socially to the latter than to the former. This strongly suggests that the birds, having learned the characteristics of the pens in which they were reared, avoided objects which they could detect as being different. We may deduce, therefore, that the sensitive period comes to an end when the birds have become familiar with input from the environment in which they are reared and can discriminate between this form of stimulation and

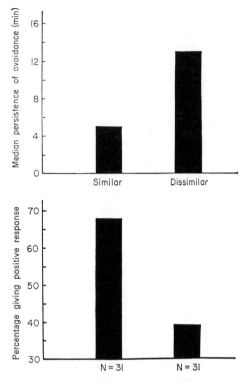

FIG. 4. The persistence with which 3-day-old chicks avoided a moving box and the percentage number responding positively (socially) to the box. Half the chicks were exposed to a box painted with a pattern similar to the pen in which they had been reared and half to one painted with a dissimilar pattern (from Bateson, 1964a).

that from the experimenter's training object. Lest "discriminate" should give difficulty here, it is as well to point out that the ability to discriminate between two stimuli and the preference for one of them cannot be distinguished operationally since they are both measured in the same way (Irwin, 1958). In other words, the end of the sensitive period can also be said to reflect the development of a preference. It does not necessarily mark the end of imprinting because the birds may, and almost certainly will, go on to learn further details of the preferred object.

Onset of the Sensitive Period

Although maturational changes do not seem important in terminating the sensitive period, they are strongly implicated in its onset. In tackling the problem Gottlieb (1961) made use of the fact that birds hatch at different stages of embryonic development. This is presumably because of differences in the thickness of the shell, in the position of the bird inside, and so on. He found that the sensitive period for imprinting was not so well marked if age was measured from hatching as it was if age was measured from the beginning of embryonic development. We may suppose that the birds hatching relatively early in development do not initially take notice of things about them and that they and the later-hatching birds both begin to develop a preference for input from their immediate environment at about the same developmental age. How can we account for the increase in sensitivity as the birds get older?

Hess (1959b), having found that older chicks rejoin their siblings more quickly than birds that are a few hours younger, suggested that the onset of sensitivity is due to the development of locomotor ability. While the changes which he observed could have been due to a variety of perceptual or motivational changes, independent evidence suggests that locomotor ability improves with age. For example, although the proportion of birds that follow a strange moving object declines with age, the amount of time spent following by those birds that do it increases with age (Bateson, 1964b).

Changes in the visual system have also been implicated in the increase in sensitivity (e.g., Sackett, 1963). Paulson (1965) measured the speed with which the system responded to a flashing light by placing electrodes at the retina, in the optic lobes and in the forebrain of Peking ducklings at different developmental ages. He found that the latencies declined markedly before hatching and, what is more interesting, continued to decline after the time when most birds hatch. In other words the visual system of the older birds responds more quickly to changes in the environment.

If we opt for a simple-minded hypothesis that a sufficient condition for imprinting is that the sensory and motor apparatus should be in working order, the evidence presented so far provides an attractive explanation for the onset of the sensitive period. Certainly the hypothesis accords well with some current theories of ontogeny (e.g. Schneirla, 1965; Kuo, 1967) which presuppose a reactive neonate rather than one which actively engages its environment. If this view were correct, the main developmental problem to be analysed would be the nature of the embryological factors affecting the increase in reactivity. However, there are signs that the evidence which we seek to explain is not quite as simple as has sometimes been made out.

A few years ago, I reared chicks in isolation in two different kinds of activity box (Bateson, 1964c). One was painted with black and white stripes and the other with a grey paint that reflected the same total amount of light. To my surprise, even on the first day after hatching the chicks reared in the plain environment were more active than those reared in the striped boxes. Since I had not actually watched the birds in this experiment, the results were not too easy to interpret but they began to make sense when I looked at undomesticated Mallard ducklings. The ducklings were reared in the dark and, about 12 hours after hatching, were placed singly in some imprinting apparatus. The experiment required that the birds be familiarized with the apparatus for a time before the conspicuous training stimulus was presented to them. During this period, far from staying still, they shuffled in disorientated fashion around the apparatus, wildly "distress" calling. I was tempted to attribute this to the fact that the temperature of the apparatus was some 25°F lower than that of the incubator from which they had just come; indeed, this was almost certainly one of the factors affecting their behaviour. However, as soon as the training stimulus, a flashing light, was turned on the "distress" calling stopped and the birds ran towards the light. Their behaviour was very similar to that of older birds which actively search for their mother when separated from her. By "searching" I mean, of course, behaving in a way which increases the likelihood of their regaining contact with the mother and ceasing to behave this way once they have done so.

These observations suggested that chicks in plain grey boxes were more active because the pattern of their environment was less effective as an imprinting stimulus; indeed, conspicuous static patterns are found to be more effective in the imprinting situation than inconspicuous ones (Bateson, 1964d). Thus it began to appear that birds which were not yet imprinted actively search for conspicuous stimuli. If stimuli that are highly effective in the imprinting situation do bring such appetitive behaviour to an end and are consummatory, they might be expected to reward the young birds.

Now there is already substantial evidence that the activities of imprinted birds can be reinforced by the presentation of the familiar object (Peterson, 1960; Campbell and Pickleman, 1961; Hoffman et al. 1966). But it does not necessarily follow that all conspicuous stimuli are reinforcing from the outset; the familiar object might acquire reinforcing properties as the result of imprinting (Moltz, 1960; Bateson, 1966). The question is, therefore, whether conspicuous objects can be used to reinforce the activities of birds that have not yet been imprinted.

Ellen Reese and I have recently attempted to tackle the problem (Bateson and Reese, 1968). In many ways it is more easily said than done, for on the first day after hatching birds do not engage in very many activities that can be reinforced. We eventually devised apparatus in which the young bird could switch on a flashing light by pressing one of two pedals in the course of moving round the apparatus (Fig. 5). The second pedal, which did not operate the light, served to measure any general changes in activity produced by the stimulus. The stimulus was a modified version of one of those flashing lights to be seen on the top of ambulances and police cars: a translucent plastic box with two of its sides blacked out, rotated round a bulb. This was highly effective in eliciting approach and other components of filial behaviour. It was positioned so that, when the birds had turned the light on, any attempts they made to approach it took them off the pedal and the light would go out. We found that on the first day after hatching both domestic chicks and wild mallard ducklings that had been reared in the dark very quickly learned to turn the light on. What was more, in the course

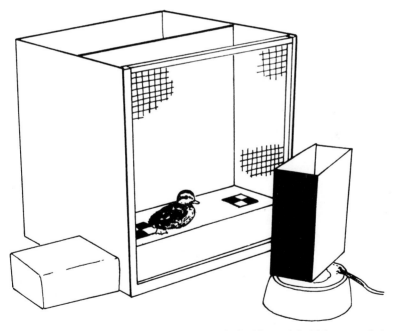

FIG. 5. Operant-conditioning apparatus in which ducklings and chicks can switch on a rotating flashing light by pressing the left-hand pedal. The right-hand pedal does not operate the light but controls for any general changes in activity.

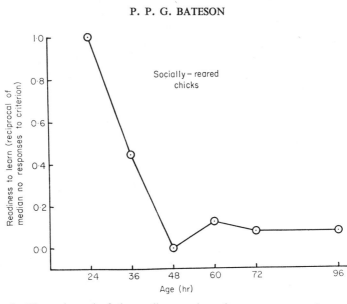

FIG. 6. The reciprocal of the median number of responses to reach an arbitrary criterion by socially reared chicks placed in the operant-conditioning apparatus at different ages after hatching (Bateson and Reese, 1969. *Anim. Behav.*, **17**, in press).

of learning to work for the light, they developed a preference for it; operant conditioning and imprinting proceeded hand in hand. Since older socially-reared birds did not learn to turn on the light anything like as readily or as quickly as the birds straight out of the incubator (Fig. 6), we may conclude that imprinting narrows down the range of stimuli that have reinforcing properties.

These results indicate that, already at the time of hatching, the birds were able actively to engage their environment and that already the behavioural machinery was fairly elaborate. It would be quite wrong to assume that the birds were passively waiting to be stimulated. This having been said, it is not difficult to see how fresh patterns of behaviour could be quickly learned, conspicuous objects being such powerful reinforcers. Furthermore since unfamiliar objects are avoided by imprinted birds it seems likely that the reinforcing properties of the familiar object are further enhanced by the imprinting process (cf. Moltz, 1960).

CONCLUSIONS

I have considered in some detail the sensitive period for imprinting because I think its analysis is relevant to a number of problems concerning ontogeny. Specifically it relates to the development of other preferences and habits occurring at particular stages in the life cycle. Although little is gained at present by basing a classification on imprinting, I do think we have learned some lessons from its study which can be applied in a wider context.

First, we must not assume that, because the way in which an animal responds in a particular situation varies with age, the change is dependent on the growth of the animal as a whole. We have seen that specific types of experience affecting the animal's behaviour can co-vary with age, and that under certain conditions it is possible to break the correlation and demonstrate the importance of that experience.

Secondly, it would be rash to suppose that wherever sensitive periods are found, the causes of the increase in responsiveness are necessarily the same as the causes of the decline.

Finally, the view (e.g. Schneirla, 1965) that behavioural homeostatic systems, such as the one which keeps young chicks within a certain distance of the mother, develop from simpler stimulus-response mechanisms may be misplaced. We may have to face up to the problem that the ontogeny of these systems simply cannot be accounted for at the behavioural level. Meanwhile, however, we need to know a great deal more about the consequences of the developing animal's activities on itself, both before and after birth.

REFERENCES

BATESON, P. P. G. 1964a. Effect of similarity between rearing and testing conditions on chicks' following and avoidance responses. *J. comp. physiol. Psychol.* **57,** 100–103.

BATESON, P. P. G. 1964b. Changes in chicks' responses to novel moving objects over the sensitive period for imprinting. *Anim. Behav.* **12,** 479–489.

BATESON, P. P. G. 1964c. Changes in the activity of isolated chicks over the first week after hatching. *Anim. Behav.* **12,** 490–492.

BATESON, P. P. G. 1964d. Relation between conspicuousness of stimuli and their effectiveness in the imprinting situation. *J. comp. physiol. Psychol.* **58,** 407–411.

BATESON, P. P. G. 1966. The characteristics and context of imprinting. *Biol. Rev.* **41,** 177–220.

BATESON, P. P. G. and REESE, E. P. 1968. Reinforcing properties of conspicuous objects before imprinting has occurred. *Psychonom. Sci.* **10,** 379–380.

CAMPBELL, B. A. and PICKLEMAN, J. R. 1961. The imprinting object as a reinforcing stimulus. *J. comp. physiol. Psychol.* **54,** 592–596.

FABRICIUS, E. 1951. Zur Ethologie junger Anatiden. *Acta zool. fenn.* **68,** 1–178.

FABRICIUS, E. 1964. Crucial periods in the development of the following response in young nidifugous birds. *Z. Tierpsychol.* **21,** 326–327.

FISCHER, G. J. and CAMPBELL, G. L. The development of passive avoidance conditioning in Leghorn chicks. *Anim. Behav.* **12,** 268–269.

Fox, M. W. 1966. Neuro-behavioral ontogeny. A synthesis of ethological and neurophysiological concepts. *Brain Research* **2**, 3–20.

Gottlieb, G. 1961. Developmental age as a baseline for determination of the critical period in imprinting. *J. comp. physiol. Psychol.* **54**, 422–427.

Guiton, P. 1959. Socialization and imprinting in Brown Leghorn chicks. *Anim. Behav.* **7**, 26–34.

Hamilton, W. R. 1940. *Mathematical papers*. Vol. 2. Cambridge University Press.

Hebb, D. O. 1946. On the nature of fear. *Psychol. Rev.* **53**, 259–276.

Hess, E. H. 1959a. Imprinting. *Science, N.Y.* **130**, 133–141.

Hess, E. H. 1959b. Two conditions limiting critical age for imprinting. *J. comp. physiol. Psychol.* **52**, 515–518.

Hinde, R. A. and Stevenson, J. G. 1969. Goals and response control. In D. S. Lehrman, J. S. Rosenblatt, and E. Tobach (Eds.), *Development and evolution of behavior*. Vol. 1. Freeman, San Francisco (in press).

Hoffman, H. S., Searle, J. L., Toffey, S., and Kozma, F., Jr. 1966. Behavioral control by an imprinted stimulus. *J. exp. Analysis Behav.* **9**, 177–189.

Irwin, F. W. 1958. An analysis of the concepts of *discrimination* and *preference*. *Am. J. Psychol.* **71**, 152–163.

James, H. and Binks, C. 1963. Escape and avoidance learning in newly hatched domestic chicks. *Science, N.Y.* **139**, 1293–1294.

Kovach, J. K. 1964. Effects of autonomic drugs on imprinting. *J. comp. physiol. Psychol.* **57**, 183–187.

Kuo, Z.-Y. 1967. *The dynamics of behavior development: an epigenetic view.* Random House, New York.

Lorenz, K. 1966. *Evolution and Modification of Behavior.* Methuen, London.

Moltz, H. 1960. Imprinting: empirical basis and theoretical significance. *Psychol. Bull.* **57**, 291–314.

Moltz, H. and Stettner, L. J. 1961. The influence of patterned-light deprivation on the critical period for imprinting. *J. comp. physiol. Psychol.* **54**, 279–283.

Paulson, G. W. 1965. Maturation of evoked responses in the duckling. *Expl Neurol.* **11**, 324–333.

Peters, J. J. and Isaacson, R. L. 1963. Acquisition of active and passive responses in two breeds of chicks. *J. comp. physiol. Psychol.* **56**, 793–796.

Peterson, N. 1960. Control of behaviour by presentation of an imprinted stimulus. *Science, N.Y.* **132**, 1395–1396.

Ramsay, A. O. and Hess, E. H. 1954. A laboratory approach to the study of imprinting. *Wilson Bull.* **66**, 196–206.

Sackett, G. P. 1963. A neural mechanism underlying unlearned, critical period, and developmental aspects of visually controlled behavior. *Psychol. Rev.* **70**, 40–50.

Salzen, E. A. 1967. Imprinting in birds and primates. *Behaviour* **28**, 232–254.

Schaller, G. B. and Emlen, J. T. 1962. The ontogeny of avoidance behaviour in some precocial birds. *Anim. Behav.* **10**, 370–381.

Schneirla, T. C. 1965. Aspects of stimulation and organization in approach/withdrawal processes underlying vertebrate behavioral development. In D. S. Lehrman, R. A. Hinde, and E. Shaw (Eds.), *Advances in the study of behavior*. Academic Press, New York.

Sluckin, W. and Salzen, E. A. 1961. Imprinting and perceptual learning. *Q. J. exp. Psychol.* **13**, 65–77.

THORPE, W. H. 1961. Sensitive periods in the learning of animals and men: a study of imprinting with special reference to the induction of cyclic behaviour. In W. H. Thorpe and O. L. Zangwill (Eds.), *Current problems in animal behaviour.* Cambridge University Press.

THORPE, W. H. 1963. *Learning and instinct in animals.* Second edition. Methuen, London.

TINBERGEN, N. 1959. Comparative studies of the behaviour of gulls (*Laridae*): a progress report. *Behaviour* **15,** 1–70.

TINBERGEN, N., BROEKHUYSEN, G. J., FEEKES, F., HOUGHTON, J. C. W., KRUUK, H., and SZULC, E. 1962. Eggshell removal by the black-headed gull, *Larus ridibundus L.*: a behaviour component of camouflage. *Behaviour* **19,** 74–117.

Discussion

Preference Learning and Avoidance

KAGAN: You seem to be suggesting that the initiation of avoidance behaviour is not dependent on maturation, but is the result of being confronted with a stimulus that is strange, relative to one that has already become familiar. Do you think that if you prevented perceptual learning you would never get an avoidance response?

BATESON: No, what I am saying is that you have got to be more sophisticated about the development of the avoidance system. Although maturation may well be involved it is clear that the determination of the kinds of things which are avoided is dependent on the preferences developed by the animal.

KAGAN: Has anyone done the extreme experiment of preventing visual experience for as long as 30 days and then testing for imprinting?

BATESON: While it is easy to keep birds in isolation, it is virtually impossible to deprive them totally of visual experience and keep them intact. Even in a sub-optimal environment some learning takes place. Nevertheless domestic chicks that have been isolated for many weeks will develop a preference for a novel object at the end of the period of isolation.

LEVINE: When you say that maturation is involved, one gets the implication that something is happening in the organism as a function of maturation. But this explains very little.

BATESON: I don't think it has very much explanatory power either. The concept of maturation is an abstraction. But it does lead one to look at other kinds of variable. It helps, in considering events that produce changes in behaviour, to distinguish between gross events in the external environment and events occurring within the organism which don't seem to be greatly dependent on external events.

FREEDMAN: You seem to be striving after an explanatory model of an interactive kind, which accounts at once for what we classically call maturation acting in combination with influences from the environment. You have been describing how variation in the exogenous situation can influence the timing at which something endogenous is set off.

BATESON: Yes. The avoidance of unfamiliar objects is a consequence of the development of a preference for a specific object. One can delay the development of this preference by rearing an animal in sub-optimal conditions, but even then learning still takes place and eventually the animal develops a preference for a sub-optimal stimulus and avoids dissimilar objects. If one plots conspicuousness of training object against rate of learning of a social preference, one finds a relationship such that the more conspicuous the object, the more quickly learning will take place. One also finds that the more inconspicuous the environment in which the animal is reared, the longer it takes for avoidance to develop. This is presumably because acquisition of a preference takes place more slowly.

GINSBURG: You're not equating avoidance with fear?

BATESON: I want to be operational about this and refer only to the kinds of thing I am measuring.

Imprinting, Preference and Attachment

LEVINE: You have mentioned that the concept of imprinting has been used in a wide variety of ways. How do you evaluate the use of this concept in the psychiatric literature?

BATESON: The concept of imprinting implies a special mechanism, but it usually refers to the development of a specific preference over a restricted part of the life cycle. Clearly there are many different mechanisms by which preferences can become established. Therefore, lumping the development of all sorts of preferences and habits in humans together with the development of social preferences in birds under the heading of imprinting can be highly misleading.

AINSWORTH: But is there no commonality in what you and I are studying? The main notion in our work is that we are studying the development of attachment, which sounds to me very much like preference. You are, in effect, talking about attachment as a consequence. Is there no basis for assuming that there is at least some similarity in what we are studying, either descriptively or in terms of mechanisms?

BATESON: I think there is a way of enquiring whether there are any similarities in the mechanisms: that is to look at the whole constellation of factors which affect the outcome at the behavioural level. In an imprinting situation there are several such factors: age of imprinting, length of exposure, number of objects to which the animal is exposed, the characteristics of the object, experience prior to imprinting, experience after it and so on. In the case of birds, study of this whole constellation of factors gives one some idea of the mechanism one is dealing with. If, in dealing with other species, one asks whether similar factors affect the development of their preferences, one may find similarities with imprinting in birds. One would then be on much safer ground in assuming that the underlying mechanisms are the same. However, until such comparisons have been made, generalizations from classical imprinting should be treated as hypotheses rather than as acceptable descriptions. The results of studies on birds certainly suggest things that can be done with other species but they do not provide a body of knowledge that can be applied indiscriminately over the whole animal kingdom.

LEVINE: In considering the development of choice in the bird, is one asking about the same thing when one asks at what age imprinting begins and at what age preference begins?

BATESON: These are two different things because birds have preferences at the outset. However, within a wide range of stimuli that are all equally effective initially, you can select one stimulus and train it to prefer that one.

LEVINE: When you are studying the development of attachment in humans, isn't one of the things you test for the response to strangers, the response to non-preferred objects?

AINSWORTH: One of the criteria we used for judging that attachment has in fact taken place was the response to a stranger in a strange situation, but I don't think it is a good criterion. This response seems to depend too much on a wide range of other variables which have not yet been properly studied. Furthermore, children who on other criteria show clear-cut signs of attachment may not show fear of strangers. Nevertheless there is some analogue between imprinting and the development of attachment in humans. Obviously in the latter the sensitive period is very much less sharp and much more extended: the development of attachment requires a lot more exposure, but the process does start off with a discrimination and, later on, fear or avoidance responses seem to join in. I can see a number of similarities and I doubt if these are just descriptive, but we don't really know what the mechanism is in humans.

KAGAN: I find the imprinting concept helpful in understanding infant development through the first 4 or 5 months. There is an interesting analogue in our data on humans which seems to arise from the fact that girls are maturationally ahead of boys; on perceptual tests in the first 3 or 4 months of life girls are better discriminators. At the same time we find that girls show anxiety to strangers a little earlier and more intensely than boys: they react to discrepancies in the human face with more avoidance. Thus, when visual functioning and perceptual learning begin early, we find that avoidance responses appear a little earlier as well.

BATESON: Ainsworth implies that, in humans, avoidance comes in later than the development of a preference. In chicks and ducklings we are dealing with very precocious animals and, because of their rapid development, these two effects may not be separate. Now it might well be that in a slowly developing species you would find the development of a preference first, with avoidance coming in later. We should also bear in mind there may be two distinct kinds of response to unfamiliar things: one is to avoid them, the other is to not respond socially as much to them as to familiar things.

Imprinting and Operant Conditioning

AINSWORTH: Hess (*Scient. Am.*, March 1958) made following more difficult by putting little hurdles in the experimental situation. He claimed that there was stronger imprinting in those birds that had to make a greater effort to follow. This appealed to me because I found, with human infants, that the ones who were permitted to be more active in their approach behaviour, that is, those in regard to which such behaviour was not prevented by the mother, also showed stronger attachment.

SCHAFFER: I understand that Hess's law of effort is, to say the least, controversial: it certainly seems to go counter to the notion that the only precondition necessary for imprinting is mere perceptual exposure. Yet the idea that such exposure will be more effective if the animal has to work for it and if it is associated with motor elements seems a reasonable one.

BATESON: Regarding this so-called law of effort, it is jolly difficult to prove a negative. A lot of people have simply confined animals and found that they developed a preference as readily as animals which, over the same period, were allowed to follow. Hess has never presented the raw data on which he based his law of effort, but even if he had done so his evidence would have been open to another interpretation. In the experiment in which he varied the length of exposure to the object, it could be equally well argued that the birds which had been exposed for longer just had more visual experience and thus more chance to learn the object's characteristics. In the experiment where he varied the speed of the training model and kept the length of training constant, there were other difficulties. First, the more rapidly moving object was a more effective stimulus; second, if the little bird could get up underneath the object it didn't have visual experience of it. Thus the argument for the law of effort is shot through with logical errors.

It is quite compelling that the animals should attend and should have some sort of interaction with the stimulus and it makes very good sense that, in order for them to learn the characteristics of the object, the animal shouldn't be sleeping! It's got to attend, and attention will be increased by locomotor activity because of the heightened arousal level.

SCHAFFER: What are your views about the relationship between imprinting and operant conditioning?

BATESON: In my experiment where the animals had to press a pedal in order to turn on the flashing light, I was struck how very quickly they developed a preference for the reinforcer. This happened much more quickly than in a situation where they were just plonked in front of the stimulus: it took only 5 to 7 minutes. What was crucial here was their alertness; the actual walking about was of secondary importance.

AINSWORTH: In the operant conditioning experiment the activity of the animal brought the reinforcer on, and the activity was caused by "anticipation" of a consequence. Now this seems very close to the sort of thing that interests me in the development of attachment in infants. When they smile something happens, and when they approach something happens. This, in a sense, is under their control and they get an immediate feedback. It is an entirely different thing when the child does something, say smiles, and nobody pays any attention.

SCHAFFER: It is also important to note, when trying to understand the strength of attachment formation, that the occurrence or non-occurrence of feedback is not entirely under the child's control and therefore not entirely predictable. The parent, under real life conditions, does not always feel like smiling back and therefore operates under a partial rather than a full reinforcement schedule. If parental responsiveness were wholly predictable it might well be that the attachments which develop would be rather less intense than otherwise.

The Limited Scope of Imprinting

BATESON: It is important to remember that imprinting does not occur to the same extent in all species of bird. There are birds, such as the curlew, which have a very restricted range of preference initially. Furthermore, in the case of the cuckoo, it seems that visual experience in early development is relatively unimportant. With regard to the development of sexual preferences, the classical imprinting theory is very far from being correct all the time. There are cases in which sexual preferences are affected by early experience, but this seems to be more the exception than the rule. There are also well documented cases in which sexual preferences are completely unaffected by early experience. In this second category there appear to be a wholly different set of developmental processes affecting sexual preferences.

In view of these facts it is sometimes asked why imprinting occurs at all, that is, why the biologically appropriate preference is not written into the genotype. There are two possibilities here, neither of which has been tested. One is that the perceptual constancies that would be required to develop this kind of thing are not developed at a very early age. The mother might appear to the young bird in all sorts of shapes and sizes and different colours and so on, and her appearance might easily not match the initial preferences of the young if they were looking for something specific. The other possibility is that, in a rapidly evolving group in which the characteristics of the plumage change, young might hatch out looking for a red mother when the mother was actually green. It might be possible to test this idea by looking at imprinting in a number of widely different species.

BRUNER: There's one other possibility. If you build it into the genotype, you would so interfere with the rest of the organization of the visual system that the bird wouldn't be able to cope in other situations.

BATESON: That may be so, but you do come across apparently highly specific responses, later on in development, given to highly specific stimuli which don't seem to be dependent on experience. The robin's reaction to the robin's red breast, for example, doesn't seem to be dependent on prior exposure to red and yet they seem to be able to cope with other visual stimuli. While one finds this later in development it is not seen early on, however.

GINSBURG: It certainly looks as though some aspects of the preferences of chicks are programmed into the genotype. If you look at the mallard duck, which is a species that has presumably developed under selection pressure in the wild up until much more recent times than the chick, you find that a much higher proportion are imprintable than in the case of chicks where selection pressure has presumably been relaxed.

I am not happy about drawing an analogy between early human development and the imprinting phenomenon. In the case of wolves and dogs, dogs develop somewhat more slowly than wolves yet the dogs are the ones which develop a one-man preference. Wolves that are socialized to human handling are, if they are thoroughly socialized, extremely gregarious. They seldom develop a total preference for a specific person. In making comparisons between different species, let alone between birds and humans, there is a real danger that any analogy is based on superficial conditions. As Pat (Bateson) pointed out, because in several species of bird one finds correlations, say, between perceptual development and some aspects of behaviour, one is tempted to infer that this will happen at other phyletic levels. One also infers similarities of mechanism. On the basis of our data I could explain social bond function negatively by saying that, since wolves seem able to generalize much more than dogs do, it is the lack of ability to generalize in a less intelligent animal that is responsible for what appears to be a social bond to a particular person.

DENENBERG: When you imprint a bird right after hatching, unlike manipulating rodents, it may not have many emotional connotations. You have an organism which is built to learn very rapidly; it acquires information from its environment in the first few hours of life, and this has perhaps a certain survival value for it. Certain elements that are most conspicuous are more likely to be learned than others. You have indicated that if one were to keep this organism in a behavioural vacuum one could postpone this learning. But what you have, it seems to me, is a nervous system which very rapidly will acquire certain limited amounts of information and, once it has acquired this information, all other information is by definition unfamiliar. What you get then is not the fear response. It isn't fear, it's just that the organism will not approach the things that it's not familiar with, whereas it does approach what it is familiar with. Why I'm so opposed to the analogy between imprinting in birds and human attachment behaviour is that your birds are a precocious species. They have a nervous system built for rapid acquisition of information that is necessary for survival. A human infant isn't built that way. We acquire information by a very slow continuous process. I'm not sure that the analogies we make by semantic manipulation are at all valid.

BATESON: I would certainly agree with your cautious approach. As I said in my paper, until one has looked at the whole constellation of variables at both levels, one is not really safe in making any kind of comparison. I think the imprinting work with birds does suggest certain kinds of procedure which one can use in studying human development, and certain kinds of thing that may be worth looking for. But I would emphasize two ways in which the popular conception of imprinting is misleading. First, preferences in birds are shown right from the time of hatching. Immediately after hatching they respond more readily to some stimuli than to others. In general we find that those stimuli which are more conspicuous to the human eye—and one might infer also to the avian eye—are more effective. Second, at hatching there is a very elaborate behavioural homeostatic system already present. What happens in imprinting is that there is a restriction of the bias on this homeostat. But the machinery is already there.

BRUNER: I should just like to back up one major point Denenberg was driving at. As one looks at the behaviour of the human infant during the first 4 or 5 months, 4 months particularly, one is struck by the fact that not only is he a system that develops very slowly, there is also a very striking disjunction between the sensory pattern and the motor pattern. The interesting thing is that, while the eyes are capable of doing a nearly adult job of scanning the environment, the whole motoric system is essentially shielded from any action by the infant's own motor immaturity. A visual scheme is being built up but there is very little motor response to it. The striking thing about young birds and the type of imprinting that has been described is that there is an immediate emission of behaviour that corresponds to the discrimination the animal can make. You just don't find this in the human species. Indeed, the whole picture we now have of how the primate nervous system develops precludes any correlation between response pattern and stimulus discrimination pattern. So I am very wary of bird-human analogies.

Some Contemporary Patterns of Mother–Infant Interaction in the Feeding Situation[1]

M. D. SALTER AINSWORTH AND S. M. BELL

Johns Hopkins University

INTRODUCTION .

Reviews of research into the effects of different methods of infant care (e.g. Orlansky, 1949; Caldwell, 1964) present no clear evidence that the way in which an infant is fed—either by breast or bottle, on schedule or demand, with early or late weaning—significantly affects his development. As Caldwell points out, research methodology in most of these studies was inadequate to handle the complexity of the variables and the interactions between them. Among the obvious short-comings were the use of secondhand and often retrospective reports about feeding variables; crude classifications which masked what might have been significant variations in practices; and isolation of a specific practice from its context—its context of maternal attitudes and style, of other infant-care practices, and of mother-infant interaction to which the infant himself makes a significant contribution.

Most of the studies examined in these reviews were concerned with the long-term effects of early feeding practices rather than with the infant's responses to them at the time. Exclusive interest in long-term effects was due undoubtedly to the psychoanalytic hypothesis (Freud, 1905; Abraham, 1921) that fixation, attributable to early frustration or

[1] An earlier version of this paper was presented at the biennial meeting of the Society for Research in Child Development in New York on March 29, 1967. The extended project which yielded data for this study has been supported by Grant No. 62-244 of the Foundations' Fund for Research in Psychiatry, and by Grant No. 1 R01 HD 01712 from the United States Public Health Service.

overgratification of instinctual drives, results in the formation of character traits which resist modification through later experiences.

Within the past decade or two research into the effects of early experience upon later personality development has shifted away from preoccupation with the fixation hypothesis towards an examination of mother-infant interaction. Impetus for this shift has come from several sources—from new developments in the study of animal behaviour, from Piagetian cognitive theory (by extrapolation), from developments within psychoanalytic theory itself, and also as a consequence of studies of the responses of infants and young children to mother-child separation and to deprivation of maternal care. The implication is still that there is continuity of development from infancy to later years and that patterns of reaction established in infancy may profoundly influence later development. There has, however, been a subtle shift from the hypothesis that an unalterable personality structure is fashioned through experience in the earliest years to the hypothesis that neonatal, neurophysiological, and behavioural structures are transformed through the infant's earliest transactions with his environment and bias his perceptions, and action patterns so that he responds to subsequent situations at least initially, in the light of the earlier experience. Although these inner structures are assumed to be more or less modifiable through experience, experience itself is held to be influenced by inner structure. It cannot therefore be assumed either that early structuring is the sole or major determiner of later outcomes or that its influence is so attenuated through later transformations as to be negligible.

This shift of emphasis has made it seem worthwhile to examine infant behaviour carefully and in rich detail, in the belief that the starting point influences what comes afterwards and that the significant endeavour is to understand how it is that different patterns of experience set up different patterns of perceiving and behaving. This is a different approach from that of attempting to prove that early experiences have long-term effects massive enough to resist blurring by the multifarious experiences of intervening years.

The present report deals with mother-infant interaction in the first 3 months of life, and focuses especially on interaction pertaining to feeding. This focus does not imply an hypothesis that the hunger drive or oral gratification is prepotent in structuring the basis for interpersonal interaction. It reflects the fact that during the earliest weeks the largest proportion of interaction between an infant and his mother has reference to feeding. Moreover, as suggested by Brody (1956), ". . . most things that a mother does with her infant, however unrelated in style they may be to each other, are related to her style of feeding behaviour with him."

In examining mother-infant interaction in the feeding situation we were guided specifically by several considerations stemming from earlier research. Levy's study of mother-neonate interaction (1959) strongly suggested that the baby's arousal level at the time he was brought to his mother for feeding determined not only his feeding activity but also his mother's response to him, and hence their interaction. Sander (1962) specified that the first issue to be resolved in the course of development of mother-infant interaction is the regulation of the baby's rhythms—an issue which is normally resolved by the end of the first 3 months of life. The later study of infant rhythms by Sander and Julia (1966) further suggested the hypothesis that the points at which feeding interventions occur in the baby's rhythmic cycle of activity-quiescence might do much to regularize or to disorganize the rhythms themselves. Ainsworth's study of the development of the attachment of Ganda infants to their mothers (1963, 1964, 1967) suggested that differences between infants fed on thoroughgoing demand in contrast to those fed otherwise might be attributable in part to the different degrees of initiative permitted to them in feeding. Later work with American infants (Ainsworth and Wittig, 1969) led to the hypothesis that the degree of the mother's sensitivity and responsiveness to the baby's signals, both in feeding and more pervasively, were potent in influencing the course of development of his attachment to her.

GENERAL PROCEDURES

The larger project which yields the findings reported here is a short-term longitudinal study of the development of infant-mother interaction during the first year of life, with particular focus on the development of infant-mother attachment. The sample to date consists of 26 babies of white, middle-class, Baltimore families, the participating families having been reached through paediatricians in private practice. These babies have been observed in their own homes in the course of repeated visits, and their mothers have been interviewed about their infant-care practices. The first 15 in the sample were visited for 4 hours every 3 weeks, visits beginning at 3 weeks of age. The remaining 11 were visited at weekly intervals for the first month, then at 6 weeks of age, and every 3 weeks thereafter, with the first four visits being of about 2 hours' duration. Four of the babies were breast fed for at least 3 months, the rest bottle fed. Two of the mothers had part-time work during part of the early period; the rest were full-time mothers.

The raw data consist of narrative reports of observations and interview findings obtained on each visit.[2] These narrative reports are being subjected to analysis by a variety of procedures, including codings, ratings, and classifications. It is the classification of patterns of interaction in feeding that concerns us here, a classification which deals with the first 3 months only.

CLASSIFICATION OF PATTERNS OF MOTHER-INFANT INTERACTION IN FEEDING

As may be seen in Table I, the classification was based on a cluster analysis of a multiplicity of features of the feeding interaction. These may be reduced to four chief aspects.[3]

The Timing of Feedings

When did the mother feed her baby, how often, and at what intervals? Did she time the feedings in response to the baby's signals? After how much delay? Was the period of delay filled with interventions intended to stave the baby off and, if so, what kind of interventions? If there was a schedule, was it rigid or flexible? Would the mother wake the baby to feed him? Would she advance the feeding if the baby was obviously hungry, and, if so, how much?

Determination of the Amount of Food Ingested and the End of the Feeding

Was the baby allowed to determine the amount of food he ingested, and to terminate the feedings himself? Or did his mother try to determine both and, if so, was it by coaxing or by forcing? Or was she impatient, discontinuing feeding at the first sign of dawdling? Finally, did she overfeed or underfeed the baby, and if so, with what intent?

Mother's Handling of the Baby's Preference in Kind of Food

When solids were introduced, how tactfully did the mother present them? How did she handle rejections of new or disliked foods?

[2] Grateful acknowledgement is made to Barbara A. Wittig, George D. Allyn, and Robert S. Marvin II, who conducted the visits and prepared the narrative reports for 21 of the 26 infants.

[3] The problems related to feeding, listed in the right-hand column, were not included in the cluster analysis upon which the classification was based. These problems may be considered correlates of the classifications. Overweight and underweight judgments are based on paediatricians' records.

TABLE I. PATTERNS OF MOTHER-INFANT INTERACTION IN THE FEEDING SITUATION

Case no.	Sex	Birth order	Type of Feeding	Timing of feedings by M	Determination of amount of food and end of feeding	[a]M's handling of [b]B's preferences in kind of food	Pacing of B's intake	Problems related to feeding
I. DEMAND: THOROUGHGOING AND CONSISTENT								
1	♀	2	Breast; cereal (5 wks)	Feeds on slight signals and for comfort; never wakes to feed	Terminated by B	B dislikes solids; M tactful, did not press	B paces self; can pause and drowse; initiative encouraged	Some colic to 9 wks
II. SCHEDULE: FLEXIBLE								
8	♂	3	Bottle; cereal (6 wks)	Staves-off tactfully; will advance feeding; sometimes wakes, not at night; instalment feedings	M gently persists in coaxing B; very prolonged feedings	No information	Many pauses while B drowses	None
10	♂	4	Bottle; cereal (2 wks)	Staves-off tactfully; will advance feeding; often wakes, not at night	M coaxes little; stops on B's cues	Bottle first; new solids introduced tactfully: flexible interspersion of bottle and solids	B can loaf, drowse; M feeds solids so B has initiative	None
19	♂	1	Breast; cereal (?8 wks)	Staves-off tactfully; will advance feeding or give "snacks" yet presses schedule	M coaxes little; feeding seems to end naturally	Breast (or relief bottle) first; solids no problem	B can loaf, drowse; M feeds solids very skilfully	Colic for first week or so

[a] M = mother [b] B = baby

TABLE I—continued

Case no.	Sex	Birth order	Type of Feeding	Timing of feedings by M	Determination of amount of food and end of feeding	"M's handling of ᵇB's preferences in kind of food	Pacing of B's intake	Problems related to feeding
SCHEDULE FLEXIBLE (CONTINUED):								
21	♀	2	Bottle; cereal (5 wks)	Rigid schedule till 7 wks; then flexible; occasionally wakes to feed; not at night	Amount small and controlled till 7 wks; M avoids overfeeding	Solids introduced very gradually and in small quantities "to learn the taste"	B very eager protests interruptions to 7 wks; frequent long burping necessary	Neonatal pyloric spasm; much improved by 7 wks; overcome later
22	♂	8	Bottle; cereal (3 wks)	Staves-off briefly; sometimes will advance; sometimes wakes; instalment feedings	M coaxes slightly; stops on B's cues	Bottle first; new solids introduced tactfully; flexible interspersion of bottle and solids	B can loaf, drowse; B paces self; B has initiative in taking solids	Slightly underweight
23	♂	1	Bottle; cereal (7 wks)	Staves-off briefly; often wakes to feed; demand feeding at night	M stops on B's cues	Bottle first; new solids interspersed tactfully; disliked food not given	M very delicate in pacing feeding to B's cues	None
III. DEMAND: OVERFEEDING TO GRATIFY THE BABY								
6	♂	3	Bottle; cereal (2 wks)	Demand; little delay; never wakes to feed; instalment feedings	M coaxes and feeds soon again; overfeeding to gratify B	Solids fed first; B likes them	B feeds very fast and M complies	Colic to 6 wks; spitting up; oversleeping; overweight; irregularity

14	♀	3	Bottle; cereal (6 wks)	Demand; short delay; never wakes to feed; instalment feedings	M coaxes and feeds soon again; over-feeding to gratify B	M switches to bottle if B fusses with solids	Delicate pacing to B's slight signals; B wants solids very fast; M complies	Spitting up; gastric distress; oversleeping; overweight; irregularity
IV. SCHEDULE: OVERFEEDING TO GRATIFY THE BABY								
2	♂	2	Bottle; cereal (4 wks)	Usually wakes to feed; some instalment feedings; 3 meals by 9 wks	B falls asleep; M coaxes; very long feedings; overfeeding to gratify B	Solids first; some struggle with disliked foods; sometimes B takes too fast and chokes	B can loaf, drowse; B protests all interruptions; pacing of solid foods fairly good	Spitting up; oversleeping; overweight
25	♂	4	Bottle; cereal (4 wks)	Usually wakes to feed; 3 meals by 4 wks	B falls asleep; M coaxes long; long feedings; overfeeding to gratify B	Bottle first, then solids, then bottle again	B can loaf, drowse; B very hungry and wants solids very fast	Spitting up; oversleeping; overweight
V. SCHEDULE: TOO MUCH STAVING-OFF								
3	♂	2	Bottle; cereal (4 wks)	Prolonged staving-off; many interventions; M denies B's hunger; occasionally B falls asleep; wakes to feed	M coaxes bottle, forces solids	Bottle first; intersperses it with force feeding solids; much struggle	Good pacing of bottle feeding; bad pacing of solids; B protests all interruptions	Unhappy feedings; spitting up; M finds schedule inconvenient
7	♂	3	Breast; cereal (6 wks)	Prolonged staving-off; many interventions; M shifts schedule about; M resents B's demands	M impatient; terminates breast feeding too soon; brief feedings	Breast first; B takes solids well	B can't loaf; M interrupts for social interaction; B protests all interruptions	Unhappy feedings; spitting up; M finds schedule inconvenient

TABLE I—*continued*

Case no.	Sex	Birth order	Type of feeding	Timing of feedings by M	Determination of amount of food and end of feeding	[a]M's handling of [b]B's preferences in kind of food	Pacing of B's intake	Problems related to feeding
SCHEDULE: TO MUCH STAVING-OFF (CONTINUED)								
24	♂	2	Bottle; cereal (1 wk)	Fairly prolonged staving-off; occasionally B falls asleep; wakes to feed	M coaxes bottle, oral stimulation; sometimes forces solids	B dislikes food fed first and persistently; M restrains B who struggles	Milk comes too fast; B protests burping; M coaxes when B loafs	Unhappy feedings
VI. PSEUDO-DEMAND: MOTHER IMPATIENT								
9	♀	5	Bottle; cereal (6 wks)	B must cry to be fed and must cry to be fed enough; instalment feeding	M impatient; discontinues feeding, then feeds again; brief feedings; underfeeding	Solids interspersed with bottle, but not tactfully	Pacing very bad; B can't loaf; nipple too fast; B chokes; interruptions	Much spitting up; unhappy feedings; underfed
11	♀	2	Bottle; cereal (8 wks)	B fed briefly when B fusses; fed off and on in instalments; prolonged delays and B falls asleep and must be wakened	M distracted; forgets feeding till B fusses again; brief feedings; underfeeding	B sometimes rejects solids; struggles, gags, and is too upset to take bottle	Pacing very bad; nipple too fast; B chokes; interruptions	Spitting up; unhappy feedings; underfed
15	♂	1	Breast; relief bottle; cereal (6 wks)	B must cry to be fed; sometimes prolonged delay; instalment feedings	M discontinues too soon; B cries again and is fed again	B is eager for food; order does not matter	M won't tolerate pauses but often interrupts herself; relief bottle too fast; B chokes	Spitting up; unhappy feedings

16	♀	3	Bottle; cereal (8 wks)	Usually long crying before feeding; M sometimes wakes B; some instalment feedings	M impatient; discontinues too soon; brief feedings; underfeeding	Solids first; B can't get them fast enough	Pacing bad; interruptions; nipple too fast; burpings too long; M won't tolerate pause	Thumb-sucking; spitting up; underweight; gastric distress
VII. PSEUDO-DEMAND: OVERFEEDING TO MAKE BABY SLEEP LONG								
13	♀	4	Bottle; cereal (2 wks)	M feeds after B wakes; delay usual, sometimes long; never wakes to feed	M coaxes bottle, forces solids; very long feedings; overfeeding to make B sleep long	Solids first; B struggles and chokes; M force feeds	M paces bottle feeding well; forces solids; B not allowed to be active	Oversleeping; irregularity; unhappy feedings
17	♀	2	Bottle; cereal (2 wks)	M feeds "on demand," but interprets all fussing as hunger; some staving off with pacifier	M coaxes bottle, forces solids; long feedings; overfeeding to make B sleep long, plus phenobarb.	Solids first; B struggles; M force feeds and intersperses bottle in forcing way	M stimulates to speed sucking; forces solids; B not allowed to be active	Overweight; spitting up; gastric distress; unhappy feedings
VIII. SCHEDULE: RIGID, BY THE CLOCK								
26	♂	1	Bottle; solids (?7 wks)	Wakes to feed or staves off; 3 meals by 10 wks	At first M impatient; discontinues too soon; later much coaxing	Bottle first; solids disliked and discontinued; later B liked them	Pacing smooth at first; M later impatient with pauses	Thumb-sucking

TABLE I—continued

Case No.	Sex	Birth order	Type of feeding	Timing of feedings by M	Determination of amounts of food and end of feeding	[a]M's handling of [b]B's preferences in kind of food	Pacing of B's intake	Problems related to feeding
IX. ARBITRARY FEEDING								
4	♀	2	Bottle; cereal (6 wks)	Prolonged delays; sometimes very prolonged; M doesn't perceive B's hunger; M detached; teases with pacifier; 3 meals by 9 wks	M sometimes coaxes to noxious point; sometimes M tries to discontinue too soon and B struggles for more	Solids first; B struggles, cries; chokes, spits up; M forces	Pacing very arbitrary; M forces solids and pace of bottle feeding; M teases by withholding bottle	Gastric distress; much spitting up; feeding is a battle
5	♂	4	Bottle; cereal (3 wks)	Very prolonged delays; B must cry frantically; M denies B's crying; M distracted, fragmented; arbitrary; irregular feeding	M reports little coaxing or forcing; at 18 wks both coaxing and forcing were observed	M reports B screams with solids; feeding not observed till 18 wks; solids forced	At 18 wks milk came too fast; solids forced	Gastric distress; feeding at 18 wks unhappy
12	♀	2	Bottle; cereal (9 wks)	Very prolonged delays; M doesn't perceive B's hunger; M fragmented; arbitrary, erratic, feedings, sometimes in instalments	B can consume little, falls asleep; M coaxes to noxious point	Bottle first; coaxes solids; intersperses bottle tactlessly	Pacing fair with bottle feeding; poor with solids	Gastric distress; very underfed; very underweight

| 18 | ♂ | 1 | Bottle; cereal (6 wks) | Sometimes long delays; sometimes wakes to feed; M denies B's hunger; instalment feedings; erratic schedule; arbitrary 3 meals with juice by 9 wks | M keeps B awake by noxious stimulation; forcing | Solids first, with forced feeding and forcing kind of interspersing with bottle | Pacing extremely bad; M forces pace of bottle feeding as well as solids | Feeding is a battle; spitting up |
| 20 | ♂ | 1 | Bottle; cereal (8 wks) | Sometimes delays; sometimes wakes to feed; M feeds at her time, plays music to drown out B's crying; M teases hungry B with fingers in mouth | B terminates own feeding; M tries to wake by noxious stimulation, but B will not wake | Dislikes foods first; B gags; M intersperses bottle and solids | B saves milk in cheeks; M forces to swallow; B protests burpings; M teases during feeding; M does not force but B gags, cries, swallows; M can't give liked solids fast enough | Gastric distress; spitting up; unhappy feedings |

Pacing of the Rate of the Baby's Intake

To what extent did the mother allow the baby to proceed at his own rate? Did she permit him to slow down or drowse during sucking? Did the milk come too fast for him to swallow it easily? To what extent was spoonfeeding geared to his pace, and to what extent was he allowed to be an active participant in feeding?

Nine patterns of mother-infant interaction pertinent to feeding were identified. Four patterns are designated as feeding on demand, four as feeding according to schedule, and one as arbitrary. The patterns set out below and in Table I are ordered, however, in accordance with an intuitive judgment of the extent to which the baby was permitted to determine the timing of the feedings, the amount he ingested, the order in which solids were given, and the pacing of his rate of intake. Needless to say, this order is considered only as a first rough approximation. In the patterns at the top of the list the baby was an active partner; in those towards the end of the list the mother was more and more dominant in their transactions.

I. *Demand: thoroughgoing and consistent.* Only one mother-infant pair in this sample was characterized by thoroughgoing and consistent demand feeding. This mother consistently fed her little girl when her signals suggested that she wished to go to the breast, and sometimes this was merely for comfort. No consideration was given to the lapse of time since the last feeding. Perhaps because breast fed, the baby did not get too much. She was allowed to drowse at the breast and then to resume sucking. By 6 weeks of age she could release the nipple voluntarily and find it again, and she was very active in her participation in feeding. Her mother was vague in her recall of timing, but by the end of the first quarter, her impression was that the baby usually signalled for the breast about every 4 hours.

II. *Schedule: flexible.* Six babies were fed according to a schedule flexibly regulated by mothers highly sensitive to their signals. All these mothers intended from the beginning to establish a schedule, but there were gentle nudgings towards regularity rather than rigid control. The least flexible of the group were mothers no. 19 and no. 21. While giving prime emphasis to gratifying the baby, mother no. 19 was striving for spacing that would suit her working hours, and mother no. 21 had been cautioned not to feed her baby more often than every 3 hours because of a congenital gastric disorder in the baby.

These mothers sometimes woke their babies to feed them, and sometimes tried to stave them off. This staving-off was usually carried out in a sociable way intended to give the baby pleasure. If the baby could not be beguiled into happy activity, then he would be fed without further delay. Yet none of these mothers hesitated to let their babies fuss a little. They believed it to be good for the baby to wait long enough to be genuinely hungry so that he would enjoy his food. But none ever wittingly let tension mount until the baby was frantic.

The most conspicuous feature of the feeding interaction of these mother-infant pairs was the pacing of the feeding, especially the feeding of the solid food. These mothers had skilful techniques of spoonfeeding which presented the food so that the baby could take it easily and could show some initiative in sucking or gumming it from the spoon. All of them built up the feeding interaction into a smooth and harmonious process, and feeding was an occasion for reciprocal exchanges of smiling and vocalization.

Finally, it should be noted that three of the six mothers used some version of instalment feeding, in which an unfinished bottle or juice would be given if the baby seemed to want something between scheduled feedings. Without a statement of the mother's intent it would have been difficult to distinguish between flexible-schedule feeding and demand feeding.

III. *Demand: overfeeding to gratify the baby.* There were two feeding patterns, labelled "demand feeding" by the mothers, in which the babies were conspicuously overfed—pattern VII and this one. In pattern III the babies were overfed in an attempt to gratify them; in pattern VII the mothers undoubtedly intended to stuff the baby so full that he would sleep a long time and demand little attention. This distinction in intent seems important.

The two mothers showing pattern III wanted their babies to be happy, but tended to treat too broad a spectrum of cues as signals of hunger. Each mother held her baby for a long time after he seemed to have finished feeding, herself enjoying the contact, and occasionally she coaxed him to take more. If he failed to do so she played with him, and then came back to the feeding later—a kind of instalment feeding. If he did not finish his bottle even then, but later began to move his mouth or to fuss, his mother reheated the contents of the bottle and offered it again. Finally, when the baby was completely satiated, having taken a very large amount of food over an extended period, he slept for an excessively long time. Both mothers worried about these long sleeps, but neither ever woke the baby in an attempt to get his rhythms more regular. When the baby finally awoke after a marathon sleep he was ravenous, demanding, and protested at any delay in feeding. These babies fed fast at first and, probably because they ingested too much, both had considerable gastric discomfort and spitting up.

IV. *Schedule: overfeeding to gratify the baby.* The two babies of this pattern both seemed constitutionally to have a high threshold for arousal. Throughout most of the first 3 months they slept virtually all the time they were not being fed. Their spontaneous awakenings were so erratic and after such long intervals that their mothers abandoned demand feeding and woke them according to a schedule; but the schedule was a widely spaced one, for both babies were down to three meals a day in short order. Once awake, both were eager for food and fed fast. After solids had been begun the mothers complied with the babies' demands by fast spoon feeding. During bottle feeding, however, both babies tended to fall asleep before they had finished the bottle. The mother let the baby drowse for a while, but then repeatedly coaxed him to take more, interpreting any mouth movement as a sign of hunger. Consequently the babies were overfed, although both mother and baby seemed to enjoy the prolonged contact. It seems likely that the overfeeding interacted with the constitutional disposition towards oversleeping.

V. *Schedule: too much staving-off.* The three mothers who showed this pattern of interaction would have been delighted to get their babies down to three meals a day, and indeed strove constantly to do so, but their babies did not oblige them by oversleeping. On the contrary, these were alert babies who slept little and seemed hungry and fussy much of the time. These mothers all declared their intention to feed on demand—meaning they would not wake the baby to feed him, which seemed to be the chief criterion of demand feeding for the mothers in this sample. But they referred frequently enough to their hope that the baby would get onto a schedule that it is no real distortion to class this pattern as schedule feeding. They maintained the fiction of demand feeding by mechanisms of denial. They refused to recognize hunger signals when they occurred. Their staving-off activities often began within 2 hours of the previous feeding and lasted sometimes as long as 3 more hours; meanwhile the baby fussed intermittently. Saying "I can't imagine what he wants", the mother tried a series of interventions —pacifier, change of position, toys, nap, bath, and sometimes social interaction—and ended by feeling frustrated and irritable when the baby refused to co-operate in a sustained way. These were mothers who later proved themselves capable of delight in reciprocal exchanges of vocalization and smiling, and they would have been pleased to make feeding a happy time. But, probably because the babies were too hungry and upset when they were finally fed, feedings were tense and unhappy.

VI. *Pseudo-demand: mother impatient.* The mothers in the four pairs who showed this pattern used feeding practices which had some of the characteristics of demand feeding, but these departed enough from a sensitive responsiveness to the baby's signals for the pattern to be labelled "pseudo-demand"—as was pattern VII also.

The babies were fed when they were hungry and cried, after more or less delay, but the feedings were disorganized and inconsistent because of the mother's failure to satisfy the baby. None of the four women could tolerate pauses, and all discontinued the feeding far too soon. In truth, none of the four was sufficiently patient in any transactions with the baby to get sustained chains of interaction. The baby behaved as though the feeding situation was an occasion for social interaction—for the looking, smiling and vocalizing for which the mother otherwise had too little time. When the baby smiled and paused in feeding, his mother concluded that he had finished. The baby, having been put down half fed, soon fussed again, and if he was insistent enough, his mother would feed him in a second or even third instalment. Perhaps as an unconscious reflection of the mother's desire to have the feeding over quickly, all these babies had bottles with nipple holes so large that the milk came too fast. Unless the baby swallowed very quickly, he choked, coughed or gagged, and this, in itself, made for a pause and provided an excuse for the mother to discontinue. Spitting up was a great problem with all four babies, and three were underfed enough to cause the paediatrician concern.

VII. *Pseudo-demand: overfeeding to make the baby sleep long.* Two mothers, who also claimed to feed according to demand, deliberately stuffed their babies so full that they would sleep a long time and demand little attention. The feedings were very long. In one case the baby, aged 3 weeks, was induced to ingest 7 ounces of formula over a period of 2 hours. Both babies were given cereal almost from the beginning, but neither accepted it well. They spat it out, struggled, and tried to avert their heads, but both mothers were determined to get the food in and they did. Needless to say, the feedings were tense and anxious. Neither baby was well regulated in rhythms by the end of the first 3 months, and neither was permitted to be an active participant in feeding.

VIII. *Schedule: rigid, by the clock.* Only one mother in this sample fed strictly by the clock. She adhered to a progressively more stringent and more widely spaced schedule of feedings, until by the time the baby was 10 weeks old he was on three meals a day. He adapted himself reasonably well to this regime during his first 3 months. On the face of it, it seemed a fairly harmonious partnership. But this pattern is placed low on the list because this mother was almost completely impervious to the baby's signals, and she fed him almost entirely at her own timing.

IX. *Arbitrary feeding*. Finally, there were five cases in which feeding was arbitrary either in the time of feedings or in the pacing of intake or both. In each case, the pattern of feeding stemmed directly from the mother's disturbed personality. The mother in pair no. 4 had a post-partum reaction; she was detached and very insensitive to the baby's signals, although she improved suddenly when the baby was about 12 weeks old. Mothers no. 5 and no. 12 were both very anxious and frag-mented. They put their babies away for long periods and either "tuned out" the crying or failed to perceive it as a signal of hunger. Mother no. 18 was anxious, and the only way in which she could stem her anxiety was to control everything and everybody in a compulsive and sometimes sadistic way. She could not bear the way her baby defied her by refusing to sleep, wake, feed, and smile in accordance with her will. The timing of feedings was erratic, but the most conspicuous feature was the forced nature of the feeding—both of milk and of solids—which had to be seen to be believed. Mother no. 20 was less obviously disturbed, and less arbitrary in her feeding practices than the others. She treated her baby as a plaything—sometimes charming, but sometimes tiresome and to be put away and ignored. Her trans-actions with him were always at her own whim, and consequently, in her own way, she was as arbitrary as the other more disturbed mothers.

CORRELATES OF THE FEEDING PATTERNS

Three sets of correlates of the feeding patterns will be considered here. These have been selected as the only ones which our current stage of data analysis made available, and certainly not as the only ones which might be correlated with early patterns of interaction in feeding. The first two of these are contemporaneous, referring to the first 3 months of life: the baby's amount and pattern of crying, and the mother's attitudes and infant-care practices. The third correlate is the baby's behaviour in a strange situation experimentally introduced at the end of the first year.

Crying in the First 3 Months

Each episode of crying which occurred during visits in the first 3 months was coded.[4] This coding was done entirely independently of the other analyses, although it was, of course, based on the same narrative reports. The quantification of the coded crying includes two types of measures: the number of episodes of crying, and the duration of each episode of crying. Precise timing of the duration of a cry was only rarely reported by the visitor, so these measures have had to be rough estimates made by the coder; the absolute figures must therefore be taken as only approximate, although the relative figures are of interest. Corrections were made to adjust for the difference between the two sub-samples in the schedule of visits, and for the differences between cases in the amount of time that the baby was actually under observation.[5] Some of the measures dealt with crying specifically related to feeding; others dealt with crying which took place at any time during the visit. The three measures of crying related to feeding were: (a) the mean frequency of crying episodes per hour in the period "before feeding"—a period which was deemed to begin 180 minutes after the previous feeding and to end when the next feeding began; (b) the mean duration of "prolonged" crying in the period before feeding, in minutes per hour—a "prolonged cry" being defined as anything not specified in the narrative report as a brief cry, and in general as a cry lasting 20 seconds or more; (c) the mean frequency per feeding of crying episodes during feeding. The three measures concerned with overall crying were: (d) the mean frequency of crying episodes per hour; (e) the mean frequency of brief crying episodes per hour—a brief cry being defined as one characterized as "brief" or any short burst lasting no more than 19 seconds; (f) the mean duration in minutes per hour of "prolonged" crying. (For measure (d), the total number of episodes counted includes a few episodes of intermittent crying that could not be classified as either "brief" or "prolonged"; none of these occurred "before feeding" or "during feeding".) These various scores

---

[4] Grateful acknowledgement is made to Robert S. Marvin II, John Conklin, Ross Conner, Terence Leveck, and Herbert Markley for their painstaking efforts in the task of coding.

[5] Since 11 of the babies had been visited four times during the first month and the other 15 only once, the various crying measures for these 11 were adjusted so that crying during the first month (which, in frequency, may well have exceeded later crying) was given equal weight to crying in the subsequent three visits—as it was for the other 15. Each measure then was divided by actual observation time in minutes, and multiplied by 60, and thus expressed in episodes per hour of observation, or duration in minutes for each hour of observation.

TABLE II. FREQUENCY AND DURATION OF CRYING EPISODES

Feeding pattern	Case no.	Crying related to feeding			Crying overall		
		Mean frequency of crying episodes per hour before feeding	Mean duration of "prolonged" crying before feeding (min/hr)	Mean frequency of crying episodes during feeding per feeding	Mean frequency of crying episodes per hour	Mean frequency of brief crying episodes per hour	Mean duration of "prolonged" crying (min/hr)
I	1	0·7 (1)ᵃ	0·2 (1)ᵃ	1·0 (2)ᵃ	2·2 (1)ᵃ	1·4 (1)ᵃ	1·8 (1)ᵃ
II	8	1·6 (4)	0·5 (2)	0 (1)	2·8 (2)	2·1 (2)	3·1 (2)
	10	1·1 (3)	0 (1)	0·5 (1)	3·2 (2)	2·5 (3)	1·4 (1)
	19	1·3 (4)	2·7 (3)	0·7 (2)	3·2 (2)	2·4 (3)	3·3 (2)
	21	1·6 (4)	0·4 (1)	0·3 (1)	5·4 (5)	4·9 (5)	0·9 (1)
	22	0·3 (1)	0·2 (1)	1·2 (2)	4·3 (4)	3·6 (4)	3·7 (3)
	23	0·5 (1)	0·2 (1)	0 (1)	3·6 (3)	2·6 (4)	0·7 (1)
III	6	0·9 (2)	1·5 (3)	2·0 (4)	3·6 (3)	1·7 (2)	3·2 (2)
	14	1·2 (3)	2·8 (4)	1·3 (2)	2·8 (2)	1·6 (1)	3·5 (3)
IV	2	0·4 (1)	0·4 (1)	0·5 (1)	2·2 (1)	1·6 (1)	2·0 (1)
	25	1·1 (3)	1·1 (2)	1·5 (3)	2·5 (1)	1·6 (1)	3·0 (2)
V	3	1·3 (4)	3·0 (4)	2·5 (5)	5·1 (5)	3·8 (5)	4·4 (4)
	7	2·9 (5)	3·4 (4)	2·3 (5)	5·1 (5)	3·7 (4)	5·6 (4)
	24	1·6 (4)	2·0 (3)	1·8 (3)	5·6 (5)	4·6 (5)	3·0 (2)

VI	9	0·3 (1)	2·1 (3)	2·0 (4)	3·6 (3)	2·2 (3)	6·6 (4)
	11	0·9 (2)	0·7 (2)	2·3 (5)	3·7 (4)	2·7 (4)	4·4 (4)
	15	1·0 (3)	0·9 (3)	3·3 (5)	3·6 (3)	1·8 (2)	6·2 (4)
	16	3·4 (5)	3·4 (5)	1·4 (3)	7·9 (5)	6·4 (5)	4·3 (3)
VII	13	0·5 (1)	1·0 (2)	1·5 (3)	2·8 (2)	1·7 (2)	4·2 (3)
	17	0·8 (2)	1·8 (3)	1·6 (3)	2·3 (1)	1·3 (1)	7·6 (5)
VIII	26	2·6 (5)	3·0 (4)	0·3 (1)	2·3 (1)	1·4 (1)	5·5 (4)
IX	4	1·1 (3)	6·9 (5)	2·0 (4)	3·2 (2)	2·4 (3)	8·2 (5)
	5	0·9 (2)	16·7 (5)	b	3·9 (4)	2·1 (2)	20·6 (5)
	12	1·7 (5)	14·7 (5)	2·5 (5)	4·7 (4)	2·5 (3)	15·4 (5)
	18	1·1 (3)	4·6 (5)	2·1 (4)	3·4 (3)	2·7 (4)	4·0 (3)
	20	3·0 (5)	4·1 (5)	3·6 (5)	9·6 (5)	6·7 (5)	11·5 (5)

a The figures in parentheses refer to quintile ranks.
b This baby was visited only three times in the first 3 months. Once he was fed by the observer, but twice he was not fed. "Before feeding" time was sampled, but no observations were made of feeding by the mother.

for each of the babies, together with the quintile rank of each score, are shown in Table II.

This table shows that the first two patterns of feeding interaction are the two associated with the least crying. The babies in these two groups (consistent-demand feeding and flexible-schedule feeding) are conspicuous for the little amount of crying during feeding, and this seems to be related to the sensitive pacing and the prompt response to signals which characterized the mothers' feeding practices. They also tended to have a relatively short duration of crying before feeding, except for no. 19 whose mother was "pushing a schedule". They had a relatively short duration of crying overall, although some of them had frequent episodes of brief crying. These findings reflect the fact that their mothers intervened promptly and appropriately enough to limit cries to short duration; they also suggest that these babies were learning to use brief cries as modes of communication rather than merely as modes of expression of state.

Feeding pattern IX, arbitrary feeding, is especially associated with long duration of prolonged crying before feeding, despite the fact that these babies do not tend consistently to have a high frequency of separate episodes of crying before feeding. This reflects the fact that the mothers of these babies tended to be very slow in responding to hunger cues. They were also slow to respond to crying generally; the overall cries tend to become very prolonged, especially in cases no. 5, no. 12, and no. 20.

The babies in pattern V, in which there was a long period of staving-off the feeding with many ineffective interventions, tended to have relatively frequent episodes of crying, especially brief episodes, although they did not have cries of long duration until the period before feeding. These babies also tended to have a relatively high frequency of crying during feeding, presumably because they were too hungry and upset when they were finally fed.

Feeding pattern VI, in which the mothers were impatient and discontinued feeding too soon, is characterized by a relatively high frequency of crying during feeding. This reflects the fact that the feedings tended to come in several instalments, each instalment being given in response to the baby's cry.

It is not possible to discuss further details here, but attention is drawn to the last column in Table II, which lists the mean time per hour spent in prolonged crying. It is evident that the first four feeding patterns, in which the mothers were relatively sensitive and responsive to the babies' signals and communications, are associated with relatively little crying, while the other five feeding patterns in which the mothers were relatively insensitive or unresponsive, are associated with a relatively large amount of crying.

Maternal-Care Variables in the First 3 Months

Twenty-two 9-point rating scales were devised to assess a number of different aspects of maternal care during the first 3 months of life. Each mother was rated by two or more judges[6], and the scores given in Table III are the final ratings agreed on by the judges in conference. Six[7] of the scales have been selected to illustrate the relationships between the ratings of the mothers and the kinds of interaction these mothers established with their infants in the feeding situation. These six scales deal with the following variables.

Mother's perception of the baby. The low end of the scale reflects perceptions that are distorted by projection, denial, or other defensive operations by the mother. The high end of the scale reflects perceptions that are realistic and accurate, because the mother is capable of seeing things from the baby's point of view.[8]

Mother's delight in the baby. Delight here is defined as situation-specific or behaviour-specific; it is experienced and expressed in response to the baby himself, and to be distinguished from the pleasure of pride.

Mother's acceptance of the baby. This scale deals chiefly with the mother's degree of acceptance or rejection of the baby in terms of the extent to which she feels that he interferes with her own autonomy.

Appropriateness of mother's interaction with the baby. This scale refers to social advances and interaction. Appropriateness is deemed a matter of the mother's timing of her interventions in the baby's state and current activity, the matching of stimulation to the baby's capabilities, and knowing when to desist from stimulation. Both over-stimulation and understimulation are considered inappropriate.

Amount of physical contact between mother and baby, especially that which occurs outside the context of routine care.

[6] We thank George D. Allyn and Robert S. Marvin II for their ratings and for their participation in the construction of the rating scales, and also Barbara A. Wittig, whose preliminary work was helpful in the construction of the present scales.

[7] The ratings of four variables of feeding practices are not reported here, since the scales were revised and the cases re-rated as a consequence of the analysis of the feeding interactions that are reported. The six scales selected for this report deal with variables not specifically related to feeding, and were devised before the analysis of feeding interaction; ratings on these were entirely independent of that analysis.

[8] Jan Smedslund suggested the happy phrase "seeing things from the baby's point of view", as the antithesis of "egocentric" perception in a Piagetian sense.

TABLE III. RATINGS OF SELECTED MATERNAL-CARE VARIABLES AND CLASSIFICATIONS OF STRANGE-SITUATION BEHAVIOUR

Feeding pattern	Case no.	^{a}M's perception of B^b	M's delight in B	M's acceptance of B	Appropriateness of M's interaction with B	Amount of physical contact	Effectiveness of M's response to B's cry	Classification of B's behaviour in strange situation
I	1	8·0	6·5	9·0	6·5	7·5	8·0	B₃
II	8	7·0	7·3	8·5	7·5	8·0	6·5	B₃
	10	9·0	9·0	9·0	9·0	7·8	7·5	B₃
	19	7·5	9·0	8·0	7·0	7·0	6·0	B₃
	21	9·0	7·0	8·0	8·0	6·5	7·0	B₃
	22	9·0	7·0	8·0	6·5	5·0	7·5	B₃
	23	7·0	5·5	6·0	7·0	6·5	6·5	B₂
III	6	7·0	6·0	7·5	7·0	7·0	6·0	B₃
	14	7·0	6·5	7·0	7·0	7·0	6·0	B₃
IV	2	6·5	7·0	7·0	7·0	5·0	5·5	B₃
	25	7·0	8·5	8·0	6·0	7·0	7·5	B₂
V	3	3·0	3·5	3·5	3·5	3·0	3·5	—
	7	6·5	6·5	5·5	6·0	6·5	3·5	B₂
	24	4·0	3·0	4·0	3·5	4·5	3·5	A₁
VI	9	2·5	3·0	3·0	3·5	3·0	4·0	A₂
	11	2·0	4·0	5·3	3·5	5·0	5·0	C₁
	15	4·0	4·0	4·5	3·0	4·0	3·5	—
	16	3·5	3·0	3·0	3·5	2·5	2·0	A₂

VII	13	4·5	1·0	4·0	3·0	3·5	3·5	C₁
	17	4·0	2·0	3·0	4·0	4·5	6·0	—
VIII	26	2·5	1·0	3·0	1·5	2·0	2·0	A₁
IX	4	3·5	4·0	3·5	4·0	4·0	3·0	B₁
	5	2·0	2·5	3·0	3·5	3·5	2·0	C₂
	12	1·0	1·5	2·5	1·0	1·0	1·0	C₂
	18	1·0	1·0	1·0	1·0	1·0	1·0	A₁
	20	2·5	2·0	1·5	3·0	3·0	1·5	A₁

^a M = mother.
^b B = baby.

Effectiveness of mother's response to baby's crying. This scale deals with three main facets of maternal behaviour: heeding the baby's cry, interpreting the cause of the crying correctly, and responding appropriately.

The reliability of these scales seems to fall within acceptable limits.[9]

The ratings of each of the mothers on each of the six scales are shown in Table III. Inspection shows that the highest ratings are associated with feeding patterns I, II, III, and IV,—the thoroughgoing-demand, the flexible-schedule, and the two overfeeding-to-gratify patterns. These are all patterns in which sensitivity to the baby's signals and a desire to gratify him are prominent. These mothers tended to be able to see things from the baby's point of view, to take delight in his behaviour, and to accept him with little regret over the temporary surrender of their autonomy. They tended to respond promptly and appropriately to the baby's crying, thus terminating the cry. In their social interaction as well as in their feeding interaction they were sensitive to the baby's state and wishes. They tended to give their babies a relatively large amount of physical contact beyond that required by routine care.

The lower ratings are associated with the other feeding patterns, patterns VIII and IX having the lowest ratings. The mothers in these last two patterns tended to be distorted in their perceptions of the baby, to take little or no delight in his behaviour, and to resent overtly or covertly the infringement of their autonomy by his demands. They were unresponsive to the baby's crying, or inappropriate in their response to it. They were similarly inappropriate in their social interactions with him, and tended grossly to understimulate, or to tease or torment, or to be inappropriate in their timing. Finally, they tended to give the baby little physical contact other than that in routine care.

Behaviour in a Strange Situation at 12 Months

At the end of the first year all but one of the 26 babies were introduced to a standardized strange situation, which has been described in detail elsewhere (Ainsworth and Wittig, 1969). In brief, we were interested in (a) exploratory behaviour in the strange situation and whether the child could use his mother as a secure base from which to explore it; (b) the responses of the child to two brief separations from his mother, during the first of which he was left with a stranger, and

---

[9] As an illustration of the reliability of rating, the following are product-moment correlation coefficients of the 6 scales, based on the 12 cases which the authors both judged: 0·93, 0·97, 0·94, 0·89, 0·89, and 0·86.

during the second of which he was left alone; (c) his responses to his mother when reunited with her after separation. (We were also interested in the child's responses to the stranger *per se*, although this is not especially relevant here.)

The babies were classified into three main groups and seven subgroups on the basis of their behaviour in the strange situation— especially their behaviour in interaction with the mother upon her return after two brief absences.[10] (Two of the babies were not included because they were ill when brought to the strange situation, so that only 23 of the present sample were classified.) The characteristics of the various groups and subgroups may be summarized as follows.

Group A babies showed little or no tendency to seek proximity, interaction or contact with the mother, and little or no tendency to cling when picked up or to resist being released. They tended either to ignore the mother on her return, to go away from her, or to turn away. They tended to be as responsive to the stranger as to the mother, sometimes more so, and did not protest at the mother's absence if the stranger was present. *Subgroup A_1* particularly lacked interest in regaining and maintaining contact with the mother, and ignored her return. *Subgroup A_2* showed some interest in contact but it was intermingled with a marked tendency to turn away, move away, or look away from the mother when she returned after an absence.

Group B babies, by contrast, had a clear-cut tendency to seek proximity, interaction or contact with the mother, and were obviously more interested in her than in the stranger. Not all were distressed during the mother's absences; if they were distressed, however, it was clearly related to her absence and not merely to being alone. Those in *Subgroup B_1* sought interaction with the mother, but did not especially seek physical contact. Those in *Subgroup B_2* sought to regain and to maintain contact with the mother, although to a lesser extent than those in *Subgroup B_3*, in which an active effort to gain and to maintain contact was especially conspicuous. Furthermore, the babies in *Subgroups B_1* and B_2 resembled each other in displaying little or no distress in the separation episodes whereas most, although not all, of the babies in *Subgroup B_3* were highly distressed.

Group C babies tended to resemble those of *Subgroup B_3* in their interest in regaining and maintaining contact, and in their distress

[10] The classificatory system differs from that tentatively formulated for the first 14 infants in the sample (described by Ainsworth and Wittig, 1969). The present system was formulated on the basis of a total sample of 56 infants, and will be described in detail in a future publication.

upon separation, but differed from them in several respects. They showed less ability to use the mother as a secure base from which they could enjoy exploring the strange environment. They tended to intermingle resistance to contact with the mother with their contact-seeking behaviour by, for example, both reaching for her and pushing her away. They generally displayed more maladaptive behaviour throughout the strange situation. *Subgroup C_1* babies were conspicuous for highly ambivalent behaviour to the mother, resistance to the stranger, and angry, aggressive behaviour with both. *Subgroup C_2* babies, while also ambivalent, were strikingly passive, withdrawn, or detached in much of their behaviour.

Table III shows that all but two of the babies classified in the first four feeding patterns fall into *Subgroup B_3*—the two exceptions being in *Subgroup B_2*—in regard to their behaviour in the strange situation at the end of the first year. Babies whose mothers were especially sensitive and responsive to them in the early feeding situation, and indeed generally, manifested attachment to their mothers (without conspicuous behavioural disturbance) through active efforts both to regain contact after a brief separation and to maintain contact once gained by clinging and resisting release. All but two of the babies classified in the other five feeding patterns fall either into *Group A* or *Group C*. Babies whose mothers were relatively insensitive and unresponsive to them in the early feeding situation, tended, at the end of the first year, either to lack interest in regaining and in maintaining contact with their mothers when reunited after an absence, or to intermingle contact-seeking behaviour with rejection of her—either tending to go away and to look away from her or to angrily push her away or to push away the toys offered by her. The two *Group B* babies whose mothers were relatively insensitive in the early feeding situation were classified in *Subgroups B_1* and *B_2*; neither was in *B_3*, in which active contact-seeking behaviour was especially marked. It is especially interesting to note that the two babies of *Subgroup C_2*, whose passivity was marked at 12 months, had earlier been fed arbitrarily, cried much, and had mothers with consistently low maternal-care ratings.

SUMMARY

The cause-effect relations implicit in these findings are by no means clear-cut or unidirectional. This is a study with a multiplicity of variables. Even assuming that we were successful in our efforts to be objective in all our ratings and classifications and to keep our judg-

TABLE IV. PRODUCT-MOMENT CORRELATIONS BETWEEN RATINGS OF SIX MATERNAL-CARE VARIABLES

	[a]M's perception of B[b]	M's delight in B	M's acceptance of B	Appropriateness of M's interaction with B	Amount of physical contact	Effectiveness of M's response to B's crying
M's perception of B	—	0·879	0·922	0·936	0·842	0·872
M's delight in B	0·879	—	0·924	0·918	0·870	0·806
M's acceptance of B	0·922	0·924	—	0·908	0·908	0·900
Appropriateness of M's interaction with B	0·936	0·918	0·908	—	0·883	0·859
Amount of physical contact	0·842	0·870	0·908	0·883	—	0·834
Effectiveness of M's response to B's crying	0·872	0·806	0·900	0·859	0·834	—

[a] M = mother
[b] B = baby

ments of each variable independent of our judgments of the others, there is nevertheless much confounding among the variables. The 6 rating scales yield positively correlated measures of the mothers' attitudes and infant-care practices, and most of the correlations are high (Table IV). The classification of interaction in the feeding situation emphasizes sensitivity of the mother to the baby's rhythms, signals, pacing and preferences as a pervasive theme, but this same sensitivity is reflected in a number of the rating scales, even those having no explicit relationship to feeding. In general, one could say that those mothers who could see things from the baby's point of view tended to adopt infant-care practices which led to harmonious interaction not only in feeding but generally. One could say further that babies whose behaviour, social and otherwise, gave rise to consistently gratifying or interesting feedback tended to cry less, to learn modes of communication other than hard expressive crying, and to gain more frustration tolerance and more regular and predictable rhythms than babies whose behaviour made little or no difference in determining what happened to them.

On the other hand, it is reasonable to believe that it is easier for a mother to interact harmoniously with a baby who is relatively easy to understand and to predict, and who responds with pleasure and interest rather than with frustration and distress. From the beginning, some of the babies in our sample may have been more difficult than others, for example, baby no. 12 who had perinatal pathology. Certainly, in the case of feeding pattern IV there were two babies whose high threshold for arousal seemed to interact with overfeeding to produce long periods of sleeping and little fussiness. The mothers of feeding pattern VII who tried to accomplish the same end by deliberate overfeeding, had much less success, perhaps in part because their babies were different constitutionally, but probably also because the feeding interaction was controlled by the mothers rather than being geared to the babies' signals. Whatever role may be played by the baby's constitutional characteristics in establishing the initial pattern of mother-infant interaction, it seems quite clear that the mother's contribution to the interaction and the baby's contribution are caught up in an interacting spiral. It is because of these spiral effects—some "vicious" and some "virtuous"—that the variables are so confounded that it is not possible to distinguish independent from dependent variables.

Let us now turn to a brief discussion of the specifics of feeding practices. The findings here presented suggest that the central issue in the controversy between demand and scheduled feeding is of some significance, and that it is a question of the programming of the whole sequence of interventions in reasonable synchrony with the baby's rhythms, signals and behaviours. There is no easy rubric for a paediatrician to use when instructing mothers about feeding practices, nor for an interviewer to use when trying to elicit accurate information about methods of feeding. There is clear support for the conclusion of previous investigators (e.g., Heinstein, 1963) that the mother's attitude is important, but the present findings suggest that it not only modulates the effect of her practice, but plays a crucial role both in her initial choice of practice and in shaping the specifics of the practice itself.

Feeding practices which have as objectives, explicitly or implicitly, both the gratification of the baby and the regulation of his rhythms seem to succeed irrespective of whether these practices are labelled "demand" or "schedule". They also succeed in a third aim, which seems important, and that is to allow the baby to be an active participant in feeding rather than merely a passive recipient. Active participation in determining timing and pacing of feeding seems very likely to facilitate the establishment of smooth and mutually gratifying mother-infant interaction. Initiative in determining the amount to be ingested and the termination of feeding seems crucial in facilitating the early regulation of rhythms. Furthermore, what can be extrapolated from animal research into the mechanisms regulating feeding behaviour (e.g. Stellar, 1967) suggests that it is important to allow an infant to pace himself in rate of feeding; it is likely that interference with his own pace tends to disrupt the feedback mechanisms which regulate normal feeding behaviour. Finally, this leads us to an hypothesis which has been discussed more fully elsewhere (Ainsworth, 1967, especially pp. 445–449). Through the favourable feedback which a baby obtains to his various signals, actions, and communications he may build up confidence in his ability to influence what happens to him, or, in terms used by White (1963), feelings of efficacy would lead to a sense of competence. Although for most babies the feeding situation has become a relatively unimportant occasion for mother-infant interaction by the end of the first year, the baby's experience in influencing his mother's behaviour through his own actions—an experience which begins in the earliest weeks of life—seems likely to influence the nature of his attachment to her.

This brings us to the impressive relationship shown by the present study between mother-infant interaction in the first 3 months and infants' behaviour at the end of the first year. This does not necessarily imply that early feeding experience has a direct effect on later attachment behaviour. Firstly, it seems very likely that the kinds of mother-infant interaction characteristic of the early feeding situation would persist beyond the first 3 months of life, which was a termination point set arbitrarily by us, and that they would continue to exert an influence. Secondly, it seems very unlikely that nothing else of consequence could happen in the last 9 months of the first year to influence the 1-year-old's attachment to his mother. Indeed, to demonstrate this kind of relationship between antecedent and consequent does not, of course, prove a cause-effect relationship at all. The important step of identifying and following through the developmental processes which link antecedent and consequent has yet to be undertaken. In this context, the lack of obvious phenotypical resemblance between antecedent and consequent behaviour need not be dismaying. On the contrary, epigenetic considerations lead us to expect that behaviour in one phase of development may depend upon the completion of the developmental "task" of an earlier phase without any apparent continuity in the behaviours themselves.

Nevertheless, it is submitted that the findings here presented suggest that early experience can have a significant effect on later development. It is also submitted that early experience exerts its influence through setting up patterns of perception, expectation, and action which interact with further environmental influences: these patterns, in the absence of gross changes in either the nature of the environment or the structure of the organism, can make for underlying continuities in developmental processes across wide segments of the developmental years.

REFERENCES

ABRAHAM, K. 1921. Contributions to the theory of the anal character. Reprinted 1949 in *Selected papers*. Hogarth Press, London. Pp. 370–392.

AINSWORTH, M. D. S. 1963. Development of infant mother-interaction among the Ganda. In B. M. Foss (Ed.), *Determinants of infant behaviour II*. Methuen, London. Pp. 67–104.

AINSWORTH, M. D. S. 1964. Patterns of attachment behavior shown by the infant in interaction with his mother. *Merrill-Palmer Q.* **10**, 51–58.

AINSWORTH, M. D. S. 1967. *Infancy in Uganda: infant care and the growth of love*. Johns Hopkins University Press, Baltimore.

AINSWORTH, M. D. S. and WITTIG, B. A. 1969. Attachment and exploratory behavior of one-year-olds in a strange situation. In B. M. Foss (Ed.), *Determinants of infant behaviour IV*. Methuen, London. Pp. 111–136.

BRODY, S. 1956. *Patterns of mothering*. International Universities Press, New York.

CALDWELL, B. M. 1964. The effects of infant care. In M. L. Hoffman and L. W. Hoffman (Eds.), *Review of child development research. Vol. 1*. Russell Sage Foundation, New York. Pp. 9–88.

FREUD, S. 1905. *Three essays on the theory of sexuality.* Reprinted 1953 in *The standard edition of the complete psychological works of Sigmund Freud. Vol. 7.* Hogarth Press, London. Pp. 125–245.

HEINSTEIN. M. I. 1963. Behavioral correlates of breast-bottle regimes under varying parent-infant relationships. *Monogr. Soc. Res. Child Develop.* **28,** No. 88.

LEVY, D. M. 1959. *The demonstration clinic.* C. C. Thomas, Springfield, Ill.

ORLANSKY, H. 1949. Infant care and personality. *Psychol. Bull.* **46,** 1–48.

SANDER, L. W. 1962. Issues in early mother-child interaction. *J. Am. Acad. Child Psychiat.* **1,** 141–166.

SANDER, L. W. and JULIA, H. L. 1966. Continuous interactional monitoring in the neonate. *Psychosom. Med.* **28,** 822–835.

STELLAR, E. 1967. Hunger in man: comparative and physiological studies. *Am. Psychol.* **22,** 105–117.

WHITE, R. W. 1963. *Ego and reality in psychoanalytic theory.* International Universities Press, New York.

Discussion

Possibility of Sex Differences in Infant Signalling Ability

HAMBURG: For babies who were fed according to a given pattern of interaction, do you know whether the frequency or duration of their crying in a nonfeeding context has any relation to that shown in the feeding context?

AINSWORTH: The measure of crying that related most to feeding patterns was the mean duration of prolonged crying: this included both feeding-related crying and nonfeeding-related crying. The difficulty is that the mothers who are sensitive to the baby's hunger signals are sensitive to all his other signals too, and I couldn't split this sensitivity variable apart.

SCHAFFER: You seem to be suggesting that differences in crying are due to differences in maternal sensitivities. We ought, however, to bear in mind the possibility that it may be due, at least partly, to differences in the signalling abilities of the children, and that there might conceivably be sex differences in this respect.

AINSWORTH: That's right; there appears to be an interaction. In our sample boys outnumber girls, and there is no evidence of significant sex differences in crying. Nevertheless I think there is a general tendency for mothers to treat infant boys differently from infant girls. I don't know what the interpretation of this is. Perhaps Freud was right in saying that boys attract mothers more than do girls, because the boy is a sort of phallic symbol.

KAGAN: I think that's unnecessary. One could just say that psycho-dynamically a mother knows about girls. When she has a girl she begins to project onto this baby. When she has a boy, on the other hand, she is not sure she understands him; he is more like a pet and she has to wait for clues to tell her how to handle him.

LEVINE: There is a completely different alternative explanation. This is that there is something intrinsically different about the male and female at birth regarding their signalling capacity.

AINSWORTH: This is also what Howard Moss (1967. *Merrill-Palmer Quart.*, **13,** 19) says: the boys cry more.

Overweight Babies

GINSBURG: I noticed that your only two cases of colic, other than the one that was involved in over-feeding, were breast fed babies. I was wondering also whether the two mothers who had overweight babies, which they were over-feeding, were themselves overweight.

AINSWORTH: There were six over-fed babies and two of the mothers themselves had weight problems. Two of the four breast fed babies had colic, but two of them showed no evidence of gastric distress. Nevertheless, I wondered whether the colic of the first two, who fell in feeding patterns I and II respectively, might have been related to breast milk, since I understand that initially it disagrees with some babies.

GINSBURG: Did babies in pattern III maintain the overweight later on and did their mothers persist in over-feeding them?

AINSWORTH: Yes, throughout the first year. Yet neither of these two mothers was plump.

Description of Maternal Delight

GINSBURG: Was the mother's interaction with the baby, in terms of her delight in him, ever related to abnormality in her? For example, could not a mother who was sadistic be said to delight in her baby in that she used it to satisfy her particular needs?

AINSWORTH: Yes, but we rule out this kind of delight. We define delight in terms of "isn't he cute", "isn't he adorable", "laughs at something the baby did". Some of the mothers showed delight by saying such things as "look how mad he is", "look how he wrinkles up his nose", "look how vigorous he is". This is a very specific delight in the baby's behaviour.

BATESON: Was your measure of delight one of frequency, or did you use other criteria as well?

AINSWORTH: Besides frequency we also rated for quality of delight. For example, a mother who showed quite a lot of pleasure in having a baby and pride in the whole situation, but who lacked the behaviour-specific delight, might be given a rating of 3 or 4, whereas the mother that was 1 or 2 showed no delight, or only a bland, mild, positive feeling that lacked the appropriate-to-situation quality of delight.

Description of Passivity and Aggression

BATESON: Can you elaborate on what you mean by passivity and by aggression, which you use in distinguishing babies?

AINSWORTH: The two passive babies didn't explore, they just sat like a bump on a log: this was passivity carried to a pathological extreme. One of the babies rolled over on her back eventually and, for our sample, this was bizarre behaviour. Aggression referred to movements of pushing a toy aside, throwing it down. Also babies who did this were inclined, if picked up by either the mother or the stranger, to want to be both picked up and put down: there was a protest and struggle as well as clinging.

One of the things that we need to do next is to make a much more careful analysis of infant behaviour in two directions. One concerns the patterns of the attachment behaviour, the other concerns things like arousal level, vigour and amount of activity and so on. Some very interesting interactions may come out of this. Babies seem to be different from the beginning in such things as arousal level. We haven't any clear-cut indication of the extent to which the baby himself in his own characteristics, except perhaps for sex, contributes to the various kinds of interaction which become established between him and his mother.

Methodology

PAPOUŠEK: In selecting your sample did you look out for pathology during pregnancy?

AINSWORTH: There was only one baby out of the 26 for whom there seemed to have been any perinatal difficulty. Our babies were nearly all selected before they were born. I wanted to get a white middle-class sample rather than one from the low socio-economic level families, mostly negro, who come to prenatal clinics and with whom perinatal pathology is more frequent. What I did was to approach a number of paediatricians in private practice and say "Have you any mothers who are expecting babies within the next two months?" They would go through their case files and produce names of women who were pregnant. We contacted them and in nearly every case they agreed to participate We didn't have much of a drop-out at that level and we didn't have any drop out after we had started observations.

GINSBURG: Were your ratings of the mothers in relation to the babies done blind?

AINSWORTH: It was not done blind. I have had four assistants working on these data and a lot of undergraduate coders. The undergraduates were working blind and they were the ones who did the coding of the crying. The assistant who worked up the entire crying material did it independently: she had not visited any of the families and did not know the people at all. One set of ratings was nearly always done by a person who had visited the family at least once. Wherever possible one of the raters was the regular visitor to the family and the second and the third rater didn't know the people directly.

What we are dealing with in the study as a whole is a set of highly correlated variables. The various aspects of the data analysis were sufficiently independent for not very much of this to be attributed to subjectivity in the examiners. These are genuinely related variables and we attempted in the rating scales to rate quite distinct aspects of maternal care that we believed would define good mothering and bad mothering.

DENENBERG: The problem is that, even though there are independent judgments, they are based upon the same set of observations. You went through these and you made judgmental ratings and classifications. Someone else then went through them and did a quantification of these ratings independently. It seems that what that someone else was doing was to isolate the particular dimension which you had used in a global fashion to make an overall rating. Is that a fair way of putting it?

AINSWORTH: Yes it is. It was with some thought that I entitled this paper "Patterns of Mother-Infant Interaction". What these data show is that there are patterns of interaction that are pervasive. What you see in the feeding situation, at least in the first three months of life, is something that is very characteristic of any given mother-infant pair. The various facets of the mother's infant-caretaking are not independent or uncorrelated.

KAGAN: There's no doubt that the kids who show separation anxiety at one year are in the top three; that's an independent observation.

AINSWORTH: That's right. We did a continuous dictated account of the behaviour in the strange situation. This was subsequently coded by two people in various categories, such as how much exploration there was. The classifications, however, were mine.

DENENBERG: There is possibly a type of circularity here which perturbs me. Even though you are getting independent sets of judgments, if the theoretical position that you and the students have are the same, you will all be filtering out the same information and this selective filtering will give you a high correlation which may be independent of the raw data. For example, the statements about mother's delight in the baby, mother's acceptance of the baby and mother's perception of the baby indicate a bias towards an interactive philosophy.

PRECHTL: It would certainly be better to work with measurements of behaviour rather than with ratings of interpretations of behaviour. For example, you could measure how long the baby cries before it is picked up by the mother.

AINSWORTH: This we can get, at least roughly, but we found timing extremely difficult. There is another possibility of confounding in these data, which is that all the procedures for the codings, ratings and classifications were devised after the fact on the basis of the sample that was subsequently classified, coded and rated. One of the safeguards will be in regard to the next sub-sample we bring in: we will apply these same procedures to an entirely new group and see whether they fit and whether the addition of the new cases will disturb the pattern of findings.

BRUNER: It seems to me that there are three problems here which we risk running into each other. First, if one makes an effort to get some classification of patterns of infant-mother interaction, then bravo for the effort. I think we would all agree that the problem here is not so much a question of correlations as it is one of consistency. For dealing with this you can use a cluster analysis, discriminate function or any of the various statistical techniques; obviously you have the data to do it and you may come out with nice strong clusters. We will all benefit from it because, when bringing infants into different kinds of experiment, it is much better to be able to classify them in terms of type of interaction with the mother than to do it by social class, etc.

The second problem derives from the objective of the study. Denenberg complains that there is a selective filter in the data collection; I would urge that we do not complain about this. Obviously, you need a selective filter. You don't do classifications just for fun or out of total objectivity. You surely have some sort of theory that leads you to devise a classification. The question is, does the selectivity used pay off by enabling you to predict things about behaviour later on in a child's life?

The third problem concerns two sets of measures, independent and dependent. There are dangers, with variables of the kind used, that independence is not assured by such rating methods. Classification schemes are a kind of heuristics and one hopes that one can make them go away by getting at some of the simple structures of behaviour that underlie them. I get the feeling, as does Prechtl, that there must be some underlying level where you think there are some simpler variables. For example, you talked about intolerance of any delay on the part of the child following a scheduled feeding, so the parent has an expectancy about that. You talked about the fact that the parent was able to project and see herself in the child's behaviour: "Look how strong and vigorous he is". Things of this sort may actually be the underlying variables within the system.

To reiterate these three sets of problems, there is the problem of cluster analysis in order to see whether your classification is good, that of predictive correlation and fruitfulness, and finally that of the simpler structure underlying the classified behaviour.

AINSWORTH: The purpose of the wider project from which my paper derives was to explore the development of attachment, with particular reference to certain behaviours that I had identified in a previous study as behaviours that lead to attachment later on, and which may be considered criteria of attachment. These were such things as crying, smiling, following, clinging, crying when mother leaves the room, using the mother as a secure base from which to explore the world and using the mother as a haven of safety against a threat. I am also interested in the various kinds of condition that precede the full-blown phenomenon of attachment which affect the rate at which it develops, or which may affect the particular kinds of behaviour through which the baby mediates his attachment. For example, some babies may be able to sustain attachment behaviour across some little distance and others prefer to be in contact, and so on. In a way it's a pity that I analysed the feeding data before I analysed some of the other things, but it's one of those conditions that you would reasonably expect would have some relationship to the outcome in terms of attachment. Yet it is only part of the picture as a whole, the full significance of which I have not shown in my paper.

Predicting the Outcome of Early Patterns of Interaction

LEVINE: The subject of this study group is infantile stimulation, and it would help us if you would show how you regard your results as related to infantile stimulation, as they obviously must be.

AINSWORTH: In an environment at all similar to that in which man evolved, the main kinds of stimulation that infants get in the first year of life have always come principally from the mother.

LEVINE: Well, given the patterns of interaction you have studied, which presumably involve different kinds and amounts of stimulation, what predictions can you make? Are you able to predict that this or that kind or amount of behaviour will develop?

AINSWORTH: I am not at all sure that we are in a position to start predicting yet, and I am not just speaking for myself. One of the reasons I chose to do my kind of research was because it is congenial to me personally. Another reason is that we don't yet know enough about mother-infant interaction in the human species to know what variables to isolate.

LEVINE: But surely more is known about mother-infant interaction in the human species than in almost any other species?

AINSWORTH: No, I don't think so.

HAMBURG: Ainsworth, would you suppose that your "arbitrary feeding" category would yield a higher incidence of anxiety and depression at a later age than some of your other categories? Would it not give some basis for prediction of later disturbance?

AINSWORTH: I could not specify exactly what the pathology would be, but I would feel that as you go down the list, you get an increasing probability of pathological outcomes.

DAVID: You have described beautifully certain patterns of behaviour in feeding. Now if you were in a clinical setting, not a scientific one, surely you would feel disposed to make some clinical judgments about favourable or unfavourable outcomes: you would make some sort of prediction. The behaviours you observe in the feeding situation must relate in some way to the total behaviour in the mother-child interaction. On the basis of your categories one feels, for example, that you have some mothers who are very disturbed in their relationship with their baby in the feeding situation. Did you see these mothers in the total situation as well as in the feeding situation?

AINSWORTH: Twenty-two maternal care variables were identified and rated in an attempt to assess both feeding and other aspects of maternal care. Although we attempted to make these variables and ratings independent of one another, they are very highly correlated. Now one of the reasons why feeding is interesting in the first quarteryear of life is that the baby spends more of its time in interaction with its mother in the feeding situation than in any other kind of situation. Therefore I think that what we have got is a fair sample of the kind of relationship which these mothers and infants have over the total day.

DAVID: I agree that feeding is classically *the* situation during the first few months and I believe it has great importance theoretically. But although, from direct observation, we know that in terms of time spent together it plays a great part in mother-child interaction, other kinds of interaction can also be extremely important. I mean such things as the cleaning procedure and other things that happen outside the feeding situation. We are accustomed to make one whole thing out of this but it could be divided up, including what happens between feeds and the length of time the child is awake without any mother-child interaction.

Mother–Child Interaction and its Impact on the Child[1]

MYRIAM DAVID AND GENEVIÈVE APPELL

Institut de Service Social Pouponnière Amyot, Paris

INTRODUCTION

THE SUBJECT OF this paper is mother–child interaction at the stage when the child is aged 11 to 13 months. The material on which it is based was gathered in a follow-up study, in their own homes, of 25 children up to 4 years of age who had been in a residential nursery during the first 3 months of their life. The main purpose of that study was to assess the effects of such an early separation of the child from its mother. In attempting to compare the total experience of the children in their different homes (just as we had compared the total experience of each child in the nursery) we analysed five of the cases from the point of view of mother-child interaction. It is these analyses which I shall now present.

The names of the children are Molly, Bob, Laura, Lewis and Frank. The history of these children and a summary of our observations on them have been published elsewhere (David and Appell, 1966; David and Appell, 1967).

Within the period of 11 to 13 months of age the scope and methods of observation and recording were as follows.

PROCEDURE

Home Visits

Two visits were made to the home each month, either in the morning or in the afternoon, each visit lasting for an average of 3 hours. Natural-

[1] The research on which the paper is based was carried out under Research Grants Nos. 56-153 and 59-201 from the Foundations Fund for Research in Psychiatry, New Haven, Connecticut.

171

istic observations were made in order to obtain the widest possible view of the child's experience.

The Testing Session

At the age of 1 year each infant was brought by his mother to the office for a visit lasting 2 hours. During this period there was free play, testing, tea, and a short separation of the infant from the mother, who was asked to leave the room.

Recording

The observer took detailed notes during each visit, after which these were fully written up. Events were recorded chronologically under three headings: all that the mother said which did not directly concern the child, all that the mother said about or did to the child, and all that the child did or said.

The Observer's Orientation

The observer behaved as naturally as possible: she responded to conversation initiated by the mother and to the spontaneous approaches of the child. There was no formal interviewing but, in order to learn about the mother's attitudes, an encouraging interest was taken in all that she had to say about the child, her other children, her relationship with her husband and with her parents, and about educational and other matters. The child was observed continuously, as also were all those who directly interacted with the child.

In this paper I propose to consider three main issues. The first concerns the nature of the criteria by which patterns of mother–infant interaction can be described and by which consistencies of pattern can be revealed. The second concerns the way in which the specific configuration of consistent patterns of interaction, which were found in each mother–infant pair, are determined by predominant forms of emotional expression. The third concerns the effects of mother–child interaction on the child's behaviour.

DESCRIPTION OF INTERACTION

Analysis of the material has shown that, although interaction is a complex phenomenon, it can be defined with precision if analysed in terms of 5 different kinds of criterion. These are quantity and periodicity, initiation and termination, form, modes, and tone.

In terms of these criteria the material revealed striking consistencies in the interactions of each of the five mother–infant pairs: each case had its own specific and consistent general configuration or pattern of interaction. This pattern differed in several respects from those of the other cases.

Quantity and Periodicity

Although exact measurement of the quantity and periodicity of interaction was not possible, quantitative differences are large enough to permit the rank ordering of the cases. Interaction is almost continuous in Molly's case, but very scanty and reduced to physical care in Laura's. In the cases of George and Frank, the balance is more even between the periods with and without interaction. In Lewis's case the pattern is one of great irregularity: long sequences of interaction are followed by long periods of extreme distance, interrupted here and there by short unhappy interactions when the mother rejects the child who is trying to initiate interaction.

Initiation and Termination

The study of who starts an interaction, for what reasons, how the partner responds, and who ends the interaction is a complex matter.

(*a*) It is often far from easy to decide who initiates and terminates an interaction. However, it seems that in all five pairs, initiative, whether frequent or not, is equally shared by mother and child.

(*b*) In all cases the child always seems to respond to the mother's initiation of interaction, whereas all the mothers ignore some of the initiatives taken by the child. Even Molly's enthusiastic mother does not always respond; nevertheless she responds more often than not, whereas Laura's mother shows the opposite pattern.

(*c*) Some mothers are prompted to start or end interaction by a "signal" which comes from the child. It was found that the signals to which they respond differ greatly from one mother to another: Molly's mother responds to all signals, Bob's mostly to his play with objects, Frank's to his behaviour during baby care and to his moving and walking. For Laura's and Lewis's mothers, on the other hand, initiation and termination of interaction seems to stem from the mother's own spontaneous wishes or needs, which may have no direct connection with the child's needs or behaviour. It is interesting to notice that both their children still respond, but they do so poorly.

(*d*) In some pairs mutual consent in beginning and finishing an interaction is predominant to the extent of making it difficult to decide who is responsible for it. This is particularly so in the cases of Molly and Laura.

(*e*) Last, but not least important, some pairs, as in the case of Molly, show great eagerness to start, and reluctance to end their interaction. This leads to "pseudo ends" followed immediately by resumption of interaction. At the opposite extreme Lewis's mother shows a reluctance which expresses itself by her starting but not pursuing interaction. Consequently her continuously disappointed boy resorts to screaming, which she disregards.

Form

(*a*) The most straightforward interactions are those which take the form of a chain in which each partner reacts to the response of the other: $A \rightarrow B \rightarrow A \rightarrow B \rightarrow A \ldots$

In Bob's record these chains are scarce and short. For example: Bob hurts himself and cries → his mother, who is sewing, puts her work down and silently looks at Bob → Bob rises to his feet and comes whining towards her until he reaches her lap → without speaking she puts her hand on Bob's head → Bob goes back to his toys content. No longer chains are to be found in this case.

By contrast, Molly's record is full of seemingly endless chains. The following example is not an exceptionally long one for this case. Molly, under a table, is playing peek-a-boo with the observer and smiling at her. Her mother says to the observer, "You see she is copying Susan", and to Molly "Come along, let's go and fetch Susan" → Molly (forgetting her game with the observer) promptly comes out of the hiding place, responds to her mother with happy sounds, takes her hand → they both go towards the door → mother asks Molly to say "good-bye" to the observer → Molly ignores this but tries to open the door → mother, wishing to stop her doing so, picks her up → Molly protests strongly → mother says "Come along, it isn't time yet" and to distract her gives her Susan's doll → Molly takes hold of the doll and speaks to it → mother puts Molly down → but Molly goes back to her mother and wants to be picked up → mother says cheerfully "Always Mummy" and gives her another doll → Molly smiles broadly at her mother → mother announces reluctantly "I won't look any more" → Molly seems content and retires to play under the table → mother looks down at her and asks "What are you doing there?" → Molly comes out and stands up . . . etc.

(*b*) Interaction can be one-way only, when the partner does not respond to the other's initiative: $A \rightarrow B; B \leftarrow A$.

This happens quite often in Laura's case when, for instance, Laura greets her mother's entrance to the room by a broad smile which is unnoticed and unanswered. Another example of this is from Bob's case, in which one partner takes pleasure in watching the other without getting any response. The mother often watches her son's play but no other direct interaction emerges. The same is true with Bob when he watches his mother moving about. In Molly's case this never happens, since each time one partner notices something the other is doing she intervenes and turns the situation into a chain interaction.

(*c*) Another form of interaction is indirect interaction via the environment and objects (A → 0; 0 → B). In this form, the environment serves as a medium between the two partners: one of them interacts with something in the environment, the other then interacts with the same thing, but this does not lead to any direct interaction between the partners.

Together with direct visual interaction, this is a predominant form in Bob's case. His mother holds the belief that it is good for a child to be provided with a variety of objects, toys and friends. Bob is delighted and uses all that his mother provides for him, but in an independent play in which she does not intervene. In turn, the mother's great appreciation of the play abilities of her son stimulates her to provide still more possibilities.

Modes

The modes refer to the kinds of behaviour employed in the interactions.

For example, in Molly's case the interactions are constituted by many different kinds of sociable behaviour: looking, talking, laughing at each other, kissing, cuddling, give and take, calling for attention and giving it in all sorts of ways. In Bob's case the range is much more restricted: visual attention is the predominant mode. The same is true in Frank's case where walking is the predominant mode. In Lewis's case only primitive modes such as cuddling, mouthing and touching are used. It should be noted that modes of that kind are no longer seen in Bob, Molly and Frank.

Tone

The tone of interaction can be judged according to its intensity and its happy or unhappy quality. In the cases of Molly, Bob, Frank and Lewis, the tone is intense, whereas in Laura's case it is flat. It is happy and predominantly pleasurable in Molly's and Bob's cases, in contrast to the predominant mutual dissatisfaction in Lewis's case. With Molly it is happy and boisterous but with Bob it is happy and quiet; in both cases, however, there are occasional explosions of anger or conflict.

INTERACTION IN SPECIFIC SITUATIONS

Having shown how interaction *per se* differs from one mother–infant pair to another while remaining consistent in each case, we shall now consider how this pattern of interaction occurs in the various situations of everyday life.

The five children under study were not only of the same age, they were also approximately at the same level of development. All of them had to cope with learning to talk and understand, to walk and to play. Although they were still dependent on the mother for feeding, toiletting, etc., they were starting to do these on their own, trying to make the mother follow their wishes and to keep her close. It has been interesting to study systematically how interactions are displayed in all these situations, which for the purposes of study are classified as follows:

dependency situations, that is, situations where the child is being fed, toiletted, carried, held in arms or on the lap;

activities of the child, such as locomotor and manual activities, play and speech;

activities of the mother which are not related to the child;

the child's relationships with others such as the father, siblings, and strangers;

situations of separation and other situations which arouse frustration and/or anxiety.

Our observations led to three main findings.

Firstly in each of these situations the interactions are very different from one mother–infant pair to another. This can best be illustrated by two examples concerning toilet training and separation.

For Laura and her mother, toiletting is a very important occasion, and the only area of interaction which is invested with strong feelings, usually characterized by tension. At the opposite extreme, toiletting is one of the few things which rarely produces interaction in Molly's case. Her mother lets Molly go about in wet pants; she makes no attempt to train her, but she occasionally laughs at her and jokingly threatens her with father's punishment. With Bob and Frank it leads to very different types of pleasurable interaction. Bob's mother keeps him very clean, and Bob lends himself passively but with obvious pleasure to his mother's clever, silent, efficient handling; for Frank and his mother this, as well as all physical care, is an occasion for cheerful interchange. With Lewis, however, the mother acts on sudden impulses to change diapers and she does so in a rough and frightening way which leads to screaming; and this in turn leads her to give up.

As regards the separation situation, Molly spends all her waking hours with her mother, and the slightest sign of separation immediately leads one partner or the other to interact in order to avoid it. Molly is an early walker and follows her mother as soon as she goes out of the room; the mother looks for Molly and calls her as soon as she gets out of sight. At the opposite extreme, separation from her mother is continual in Laura's case. Her mother and grandmother leave her and her sister in one room while they do their work in the next room, out of sight and sound, with the door shut. Separation does not lead to any interaction, with Laura not reacting to her mother going out of the room or flat, and giving little if any attention to her when she returns. In Lewis's case the separation situation leads to violent interactions. His mother, actively seeking separation, leaves Lewis alone in the flat for long periods or abandons him to the next-door neighbours, Lewis yelling in despair until she comes back. In Bob's case the amount of togetherness and separation allowed by the mother is regulated on both sides by subtle and complex modes and forms of interaction which are mainly visual and indirect.

The second main finding was that for any given mother–infant pair, interaction is not evenly distributed through all five situations: there are obvious privileged and underprivileged areas of interaction. This variability refers not only to the quantity of interaction but also to its tone. For Laura, there is no interaction except that during physical care. During such caretaking the mother holds her firmly and prevents all attempts by Laura to act on her own or to learn through moving about and touching things. Very rarely there is short, insignificant, baby play in which the mother asks Laura to copy social mimics such as "good-bye", "thank you" and so on. For Lewis, interaction mainly occurs during long sessions on his mother's lap after physical care. Apart from this there are short interactions when the child tries to come near but the mother pushes him away. For Frank, the interactions are fairly evenly shared between physical care, which is pleasurable to both, and loco-motor activities, which are tinged with anxiety and frustration for both (Frank has a slight neurological disorder which is poorly tolerated by both). For Molly and Bob, interaction is greatest and richest outside dependency situations. For Molly and her mother, there is both verbal interchange and also constant intervention in each other's activities, each of them seeking for and giving attention in many different ways and circumstances. For Bob, on the other hand, the pattern of quiet, pleasurable, visual and indirect interaction relates mainly to play and social activities; speech and motor activities are hardly ever an occasion for direct or indirect interaction.

Thus for each pair there is one (or more) characteristic type of situation where interaction predominates. The particular situation selected, as well as the pattern of interaction involved, reveals strong emotional attitudes in both partners. This leads to our third finding.

In each case it seems clear that the specific characteristics of the various criteria of interaction are strongly interconnected. Each characteristic serves in its own way as a form of expression and satisfaction of strong, mutually interacting emotional trends which underlie interaction, organizing its pattern, and supplying its strength, consistency and specificity. One example will illustrate this point.

In Molly's case, the mutual search for togetherness accounts for the great amount of interaction for the avoidance of separation, and for the constant intervention in each other's activities. These patterns all converge to shape interaction, into almost endless chains, while exploiting all possible modes. In this process one finds that speech and locomotion are favoured and used by both in the service of interchange and togetherness. By contrast, play with toys and contact with other people are consistently avoided. Thus mother and child favour interactions which prevent them from getting involved elsewhere.

It appears, then, that interaction is not only a reflection of the mother–child relationship, but that it is used (unwittingly) as a mode of expression, as an acting-out and regulating device for the different facets of the relationship. Indeed, the amount of interaction reflects the amount of space which one partner invites or allows the other to occupy in his or her life: this is more or less great, includes many or few areas, and is shared or not with others. This space is controlled by the mother through her readiness or reluctance to start and end interaction or to respond to the child's initiations.

The form of interaction is a very subtle means of regulating closeness and distance: chains indicate closeness, one-way interaction ensures distance, while indirect interaction promotes a balance between these.

The modes of interaction serve several aims but mainly reflect mutual sensitivities and the emotional level of the relationship. The predominant areas of interaction, and the tone attached to them, indicate the areas of mutual love and satisfaction, frustration and anger, and conflict. The overall tone of the interactions is a powerful means by which child and mother convey the feeling of being for the other a good or a bad object.

EFFECTS OF MOTHER–CHILD INTERACTION
ON THE CHILD'S BEHAVIOUR

The individual and comparative study of these five cases leads to the hypothesis (which needs more refined formulation) that a relation exists between the quality of the mutual feelings displayed in a given area of interaction and the quality of the behavioural performance of the child in this area. This relation can be exemplified from our observations in five different ways.

Firstly, mutual pleasure creates in each partner a mutual responsiveness which leads to a kind of resonance phenomenon. This keeps interaction going and accounts for its rich variety, the pleasure of each partner reinforcing that of the other; it also induces in both an eagerness to create situations which can be mutually enjoyed. It is hard to say who leads and who follows, since each seems equally active.

Such is the case between Molly and her mother in their attitude to being together. In an infinity of ways they use all the circumstances of daily life for the purpose of being together and enjoying each other, and to ensure minimal separation. The same is seen in the mutual pleasure which Bob and his mother derive from their side-by-side, yet autonomous activities; these ensure both closeness and distance that are equally agreeable.

These mutual pleasures in each couple are to be found in those specific areas of interaction which favour mutual emotional satisfaction. Furthermore, in each of these areas the child displays high performance: for example, Molly excels in speech and locomotion, while Bob is outstanding in his constructive and imaginative play with objects and with children.

It appears also that in those cases where this deep satisfaction in each other predominates, as it does for Molly and Bob and their respective mothers, the child shows advanced development of abilities for mastery and defence, whether independently or using the mother as a prop.

For instance, when confronted with a stranger Bob controls the situation by watching the stranger. His obvious interest in her, moderated by fear, induces a cautious but progressive approach. There is prolonged and distant observation of her belongings, which he takes, not when she offers them, but later when she leaves them on the table;

he pushes his toys in her direction, so coming nearer and nearer; finally he engages in play with her. Molly, on the other hand, while showing a similar degree of interest in a stranger, displays overt fear by screaming and clinging to her mother. Only from this haven of safety does she dare to look at the stranger. Then, step by step, she leaves her mother's lap while still touching her; slowly she emerges further, always running back to her mother as soon as the unknown creature moves or makes a tentative approach. Only after a long time does she feel secure enough to dare provoking the stranger.

Secondly, at the opposite extreme, some areas of behaviour are seldom brought into use during mother-infant interaction and the performance of the child in such areas remains unimpressive. Such is the case for Molly regarding manual activity and imaginative play, and for Bob regarding locomotor activity and speech. In Bob's case, neither he nor his mother is interested in his locomotor activity. She does not comment on his abilities or disabilities in this respect, disregarding it to the extent of not even mentioning his first step; and Bob, so far ahead in play activity, is not interested either, just moving about to get what he wants, but not for pleasure. Moreover, there is an advantage for both of them in Bob's relative immobility: his mother finds it convenient to lift him from one spot to another when he wants to move and this procedure is obviously pleasurable for Bob. Thus he is not stimulated to walk. He remains clumsy, which, far from annoying his mother, makes her laugh; this clumsiness is no frustration for Bob, since he has at hand everything he needs to play with and to enjoy himself. Similarly both Laura and her mother are indifferent to her walking, moving, doing things; in all of these Laura performs poorly.

It is impossible to say whether the lack of mutual interest, by depriving the child of stimulation, promotes poor performance, or whether the poor performance is responsible for the mutual lack of interest. What is obvious, however, is the association of the three elements: lack of interest and lack of responsiveness in both mother and child, and unimpressive, low or average performance in the child. Each of these elements seems to reinforce the other two.

Thirdly, in some cases specific areas of behaviour are dominated by an overall feeling of mutual dissatisfaction and frustration. In such cases the child is found to be incapable of developing well-structured or constructive behaviour in the area invested with such feelings. Here again the mutual conflict and failure in the child reinforce each other.

Such is the case with Frank and his mother in relation to his motor behaviour, their conflict being caused by his minor neurological defect.

It is fascinating to find how the anxiety and frustration of the mother, meeting the anxiety and frustration of the child, leads over and over again to interactions which are frustrating for both and which increase the handicap. In Bob's case, where there are so many aspects of his relationship with his mother that lead to great mutual satisfaction, there is one area in which the mother was for a long time unsuccessful, namely, Bob's normal separation anxiety. Both seem unable to cope with the situation: Bob cries desperately, rocking, and developing a mild sleep problem; his mother feels upset and depressed. In Lewis's case, where mutual frustration spreads to all areas of behaviour, one finds a poorly developed, hyper-active, unstable child.

In all these instances the mother blames the child, who becomes in a specific area (Bob and Frank) or in all areas (Lewis) a heavy, tiresome burden for the mother. This arouses in her a mixture of anger and depression, to which the child reacts with corresponding feelings. Interaction in such cases seems to rub on the child's failure, and a vicious circle is created which aggravates the problem and reinforces mutual anxieties.

Fourthly, a correspondence of attitudes in the mother and child is also seen when the mother makes firm and consistent demands or regularly imposes restrictions. The child is then found to comply readily without showing any sign of frustration as if there were mutual agreement to undertake or to abandon certain types of activity.

For instance, Molly's mother, in contrast to her usual attitudes, decides very firmly when Molly must sleep: she has a way of putting Molly to bed with a bottle, leaving her alone with the door shut, and insisting that no one should stay in the room. Molly has never been observed to protest at this: she goes to sleep as soon as the bottle is empty, without asking for any attention. The same can be observed between Laura and her mother, who is surprisingly successful in restricting her little girl—in subtle but firm and consistent ways—in all areas of behaviour. Laura shows not the slightest sign of protest or frustration: she is quite content to stand and look with nothing to do and with no freedom to move about.

Fifthly, there are, on the other hand, instances in which the mother, though disapproving verbally of the child's behaviour, forbids it inconsistently. In such instances, not only does the child show protest and opposition to the frustration, there is a reinforcement of the disapproved behaviour.

This is strikingly seen, for instance, in Molly's case where the mother is critical of Molly's possessiveness which she judges to be "bad".

However, sometimes she laughs but at others she is angry and irritated and wants to prevent Molly from touching her belongings. When that happens, Molly fights back vigorously and clings even more so to her mother's belongings.

This study of the impact of the mother–child relationship on the behaviour and development of the child is far from exhaustive. It clearly shows, however, that all areas of the child's personality are deeply influenced by the child's interactions with his mother. Although mothers are not aware of it, each one of them makes consistent and significant, conscious and unconscious, choices as to how she interacts with the child. Her selection depends on whether the behaviour he shows during the interaction arouses in her pleasure, indifference, displeasure, or anxiety.

By talking to each mother, one gets a partial hypothetical understanding of the motivations which arouse her specific feelings either towards her child as a whole, or towards specific trends, areas of behaviour, developmental features or emotional problems. These motivations have links with past history, her own early parental relationship, her socio-cultural value system, her present ties to her husband, and the idiosyncratic sensitivity of her own personality make-up. Whatever the links may be, the emotions which the child arouses in the mother govern the part she plays in the relationship in all its aspects—closeness, maturity, intensity, quality, the life-space involved, and the zones of emotional investment.

It is also true that the child brings into the interaction his own special gifts and handicaps, and perhaps his own spontaneous emotional trends. These are either emphasized or restricted through interaction with his mother. Out of this process of shaping grows the child—his emotional and behavioural equipment, his ego strength, and his modes of relating to his mother.

SUMMARY

This paper has attempted to show how the study of interaction can lead to a more precise knowledge of the mother–child relationship. It has shown how, in each mother–child pair, the interactions are organized into patterns which can be described in terms of quantity, initiation and termination, form, modes, and tone. These patterns are consistent for each pair but differ from one pair to another. They are displayed in a wide variety of situations and areas of behaviour. The patterns of interaction function to regulate with great sensitivity aspects of the mother–child relationship such as closeness, maturity level, intensity, quality, the life-space involved and the zones of emotional investment.

Interaction is also a means of expression of emotional attitudes. The spontaneous impulses and behaviour of the child stir up strong feelings in the mother. She reacts more or less differentially to the various areas of the child's behaviour (speech, play, motor activity, social interplay, separation behaviour), thereby shaping their development. In all these areas the emotional attitudes of the mother and of the child tend to correspond. It is precisely these emotional attitudes to each other which organise the interactions into the specific and cohesive patterns characteristic of each pair. These interactions between mother and child act as a dynamic organizing force in the personality development of the child.

REFERENCES

DAVID, M. and APPELL, G. 1966. La relation mère-enfant. In *La Psychiatrie de l'Enfant* **IX,** Fasc. 2. Presses Universitaires de France.
DAVID, M. and APPELL, G. 1967. Mother–child relations. In J. G. Howells (Ed.). *Modern perspectives in international child psychiatry.* Oliver & Boyd, London,

Discussion

The Place of Observational, Clinical or Inductive Research and Experimental Research in the Study of Early Development

DAVID: The material I have just presented is of a very different kind from that concerned with infantile stimulation in animals and it would be interesting to consider how, if at all, the two kinds are related.

FREEDMAN: We are dealing with quite different things and I doubt if there are any parallels. Your explanatory mechanism is really a learning model, whereas the Levine-Denenberg explanatory mechanism is at the biochemical level in terms of hormones. Also the dependent variables you are working with are different.

LEVINE: I don't understand David's and Ainsworth's approach, their methods, or their conclusions. They have provided some fascinating kinds of observational, clinical reports of relationships between organisms interacting in an environment, but I'm having a great deal of trouble relating them to my own work.

BRUNER: There is a great danger in trying to find direct parallels here. Instead, we should try to find some models which would encompass both areas. I should like to suggest an approach which may help us in doing this. David's and Ainsworth's papers confirmed my conviction that, in describing the way in which the human being develops, we must try to describe the context in which stimulation occurs. Ainsworth has remarked that one of the most significant pieces of "packaging" in the stimulus world of the infant is another human being. The impact of that human being on the infant depends upon expectancies being built up in certain contexts. In order to understand what "amount of stimulation" means, we have to know what is the immediate context and also the history of that stimulation in any particular mother–child relationship. It's very difficult to get a precise model for this, but one can make this very simple and axiomatic statement: that a stimulus means nothing in terms of later development unless one thinks of it in terms of the context in which it fits. David's description of interaction in terms both of the five criteria and of the areas of activity she mentioned is a good start in providing a method for describing such a context in mother–infant relationships.

LEVINE: I could have substituted "monkey" or "rat" in all your statements. Obviously there is a stimulus context, no stimulus is without one; even when we talk about steroid chemistry it is with a stimulus context.

BRUNER: But I doubt whether the stimulus contexts in the two areas are at all of the same kind.

KAGAN: I agree strongly with Bruner that it would not be profitable at this point to try to find a liaison between the work of Ainsworth and David on the one hand, and the animal work on the other. I am not distressed that we cannot relate the rodent and human data. There seem to be three bases for our present inability to find any relation. Firstly, Dr. David has used dependent variables that have no clear animal analogue, such as laughing and language. Secondly, she is interested in the bases for the individual differences in children; the comparative psychologist is searching for nomothetic relations. Thirdly, both Ainsworth and David have implicit *a priori* ideas that are bothering Levine and Denenberg. For example, Dr. David believes that affective interaction between mother and child is important and she predicts outcomes from her implicit assumptions about this. I should like to ask what led her to look at the amount of physical contact.

DAVID: It was the material itself which highlighted it for us. To start with, I was not especially interested in mother–child interaction; I just wanted to get a global view of what was going on in the child's life. If one wants to look for effects of early mother–child separation, to begin with one doesn't know where to look so one has to take a look with a rather wide view. Later on, however, when we started to analyse the material, we thought it would be valuable if we could find a way of assessing the mother–child relationship from the material we had collected. However, we had no idea how to go about this and we did not even know if it would be possible.

The first thing which came to mind was that, whereas some cases seemed to be overloaded with many kinds of interactions between mother and child, in other cases such interaction was very limited indeed. The two most extreme cases we noticed were Molly and Bob: Molly because interaction was so obviously going on all the time and Bob because it was so completely absent. Nevertheless in Bob's case, from my clinical viewpoint as a child psychiatrist, there seemed to be a good mother–child relationship in spite of the fact that there were no chains of interaction between them. Because we felt sure that there was something going on between them, we started to look at the material in more detail and found the visual eye-to-eye interactions. We subsequently looked for this in all the cases. Eventually we came to analyse interactions in terms of whether they were direct or indirect. We still felt, however, that there were some aspects which were not adequately accounted for by this distinction. We then started to look at the modes and the tone. Thus our analyses of interactions gradually developed through progressive study of our material on the basis of our clinical outlook.

AMBROSE: I'd like to come back to the basic problem with which this study group is now confronted. This group is composed of at least three classes of people who are distinguishable in terms of the different sorts of effects of infant stimulation which they have studied. There are those who have studied the effects on emotionality, those who have studied the effects on socialization, and those who have studied the effects on learning functions. There can be little doubt that these so-called different kinds of effect overlap with each other. This study group is just the kind of group that could be expected to throw considerable light on the relations between these various aspects of the problem. The group has got into difficulty over basic issues of conceptualization and methodology which are in part related to the fact that some people here work only with animals and others work only with humans. Not only is a rat or a mouse a very different kind of organism from a human being, one can design experiments with these which you could never do with the human. At this stage, in order to see how far bridging operations are possible, I think it is important that both the people working with animals and those working with humans should each try to make clear both the level at which they are conceptualizing and the stage in the research process to which their methodology is appropriate.

DENENBERG: I would like to raise three fundamental points about methodology. First, when studying human beings, on what basis do you decide how often to take time samples? How do you arrive at the minimal amount of time per day or per week which will give you an adequate sample of the child's behaviour? Often one finds that infrequently occurring events are extraordinarily important, but if the time sampling is not right you may miss these. Second, what population does your sample of children represent? Third, what is the effect of the experimenter's presence upon the behaviour of the mother and the child? In animal research these things are critically important. Therefore, before I can talk about emotionality in the human being, I ought to know something about the basis on which the observations were made. I ought to know how substantial the data are with respect to these particular methodological questions before I can talk about concepts.

BATESON: You can't force the pace: you can't ask for precise measurements when you don't know what to measure precisely. You first have to survey the whole situation and extract temporal correlations by a sort of unconscious statistical analysis. This enables you to set up your categories, and this is what Ainsworth and David are doing at this stage. Only after decisions have been made about what is worth measuring is there any point in doing quantitative analyses and in seeing what sorts of time-sampling techniques are most suitable for producing the data.

LEVINE: This has not been done. In what has been done there are already some preconceived notions as to what to look for: there has been selective looking.

HAMBURG: I think we should be careful to avoid the implicit assumption that it's somehow better to study animals than to study people. There is inevitably some selectivity in all research. The question is to what extent the investigators are aware of this selectivity. One wants to obtain predictive power from the variables that one selects. We always select, we can't study everything. I don't think that the issue of selection in itself distinguishes animal research from human research, or is even really central to the problem.

PRECHTL: I wanted to praise and thank David for doing the first step before the second one, and for using common sense and common language in describing phenomena. Only if the first step is done properly can one then go ahead by splitting up the phenomena and looking into particular details in a quantitative way. David's work derives primarily from her interest in children, not in mechanisms.

In so much of the recent and current research the second step is carried out before the first. For example, in much of the current work on the psychophysiology of the newborn infant, researchers are not looking at the newborn, they are only recording heart-rate.

LEVINE: Let me give you an example of the point I have just made. If I put a female rat in with another female rat and then give her testosterone, she goes through a sequence of behaviours which include getting on to the rear end of the other rat and showing pelvic thrusting. Now I could describe this as mounting and thrusting behaviour, but I could also describe it as male behaviour. The moment I describe it as male behaviour I'm already adding an element of a preconceived notion as to what is male behaviour. This creates havoc in the area of sex behaviour: it is not male behaviour insofar as the female and the male both engage in such behaviours, it is essentially mounting behaviour and nothing more than that.

BRUNER: Why do you choose a particular granularity in your analysis and then say that everybody else should stick to that level?

LEVINE: I'm not trying to do that. I can talk about a piece of behaviour in terms of what that behaviour is, or I can interpret that behaviour and add connotations to it which are not necessarily meaningful.

BATESON: Yes, but you specified precisely what you meant by mounting behaviour. It was only when you saw something descriptively similar in females that you stopped calling it male behaviour. The same kind of change in labelling can take place in the human work: they derive more precise categories from their observations. They first give labels which are based on their own preconceptions; if they find that these preconceptions were wrong, they will change the labels or change their ideas and derive more precise categories. You can't expect them to employ very precise categories from the outset; that would be impossible.

DENENBERG: First, I want to make it clear that I do not hold the belief that animals are more important research subjects than humans. Second, Bruner's comment on granularity bothers me considerably. I would prefer people to get quantitative data and do inter-correlations and factor and cluster analyses: let the construct come out of the patterning of the data. I recognize how easy it is to operate with some sort of perceptual bias, but we can at least minimize this by counting events and recording numbers through the use of film or TV. We have to get clear about such methodological issues before we can talk about our preconceived notions.

KAGAN: You have noted, and I agree, that sometimes the most critical information is obtained from observations of rare and discrepant events. If you perform a factor analysis on a large corpus of events, only two of which are unique and important, they will never load on any factor.

DENENBERG: I recognize this. I also recognize fully the necessity of making excellent clinical observations. But the point comes when one has to go from clinical observation into experimental testing.

BRUNER: What you are saying now, and what Bateson said before, seems to me to be the critical point. At the start there is a role, not necessarily for clinical observation, but for induction and naturalism: I mean having a look at big chunks of behaviour. The whole ethological movement has had beneficent effects on psychology by getting us to look again at the big chunks of behaviour before we make bets on the fine-grain material. That is not a very radical thing to say but I, too, have the feeling that a lot of these issues concerning the level of analysis at which we work have to come up when we start addressing ourselves to the sorts of question that Ambrose raised concerning the relationships between these different areas. If we are to study such problems as the effects of stimulation on emotionality, and the effects of both of these on learning, cognitive capacity and social interaction, we first need to establish what kinds of variables we need to study in order to get at these relationships. The methodology we employ will follow from the nature of the task we set ourselves.

GINSBURG: David's sample contains only five cases, but the observations were thorough and covered a particular developmental stage in the life-history of the child. Many interesting questions arise from such detailed observations on individual cases. For example, is the kind of child who continues to get mostly non-verbal assurances going to look later on for very different kinds of communication, assurance and security as compared with the child who has learned to verbalize everything and gets his reinforcement that way? I think it is extremely interesting that the same behaviour can be reinforced in such very different ways. A normal child with a wide spectrum of behavioural abilities gets reinforced for certain cues and not for others: for example, verbal as against nonverbal. It seems that the particular "shaping" reinforcements that the mother uses can determine which aspect of the multivalent genetic potential of the child becomes the basis for his behavioural development in this domain.

Another point concerns my own research biases. The movement that focuses on the study of critical and sensitive periods in early behaviour has been tremendously influenced both by the work on imprinting in birds and by the work of Freud. As a result, we now tend to think of events that happen early as being necessarily determining and irreversible. Our researches, however, have led us to a different viewpoint.

A good example of this comes from our attempts to socialize wolves to humans. Socializing adult wolves to humans turned out to be easy. By contrast we found that socializing very young wolves, by handling them like pets during the first 8 months of their lives, did not produce lasting effects. If they were then placed with untamed animals and not handled for 18 to 22 months, we found that the early socialization treatment had no permanent effect. Without individual identification we would not have known which animals had received the early socialization treatment. The socialization of adult animals is, by contrast, lasting. If you use this animal model rather than some of the other ones, the implications for human studies are quite different and, from the psychiatric point of view, more hopeful. I therefore like the fact that David has not, so far, adopted any arbitrary way of selecting and analysing her data. She has given us some type-specimen observations on the basis of which there can be some free-wheeling: some thinking and probing before things jell.

HAMBURG: I think Ginsburg's comments are very helpful all round, particularly his evocation of the horrors that are potentially inherent in the mother's effect upon the child. What the Ainsworth and David papers are concerned with, centrally, is the question of whether we can find some patterns of interaction between mother and infant which will, in the long run, have a powerful effect upon the child. Now before they can get to this long-run question, they have to have some ways of reliably characterizing different patterns of interaction between mother and infant, ways of distinguishing between such patternings that would be reproducible from Palo Alto to Paris.

There was a time, not so very long ago, when we thought that this was a simple matter: that if you distinguish between the breast and bottle feeders, for example, these would show major differences in personality later on. We got rather disappointed with some of those simple, but once attractive, kinds of suggestion. The question then arises as to what are the patterns of interaction we would be willing to bet on, which would be worth the investment of a set of longitudinal studies, with all that that implies given the life span of the human subject, its mobility and so on. It would be scientifically powerful if, experimentally, we could raise an infant in near-total social isolation like Harlow does with monkeys, and I think most of us here would agree that the effects would in one way or another be quite devastating. Since we can't do that, for ethical reasons, we find ourselves restricted to a much more limited range of variation of early experience. We can only try to tease out rather small differences that distinguish mother-infant pairs from each other. We are then left with the problem of looking at the outcome of these differences in the behaviour of the grown-up, which is hard to do. It seems to me that there has been a kind of backing off from the earlier presuppositions in favour of a sort of ethological "look with open eyes" approach to see what patterns we can distinguish. I think that some of you, probably rightly, object to a lack of specification in the patterns that are observed. Many of them are still somewhat vague and, in most cases, major reliability checks have not been done. One suspects that reliability wouldn't be very high as yet because the specification isn't very great. But I think that there is a sense of working towards a greater specification which will eventually permit adequate reliability and, later on, the longitudinal determination of what, if any, are the effects of those different patterns of mother–infant interaction on personality development. It is a long sequence of research which will require a community of investigators.

Biological Functions of Infant–Mother Attachment Behaviour

GENERAL DISCUSSION

Distinguishing Different Kinds of Consequence

BATESON: In order to help us to discuss the issue of biological function fruitfully I should like to elaborate on a basic point made in my paper. We must remember that questions about the function of a piece of behaviour can be of three different kinds and that the answers to these questions may be quite independent of each other. They are all concerned in different ways with the consequences of the behaviour. The first kind of question is "What brings the behaviour to an end, or what terminates it?" For example, going back to Tinbergen's study of the gull's egg-shell removal from the nest, what ends this behaviour is dropping the shell out at sea. The second question is "What is the present survival value of the consequences of this behaviour?" In our example it turns out to be protection of the nestlings from predators. Both of these questions are subject to experimental analysis. The third question is "What was the survival value in the past of the consequences of the behaviour?" In our example the answer is probably the same as to the second question. In the case of the human being, however, whose environment has certainly changed drastically from earlier stages in his evolution, the answer to the third kind of question is likely to be very different from that to the second. It can only be obtained by the comparative study of closely related species.

Protection from Predation

FREEDMAN: With regard to imprinting we have to ask how it is adaptive for each particular species in which it occurs. For this we have to look at the context in which it occurs, because it is only in terms of this that its function becomes meaningful. Furthermore, because the context of imprinting in one species may be different from that in another we cannot necessarily generalize about the nature of its function over all species. For example, I may decide that in mallard ducks the function of imprinting is to prevent predation. The mother always lays her eggs at the side of a pond within easy reach of predators. When the predator comes along the mother takes off from the nest and the young follow her. In this way they reach a position of greater safety. Now obviously this is not a close analogy to what happens in the human being.

AINSWORTH: I think that in primates also the function of imprinting is to avoid predation. This view was originally put forward by John Bowlby in his study of the nature of the child's tie to his mother (1958. *Internat. J. Psychoanal.*, **39**, 350), and he has recently elaborated on it (1969. *Attachment and Loss*, Vol. 1. *Attachment.* Hogarth, London). I must say that I was a little puzzled when I first read about it, but it now seems to me to be sound. In the original (prehistoric) environment to which the human species had to adapt, all those behaviours that ensured the proximity of the child to its mother, both those that lured the mother to the child and also those by which the child actively maintained contact or proximity with the mother, had the same biological function, namely, to avoid predators.

AMBROSE: One of the things that influenced Bowlby in putting forward this view was that, in most or all sub-human primates, if the young lags behind or gets away from its group, or if it gets wounded, it is almost certain to be picked off quickly by a wild animal.

GINSBURG: There must certainly be a strong evolutionary basis for the infant's attachment behaviour because, in the case of the non-human primate mother, even if she pays no attention or is hostile and punishing, the primate infant will keep trying to approach her.

AINSWORTH: Bowlby also makes the good point, which we have ignored up to now, that in the primate there is a reciprocal set of behaviours on the part of the mother. These are generally classed under the heading of "retrieving": when the baby is at a distance from the mother, she goes to him, picks him up and gets him back within safe orbit. Even in the most civilized human society, if you want to see a real retrieval response, then endanger the baby! If it's out in the road and there's a car coming you get a very intense retrieval behaviour by the mother.

Achievement of Proximity between Infant and Mother

SCHAFFER: It would help if we could agree that the common ground of all infant behaviours associated with imprinting and attachment is, quite simply, proximity-seeking. At one time imprinting was defined merely in terms of learning to follow: the following response was the key element, regarded almost as synonymous with imprinting. As a result of this, various attempts were made to find the analogue to the following response among the behaviour patterns in the human being: responses such as visual following and smiling, for instance, were advanced as candidates for this role. Now, fortunately, we are getting away from this approach because we have learned that imprinting can occur without the following response ever being manifested. Imprinting is characterized, not by the occurrence of a particular motor pattern but by the opportunity to be perceptually exposed to and thus to learn the features of the parent object. In this way the emphasis has swung from the motor to the perceptual side, and this at once makes it very much easier to find common ground between animal and human phenomena in the attachment field. The task of the infant, of whatever species, is to learn perceptually to distinguish certain objects in its immediate environment in order to direct its proximity-seeking responses appropriately. The form which these responses take is another, and secondary, problem, depending on species, sensory-motor equipment and situational circumstances. What is common is the establishment of preferences.

BATESON: It makes a lot of sense if you think about it in this way, because you can then pull together the whole range of different responses which lead to the outcome of getting either the little bird or the young baby close to its mother. This includes such various responses as avoidance of the unfamiliar, searching in the absence of the mother, approaching the mother when they have wandered away from her, following her, etc.

KAGAN: Let's take the level of abstraction up a bit and talk about the infant-caretaker relationship instead of the infant-mother relationship. This will allow us to generalize a bit more, because in many species infants interact with other members of their group besides the mother.

Establishing Social and Cognitive Capacities

AMBROSE: The achievement of proximity of the infant to its mother or caretaker is the immediate consequence of an episode of attachment behaviour which brings it to an end. In asking about the biological function of attachment behaviour in any particular species, however, we have to examine the further consequences of this achievement of proximity. At the human level the further consequences that are of biological significance may not be limited just to protection from predators. While in primitive man this particular consequence must undoubtedly have played a major part in enhancing the chances of survival during infancy, other consequences such as provision of an adequate food supply and protection from cold and from disease must also have contributed to this. But whatever was or was not conducive to the survival of the individual infant, we must remember that in considering biological function we have to be concerned essentially with what is conducive to the survival, not of any particular individual, but of the species as a whole. For this, of course, survival of a sufficient number of individuals from infancy up to adulthood is essential. Species survival, however, requires that these individuals should not only survive but also be capable of behaving effectively as adults in a number of respects: as sexual partners for reproduction, as parents for child rearing, and as members of the social band or group for economic and security reasons. Now I think we know enough about the prerequisites for effective behaviour in adulthood to know that this is heavily conditional upon the individual having achieved, in the period of infancy, an adaptive organization of his drives and social capacities as well as of his perceptual and motor capacities. The whole trend of recent work on the effects of separating the young child from his mother has been to show the vital importance for the individual's social development both of adequate stimulation during early infancy and also of the establishment during infancy of a stable relationship with a single mother-figure. In other words the early proximity of the infant to his mother almost certainly has, as one of its major consequences, the optimal functioning of the individual in his various roles as an adult.

Therefore I agree that, in considering the consequences of early mother-infant proximity that are crucial for species survival, protection from predators is certainly a highly significant one. Nevertheless, this shouldn't prevent us from noticing other important consequences of this proximity which may have played a part in the natural selection of attachment behaviour during human evolution and which must therefore be included in any adequate definition of the biological functions of this behaviour.

BRUNER: I should like to expand on what Ambrose has just said. Suppose we take the view that there is a big difference between the function of the particular pattern of attachment that you get in the human species and those that you find in other primate species. Suppose we assume also that one of the functions in the human species is to keep the infant in some position which enables him to do the kind of learning that's going to make it possible for him to be a human being, that is, capable of using tools, of using language, and of using culture as an amplifier of all his powers. This is the achievement which has changed the species, by making it possible for the species to transmit information about the environment. Suppose now we take a look at the nature of the attachment and ask "What are the properties of those kinds of attachment that would not fix behaviour too firmly and too soon?"

I am interested particularly in forms of attachment that keep the child oriented towards relatively complex segments of the environment such that, when he encounters instances of them, what he does is to learn the rules that govern changes in them. Since the child is going to have to operate with language very early on, he's got to do something of this sort. So I'll take a look at the behaviour, and one of the things I find is what David reported to us: there are certain forms of mutuality that develop very early, exchange relationships, which are absolutely crucial. These have to get stabilized if the child is going to enter into the type of patterned habitat which is subsequently capable of a great deal of change. He has to have, if I may use the analogy, a carrier wave on which he is going to put his modulations in order to cope with a changing environment. A primary function of mother-child interaction in the human species is, basically, to establish for the infant a stable mutuality of relationship which is fundamental for his further development in numerous respects. I would then selectively look for data that would tell me something about how this mutuality gets established. I would not want to start off with a model from elsewhere, such as imprinting as we first learned about it in birds, which turns out to be a quite different kind of phenomenon. I would want to see what an analysis of process could tell me about the establishment of mutuality. Now there are lots of different ways in which, and degrees to which, this kind of mutuality relationship can get established. It is very important therefore to look at what happens when it doesn't get established, or when it gets interrupted. If you look at the slum home, where the parent is rarely at home, you will discover that without mutuality you get a relative decline in intelligence very early on, at about the third year. By the fourth or fifth year, the decline starts to look irreversible: the language function suffers and the child's general adaptation to the environment becomes increasingly inadequate.

Species-Specific Patterns of Mutuality

LEVINE: This is a very important point. You are saying that there is a species-specific pattern of mutuality in the human infant-mother relationship. Can we make the generalization that there are certain species-specific patterns of mutuality between mother and young in almost all species, which serve the function of enabling the individuals to develop into species-characteristic adults?

HAMBURG: Yes I think so, but the species-specific patterns of mutuality show considerable differences between species. In all the Old World monkeys that have been studied, such as the baboon, that is, the monkeys which spend a great deal of their time on the ground, the clinging response is very highly developed at birth. It takes precedence over the righting response or anything else. In the field, its adaptive function is very clear indeed: when the group moves it covers a lot of ground and the infant has got to be able to keep clinging and hang on over some pretty rough going. The chimp and the gorilla provide two partial exceptions to this during the first 4 to 6 weeks of life. The clinging response in that period is not very strong, so the mother has got to help: she does a fair amount of scooping up the baby and holding it. But even in that period the clinging response is much more highly developed than in the human.

Now, when you come to man you get a radically different situation in which, first of all, the motor equipment is altogether less developed. Secondly, the human mother is essentially hairless on her body and, even if the human infant had a strong clinging apparatus, it wouldn't do much good with that kind of mother. Thirdly, the period of relative helplessness is very much extended and probably serves the kinds of learning function that Bruner has just suggested.

Infant Cues and Maternal Motivation for Proximity

HAMBURG: The evolutionary problem raised by all this is how the proximity between infant and mother is enforced so that it can serve the various functions that have to do with learning how to cope with a whole range of environmental requirements. How is it to be enforced when the infant can do so little to enforce it by the tangible method of grabbing hold and hanging on? It seems to me that the solution to the problem has relied very heavily upon the mother's motivation for care-taking functions. It is not, of course, solely a mother-infant problem: typically in the Old World monkeys and the great apes the other members of the social network take an enormous interest in the infant, but their access to it is subject to limit-setting by the social network process. We can say that there has to be motivation on the part of one or more animals to look after that infant and to provide the necessary exposures.

The particular point that intrigues me is the extent to which behaviours of the infant serve to elicit or reinforce some kind of caretaking motivation or orientation on the part of the mother or mother-figure. We talked earlier about variations in the sensitivity of the mother to cues in the infant; I think we have also to think, in some complementary fashion, about variations in the capacity of the infant to provide these cues.

SCHAFFER: Probably the most powerful cue the infant can provide is crying, and it is rather curious that this response has received so little attention from research workers. Just how powerful a signalling system it can provide is best appreciated by looking at what happens in cases of its extreme pathological absence. Let me tell you very briefly about some material which I obtained a little while ago concerning the infancy of children who in subsequent years were found to be autistic. It consists of retrospective maternal reports, with all the obvious disadvantages this implies, and concerns only a handful of infants. There are nevertheless some extremely interesting suggestions in this material which appear with a fair degree of consistency. In brief, it seems that the signalling ability of these children in the first year of life is severely impaired. The mothers usually described them as being very good children: what they meant by this was that they just never cried. These infants did not even cry for food: there were several instances where a feed had inevitably to be delayed for a lengthy period or even missed altogether, and whereas a normal infant would be screaming his head off these children did not respond at all. They were also reported as never crying either for company or for stimulation, so that they could be left alone for hours on end without protest. Again, whereas the normal infant, at the end of his feed, would turn his head away or adopt some other means to indicate that he had had enough, these infants did nothing: they remained utterly passive, and it was the mother who had to determine on her own initiative when to stop the feed. In this kind of situation we see a lack of interaction which was determined not by maternal insensitivity but by the failure of the infant to signal for certain kinds of stimulation or to signal that he wanted stimulation to be terminated. The smiling response, incidentally, was said to appear at the usual time and to manifest itself under the usual circumstances in the first half-year; it waned only subsequently when focused relationships should normally have developed. Nevertheless as far as crying is concerned, this example does serve the purpose of drawing attention to the possible existence of individual differences in "signalability" and to their contribution to the early mother-child relationship.

HAMBURG: I think this is quite fascinating. We've pulled out crying as one item of infant signalling that seems to have a powerful effect on the mother. Eye-to-eye contact is almost certainly another. Ainsworth, one of the categories of maternal behaviour you studied was "delight". Did you get any record or impressions about what categories of infant behaviour were most likely to elicit delight?

AINSWORTH: Smiling, early vocalizations (non-crying vocalizations), babbling, activity. Next to smiling, probably the most delight-arousing thing was evidence of the infant's alertness and of interaction with either a person or a physical object. I should like to underline the fact, which is familiar to almost everybody who has worked intimately in this field of mother–infant interaction, that the infant himself makes major contributions to the patterning of the interaction. We are dealing with interaction in its real sense: the mother responds to the baby's behaviour just as much as the baby responds to her behaviour, and the behaviour of both of them is chained together in spirals. It is difficult, if not impossible, to distinguish dependent from independent variables in such interaction.

AMBROSE: I agree with you absolutely about the interactional nature of what you and I have observed in the natural setting, but for the purposes of analysis it is helpful to break the interactions down into component sequences in order to gain understanding of both the causation and the function of specific units of the behaviour involved.

At this point I should like to emphasize the importance of the infant's smiling as a communication signal that has a powerful effect on the mother. In my earlier studies of this response in the natural setting I was very struck by the enormous delight shown by the mother when her baby first smiles at her face. Furthermore, if her infant doesn't smile at her when she feels it should be starting to do so, usually during the second month, some mothers go to considerable lengths in trying to elicit the response such as by tickling the sides of the mouth. When the infant's smiling responsiveness has really developed, one can see that this behaviour does increase the chances that the infant will get longer durations of playful interaction with the mother. I believe that this kind of interaction provides important sensory inputs and early cognitive structuring for the infant which are not provided adequately in the feeding situation alone.

In getting at the function of a response it is often revealing, as Bateson pointed out, to look at it comparatively in the hope of finding evidence both about its place in the evolutionary process and its functions in other species. I did this with the smiling response (J. A. Ambrose, 1960. Ph.D. thesis, University of London, p. 397) by studying the primate behaviour literature and by consulting people who have studied social behaviour in different kinds of primate directly. It appears that the smiling response, as a communication signal, is unique to man. Among the higher primates there are certainly behaviours which look like homologous movements but these do not seem to have any communication function in the early infant–mother relationship. If the smiling response, in its role as a signalling behaviour, really is unique to man then we have to ask "Why?" To answer this we have to come straight back to the species-specific nature of human infant–mother interaction, to the fact that the infant cannot cling to or follow the mother as ways of getting the kinds and amounts of early stimulation from her that are so essential for his subsequent normal development. For these, as Hamburg has said, he is dependent upon her being adequately motivated to provide them. While this motivation must be partly built up through physiological changes in the mother during pregnancy, it is also partly dependent upon stimulation from her infant. I believe it is precisely in this respect that the infant's smile serves such an important function.

KAGAN: In other species in different contexts a similar function may perhaps be served by, for example, lip-smacking in infant monkeys or by tail-wagging in puppies. There are all sorts of equivalent behaviours in different species that are different ways of getting the same result.

HAMBURG: Are there any observations on infants who, for genetic reasons, show remarkably weak smiling responses? What consequences tend to occur in such cases?

AMBROSE: There are big individual differences, at any given age, in smiling responsiveness under equivalent conditions. Since both Brackbill's (1958. *Child Devel.*, **29**, 115) and my own (1960. *op. cit.*, p. 134) studies have shown that smiling response-strength is much influenced by learning, it is not possible, at this stage, to know to what extent such differences are attributable to genetic factors. In any case, to my knowledge no studies have yet been done on the consequences of low as opposed to high smiling response-strength in young infants.

GINSBURG: The fact that blind babies smile is an argument for the response being genetically built in. What I would like to know is what happens if the response is not reinforced from the beginning, say because the mother is blind. How much individual variability would you get then?

AMBROSE: Such a study has not yet been done. All I can say about this from my own work is that smiling rapidly habituates when repeatedly elicited without reinforcement, and that there are individual differences, under standardized conditions, in the time taken to reach complete habituation.

PAPOUŠEK: I am very interested in the relation between emotional responses such as smiling, and cognitive functioning. I have seen very young infants, 2 or 3 months old, respond to success at a learning task by smiling, and to failure by fussing or crying.

BRUNER: I'd like to just mention an observation I made about smiling as I ran three babies through on a procedure for conditioning vocalization. What we did was to put up a concentrically patterned table-tennis panel at the end of the crib. If the baby vocalized then I would appear and say "coo". What we noticed along the way was that the appearance as such would lead either to one response or to two responses that were contradictory. The baby would start to vocalize; then, with the vocalization going on as a sort of pumping up and getting ready effort, there would appear an irresistible smile. This would then tense all the muscles that were necessary for vocalization and you could watch the conflict back and forth between his two signalling systems, that is between vocalization and smiling. The infant cannot both smile and vocalize properly at the same time. We haven't followed this up yet, but you begin to wonder whether there isn't a sequence of appearance of different kinds of signalling systems. The first consists of crying alone; then there comes in smiling, eye-catching and eye-responding; then comes smiling with the possibility of smiling and vocalization being phased one with the other so that they don't inhibit each other. We ought to look not just for single responses but at the development of the response repertoire as it is built up into sequences of behaviour.

Exploration Beyond the Mother

HAMBURG: I'd like to ask Bateson if he carried his study of preferences forward developmentally. I assume that, once the birds have learned to discriminate the mother, they then have to build up a cognitive map of their world. How does that come in? The process doesn't stop at establishing a preference for the familiar.

BATESON: Not a lot of work has been done on this. It looks as though once they've established a firm preference for their mother, or for others inside the group, they then start to explore the environment. If you look at a flock of chicks and measure the maximum distance that they travel away from the mother, they start to move away a bit even on the first day while they're still learning about the mother. They are quite active and do a lot of moving around, but on the first day they stay within a couple of feet of her. As the days go by the maximum distance that they travel away from her gradually increases. They travel further and further away from her as they explore the environment. At the slightest sign of a disturbance they run back to her, of course, but during this time they seem to be acquiring information about their environment. A precondition of this, however, is that they should know what to run back to. There's nothing very analytical about this; it's largely based on impression.

AINSWORTH: This all sounds very much like the primates.

FREEDMAN: That's right. We saw the same kind of thing in puppies: each week they were able to move a little further away from the nest.

Early Stimulation and Cognitive Development

Processes of Growth in Infancy

JEROME S. BRUNER

Harvard University, Massachusetts

INTRODUCTION

FIRST LET ME apologize for the incomplete experiments I shall be reporting. We are only at the beginning of our work, and, due to the variability of our data, we are still confining ourselves to the analysis of results for individual infants. I have no averages or central tendencies to report. It is work very much in progress and very much the progress of a joint effort.[1]

The previous cycle of research at our Center had been concerned with problem solving, perceptual recognition, and cognitive development in children from 12 to 13 years of age. A book entitled *Studies in Cognitive Growth* (Bruner *et al.*, 1966) came out of that work, but we were left with a sharp sense of incompleteness concerning the origins of what we had studied. Because by age 3 a repertory of skills is already well developed it was clear that the next cycle of research would have to go below that age.

I shall discuss problems of learning and the processes involved in very early learning. Before turning to our research, I should like to set forth some of the biases and presuppositions that have developed in the course of our work over the last 2 years and that have surely affected the way we approach the processes of cognitive growth in infancy.

Let me discuss these under five headings: the doctrine of functional systems, the concept of morphological order, the role of evolutionary inheritance, the doctrine of immanence, and the principle of the

[1] May I express warm appreciation to my colleagues Drs. Trevarthen, Brazelton, Jonckheere, and Richards. I am also particularly grateful to Mrs. Ilze Kalnins, Mr. Donald Hillman, and Miss Karlen Lyons, who have helped in the formulation and execution of this work.

terminus. My object will be to indicate what our biases are rather than to explore them.

Functional Systems

It is difficult, if not impossible, to conceive of an organic system without being conscious of the functions it is performing. I do not mean this in the morphological sense of differentiating the nervous system from the digestive system, but more in the fashion of systems engineering where one thinks of what is required to fulfil some function, such as delivering cargo over a particular terrain or transmitting information at a certain rate and with a certain loss, etc. So with infancy one may ask what it takes for a bipedal organism with bilateral symmetry to manage to get an object to its mouth. A series of operations is necessary to achieve some goals. How may these operations be characterized? You will recognize that I am proposing a kind of heuristic teleology, the sort of working functionalism which I believe to be more characteristic of the biologist than of the philosopher. I find it invaluable as a means of starting off our work. What is interesting about such a working functionalism is that it tends to wither away once one has made progress.

Order

As one works with infants, one is increasingly impressed by the ordered morphology that gives structure to early behaviour. It is a professional deformation of psychologists of my generation to overlook all forms of order save those that are learned through interaction with the environment. I find it necessary to divest myself of this radical empiricism when I come face-to-face with the behaviour, and particularly the learning, of infants. This is shaped, constrained, and supported by orderly organic processes that reflect the emerging morphology of the infant. That the infant will grow to be about 2 metres long, that he has eyes with an interocular distance of a few inches rather than a few feet, that the eyes move ballistically though mounted in a head that moves by guided operations, that the child will be upright and bipedal rather than crawling and quadrupedal—all these conditions make a difference to the patterns of growth and to the child's capacity to benefit more from certain experiences than from others.

Evolutionary Inheritance

Although the development of the infant does not reflect primate evolution directly, it is extraordinarily shaped by it. When one observes

the emergence of early visually guided grasping and the gradual differentiation of power and precision grips, one realizes that the pre-
adaptation affecting these phenomena follows the course of evolution. It
is a long history from the fusion of the two forms of grip in prosimians
to their gradual separation in the pongid apes to the final asymmetry
of the hands of man, in which one hand is used principally for power
and the other for precision gripping.

Immanence

I shall be talking at length about sucking, both nutritive and non-
nutritive, and the role it plays in the economy of the infant. You may
ask what this has to do with the development of cognitive activity. My
answer is very much the same as that of Dr. Papoušek. Cognition is
immanent in behaviour; for example, we can show that sucking, which
at first is mainly a reflex activity, soon patterns itself to the contin-
gencies of the environment in a way that plainly reflects a massive
amount of information processing.

Terminus

Man is a species whose powers are amplified by the use of language,
culture, tools, and technology. His uniquely human process of growth
is what makes these amplifying powers accessible to him. In observing
the patterns of growth in human infancy and childhood it is important
to bear in mind that, although there is kinship with the other primates,
there is also a uniqueness in man's capacity to avail himself of these
prosthetic devices. I believe that science must practise reductionism, but
it cannot do so at the cost of overlooking the phenomena to be explained.

PROGRAMME OF RESEARCH

Our research has centred upon five great issues concerning human
infancy. The first of these is to understand how the infant achieves
voluntary control of behaviour in a fashion governed by prediction and
anticipation. The work of von Holst and Mittelstaedt (1950), of
Sperry (1950) and of Bernstein (1967), concerned with the role of
reafference and corollary discharge, is central to our considerations.
Intention, anticipation and prediction during the first year of life
constitute prime targets in our work.

The second issue concerns the nature and growth of human skill in
infancy, and particularly its transferability and generativeness. The
growing adeptness of the hand and eye, and the manner in which

visually guided and intelligent manipulative behaviour emerges, are central to our studies.

Our third concern is with the development of hierarchy in behaviour, the means whereby the infant organism progresses from being a "one-track" enterprise to being able to carry out several activities simultaneously and under the control of an over-rule. We are therefore concentrating on the integration of activities such as sucking and looking, which originally interfere with each other but eventually become compatible.

We are concerned, fourthly, with the growth of attention, and particularly with the manner in which the control of attention shifts from external constraints to internal constraints. Increasingly with age, attention is given over to the requirements of problem solving and search, whereas in its early manifestation it seems to be more at the mercy of novelty in the environment.

Finally, we are much occupied with the study of the growth of pre-linguistic codes, particularly in the interaction of the mother and infant. Our underlying assumption is that the codes of language, while they may indeed reflect innate patterns, are first primed by a great deal of interactive code-learning of a nonsyntactic type. When certain of these pre-linguistic manifestations are understood, perhaps light will be shed on the deeper question of the nature of language as such.

MECHANISMS OF LEARNING AND ADAPTATION

The first and perhaps the most striking thing one can say about learning in the first months of life is how little of it there is, that is, if one defines learning in any usual sense of the word. Motor learning in the sense of a gradual acquisition of skill is scarcely to be found. This does not mean that there are not profound changes in motor response, for there obviously are. Rather, one observes important qualitative changes in motor pattern that reflect some interaction of innate response mechanisms and environmental stimulation. In consequence it is very rare to find any improvement in performance of a motor task despite 20, 30, or 40 exposures to it within the period of a week. In such specialized motor activities as eye movements there is little change after the first few weeks, and that change is mostly related to the development of coordination between head movements and eye movements. The issue is not so much a matter of gradual accretion of skill as of development of qualitative organization between two systems, the head and the eyes. This form of intercalation seems to go in steps and has very little to do, we believe, with the incrementing of skills over a series of short-term opportunities for practice. Finally, there seems to be very little evidence to favour the view that there is learning of sensory organization in the form of improvement through trial and error. This, too, seems to proceed in large jumps followed by reorganization.

Plainly, then, we must look for mechanisms of learning over and beyond the usual conception of the isolated response that is strengthened by reinforcement and shaped by repetition under reinforcing conditions. The initial issue in improvement of performance is the formation of responses and the development of sufficient organization to enable something approximating reinforcement to work. In the remainder of this paper we shall examine several possible mechanisms that appear to operate in the spheres of feeding behaviour, looking, and visually guided manipulation.

The first is the mechanism of *differentiation*, discussed so persuasively a generation ago by Coghill (1929) in his celebrated book *Anatomy and the Problem of Behavior*. This mechanism consists of the differentiation of gross patterns of response into sequences of finer patterns that achieve the same function with more degrees of freedom than before. The second mechanism is *modularization*, through which differentiated response segments become detachable and recombinable in a form that permits skill to become generative or productive in the sense in which linguists use those terms. Thus when the child uses its hands to reach for a seen object its reach differentiates into segments, each with relatively uniform action time. These segments can then be recombined and substituted in different acts related not only to reaching but also to manipulation generally. The third mechanism is *substitution*, whereby the child learns that one response can be substituted for another and that the task is basically to choose a response that is appropriate to the achievement of its goal. The fourth phenomenon is *sequential integration*. The privileges of occurrence rather than fixed order in a sequence are characteristic of this technique. A fifth process shall be referred to as *place-holding*. By keeping some feature of an ongoing act in operation while carrying out some other act in parenthesis, the infant reminds himself to return to the original act. The sixth process, about which I have very little to say, is what Vygotsky (1962) referred to as *internalization of action*—the ability to carry out behaviour symbolically.

That is our list: differentiation, modularization, substitution, sequential integration, place-holding, and internalization. Consider each of them now as they appear in the areas of inquiry already mentioned.

FEEDING AND LOOKING

Let me begin by describing briefly the growth of nutritive and non-nutritive sucking in the infant. At birth the infant sucks with the corners of the mouth shut, eyes closed, and pressure evenly distributed throughout the buccal cavity. A very strong pattern of rhythmic activity is observed in which regular sucking is interspersed with pauses. These pauses, although fairly widely spaced during the initial phases of feeding, also occur at regular intervals. At the outset, while not completely preempting other activities, nutritive sucking is nevertheless dominant. The child's attention can, however, be distracted and it is interesting to note that the principal form of distraction that brings sucking to an end is a novel visual stimulus.

Non-nutritive sucking is very much a part of the pattern during the first few months of life and even longer in some children. It is known to serve a mildly analgesic function and may also prevent the child from becoming overactivated. In general, the more vigorous the level of non-nutritive sucking, the more effective it is in inhibiting the baby's activity. Usually, slightly painful or distracting stimuli lead to an increase in sucking activity.

At birth sucking, swallowing, and breathing have a massive undifferentiated relationship to each other. At the outset swallowing is neatly executed by reflex response of the oesophagus to the pressure of milk; fortunately the larynx rises slightly above the passage of milk, allowing nutriment to pass the opening of the respiratory tract harmlessly and without choking the child. By the end of a few weeks the need for more subtle swallowing and better disposed breathing-sucking coordination has arisen and been solved.

By the fourth week one can observe some striking differences in the child's sucking behaviour. The corners of the mouth are now open, and there is the beginning of differentiation in the mode of sucking. Pressure is no longer evenly distributed all over the buccal cavity but is now concentrated in the rear of that cavity. The nipple is gripped differently, whether it is the mother's nipple or an artificial one, and the infant adapts his pattern of sucking to the nature of the flow of milk. One gains the impression that a more skilful form of sucking, in which discernible parts follow in sequence, has replaced what in effect was a mass movement. The infant is capable of holding the nipple while looking, and in general the pauses come more frequently; thus his feeding appears to have lost its original frenzied unity.

The studies that I shall be reporting were conducted with babies over 4 weeks of age. One of the first things examined was the way in

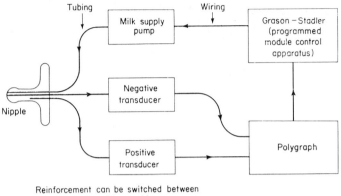

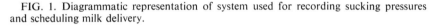

Reinforcement can be switched between
negative and positive sucking

FIG. 1. Diagrammatic representation of system used for recording sucking pressures
and scheduling milk delivery.

which the child's sucking is affected by the delivery of milk from the
nipple. In diagrammatic form the system we used is illustrated in
Fig. 1. It provides a means of measuring, on a polygraph, both suctioning pressure and the positive pressure of mouthing and pressing the
nipple with gums and tongue. At the same time it also enables us to
deliver milk directly through the nipple to the baby in response either
to his positive or negative sucking or to some combination of these,
and with whatever contingent schedule we wish to reinforce. A record
of the baby's sucking registers not only on the polygraph but also on a
programming device that can be set to activate a milk-pulsing system
each time the baby sucks in a specified way such as every other time,
every fourth time, or once every second for a specified interval of time
during which the baby has sucked. The sucking device we have used is
modelled upon similar ones that have been used in recent years by
Kron, Stein, and Goddard (1963) and by Sameroff (1965). Complicated
though it may seem, it is not really very formidable and, as Fig. 2
illustrates, to infant and mother it is for practical purposes indis-
tinguishable from an ordinary feeding bottle.

A typical sucking record at 10 weeks of age is shown in Fig. 3. The
sucking proceeds, typically, at 15 to 20 sucks per burst with pauses in
between.

Figure 4 shows the result of introducing differential reinforcement in
such a way that only the positive or mouthing component of the sucking
produces milk: negative sucking begins to disappear. At 17 weeks the

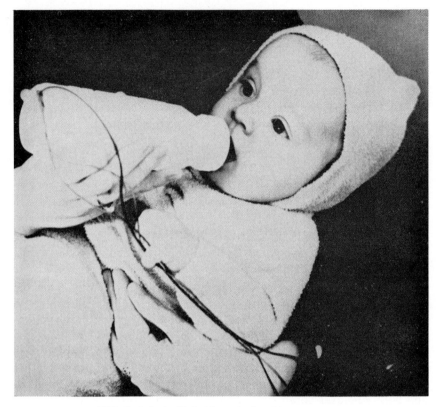

FIG. 2. Infant with bottle part of sucking apparatus.

infant's negative sucking in a session will cease within 5 minutes if positive pressure only is reinforced. If we put an infant on a fixed-interval schedule of reinforcement, with milk delivered at the end of every second provided there has been a suck during that second, then the kind of response pattern illustrated in Fig. 5 appears. The child's sucking bursts shorten and the intervals of inactivity become more frequent. The child's programme seems to be based on the hypothesis (or whatever one chooses to call it) that short bursts of sucking are more likely to be reinforced. If, however, the schedule is altered to a fixed interval of 2 seconds (i.e. the child receives milk within a 2-second period if a suck occurs during that period) then his pattern may not be a shortening of sucking bursts but either a marked arrhythmia or some other sign of distress, with increased intensity of sucking and a marked increase in length of burst. In short, he can respond subtly to a relatively

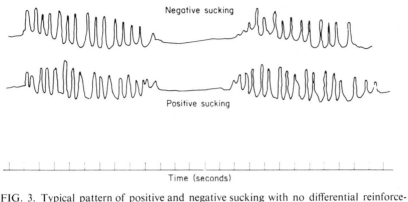

FIG. 3. Typical pattern of positive and negative sucking with no differential reinforcement; baby aged 10 weeks.

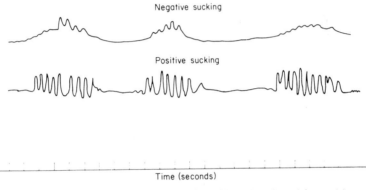

FIG. 4. Pattern of negative and positive sucking with milk delivered for positive sucking only; baby aged 10 weeks.

small range of variation; but if the range of variation exceeds certain limits then the behaviour loses its subtlety and goes back to a more intense and unlearned level. The same can be said for the differentiation of the child's sucking into positive and negative components when one or the other is reinforced. If the task becomes too difficult, differentiation disappears and the child goes back to his natural or signature sucking pattern.

Let me say a word now about the relationship between sucking and looking as it develops over time. Present an attractive visual stimulus to a 1-month-old infant who is sucking either nutritively or non-nutritively: if fixation or tracking occurs, sucking will stop. By an attractive stimulus I mean one which is concentrically organized with

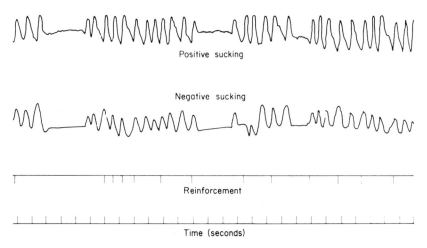

FIG. 5. Shorter bursts and longer pauses with a 1-second fixed-interval delivery of milk provided there has been a suck during that second; baby aged 13 weeks.

some highlight on it and which is moving so as to provide a parallax. At about the age of 6 weeks, however, it is possible for the child to look towards an attractive object and to continue to suck, provided there is not convergence on the object with fixed attention. Once fixed attention occurs, sucking stops.

The next phase in this development is of particular interest. The infant begins to exhibit a pattern of alternation—looking at an attractive object during the pauses and withdrawing attention during the bursts of sucking. During the sucking bursts, the infant may either look away or look vacantly at the object without convergence or accommodation; then as soon as a pause occurs again, the eyes brighten and convergence occurs.

Indeed, during this phase, if an attractive stimulus is presented or removed while the child is sucking, the pattern of sucking is almost immediately disrupted, as in Fig. 6. If on the other hand a stimulus is presented or changed during a pause then, as in Fig. 7, the sucking pattern continues without interruption. This suggests that information processing is going on during pauses. In effect, then, the infant is handling the relationship between sucking and looking by alternating the two.

In the next stage in the development of intercalation between these two systems there is another considerable step forward. When an object is presented to the child, sucking appears to go on while he looks at it

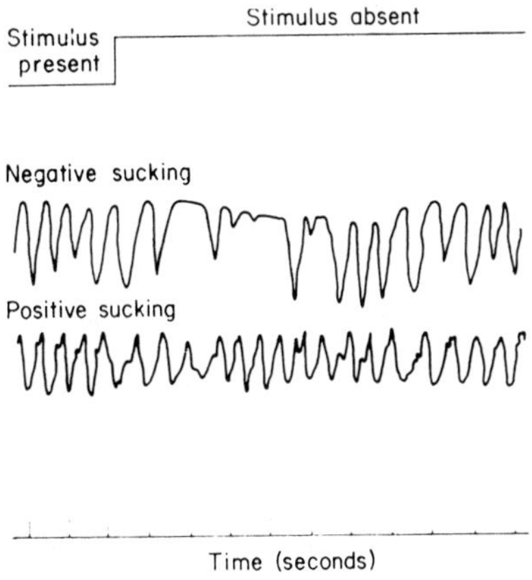

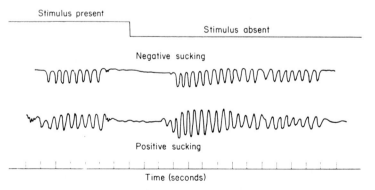

FIG. 6. Disruption of negative sucking with stimulus change during sucking burst; baby aged 9 weeks.

intently. If, however, one inspects the polygraph record it is apparent that, although positive mouthing followed its rhythmic course, negative suctioning dropped out. The infant used the positive mouthing pattern as a place-holding operation until he had looked at the object, and then he returned to suctioning so that nutritional activity could start again. Later still the child merely holds the nipple lightly in his mouth while he looks and, as soon as he has had his fill of looking, he goes back to sucking.

To restate the matter in a few words, it appears that the development of integration between the two systems of looking and sucking goes

FIG. 7. Absence of any disruption of sucking when stimulus disappears during a pause; baby aged 8 weeks.

through phases. At the outset one of them suppresses the other, and interestingly enough it is usually looking that suppresses sucking. Following this, there develops a technique whereby the child integrates by alternation. Sucking and looking succeed each other, creating the burst-pause pattern so typical of sucking in human infancy. Finally sucking and looking appear to be able to take their place in an integrated action. The system seems to go step by step from *suppression* to *succession* to *place holding* without any incremental changes between them.

An observation that we made in connection with other studies on the relation between sucking and looking has to do with the question of whether the appearance or the disappearance of an object will have the more disruptive effect on sucking. We had noticed rather to our surprise that the gradual disappearance of an object as it moved behind a screen served to alert the 6-week-old infant and to suppress his sucking. Towards $3\frac{1}{2}$ or 4 months, the infant becomes less and less disrupted by disappearance: the change now occurs in the effect of appearance. In our observations of younger children, appearance of an object had the effect, if anything, of stimulating sucking as the child grew excited. But in the infant of $3\frac{1}{2}$ or $4\frac{1}{2}$ months the appearance of an object, particularly if it is an object within the child's reaching space, serves to disrupt sucking immediately. The child's arms become activated in anti-gravitational activity stimulated by the object. The effect of the appearance of an object is to stimulate manipulatory activity, which in turn serves to suppress both nutritive and non-nutritive sucking. What the child is slowly mastering is the arrangement of response tendencies into a system of priorities. This enables him to carry out his intentions and releases him from the tyranny of each object that appears before him in the environment.

In our effort to understand the relationship between sucking and looking we have also devised an apparatus which operates in such a way that, when a child sucks at a prescribed rate (one suck per second) it brings a motion picture into focus, and when he stops sucking at the prescribed rate the picture drifts out of focus. In the control condition the child drives the picture out of focus by sucking, and permits it to come into focus by ceasing to suck. The schedule that has been used in these experiments provides that the picture will be brought from completely out of focus into full clarity within six sucks occurring within a 6-second period.

First let me say that a 6-week-old infant can, in fact, learn to suck to bring the picture into focus and to desist from sucking when his sucking has the effect of blurring the display. Infants plainly prefer visual clarity even as early as the first month of life. The strategies by which the child learns to coordinate these two ordinarily independent activities of sucking and looking are extremely interesting. Indeed, not only are sucking and looking under certain conditions independent of each other, it can also be shown that one inhibits the other. While there is a gradual increase in the amount of time the child is able either to suck or desist in order to keep the picture in focus, what is interesting is that the strategies change markedly from child to child. One child will keep a picture in focus by a series of short bursts, looking intently while the picture is clear and then averting his gaze when the picture goes out of focus. Or, with inhibition, one child will suck compulsively, looking away until the picture comes into focus, at which point he will suck and look. Another child, to the accompaniment of much wriggling, inhibits sucking completely while inspecting the picture; finally, overcome by the distress of that much inhibition, he begins to suck. Still other children will suck, bring the picture into focus, be dazzled by the picture, let it go partly out of focus, quickly recover it, etc. Most of these patterns of response have the effect of producing a clear picture, yet each of them has a complex organization of excitation, inhibition, and timing.

We know that in an ordinary situation the child's sucking is inhibited by the visual stimuli at which he looks. How is it that, as in the last experiment, the infant is able to suck in order to bring a visual stimulus into position for inspection? The answer lies in the difference between self-generated control of the environment and events imposing themselves from the outside. I put the matter in the form of a query: could self-initiated control of the environment have the effect of producing a manageable and interpretable reafference signal within the system that permits the child to regulate his behaviour more effectively? It has that effect, for example, when one tracks the self-initiated movements of one's own hand in contrast to when one tracks the movements of someone else's hand. In the former case eye-movement tracking is smooth; in the latter it is halting with discontinuities in tracking. In the present instance, what permits a coordination of sucking and looking is precisely the anticipation of change carried not only in the movement of the object, but in the correlated feedback from the action producing the movement. Also to be taken into account is the difference between a single object appearing or disappearing and, at the other extreme, a continuing motion picture which goes in and out of focus and to which the child is capable, to some extent, of habituating.

To sum the matter up, there is in infant sucking an early capacity for adaptation. Human sucking, for all its primitive mammalian origins, adapts itself from the start to the shape and tempo of nutritive supplies. From the beginning it is anticipatory and moves towards a state in which it can be fitted into multiple enterprises—even to the point of being used to produce changes in situations which before might inhibit it. Before the third month of life there is ample indication that the activity of sucking not only serves innately-determined functions such as nutrition, pain reduction and exploration, but that it can also be diverted to arbitrary and intelligent instrumental activity such as changing the focus of pictures—an activity that could not possibly have been preordained by evolution. Since the components of sucking can be shown, under suitable environmental conditions, to be separable, the capacity for differentiation is built into the system early on. Sucking seems to become related to other enterprises first by mutual inhibition, next by a pattern of alternation, and finally by a technique for holding its place within a larger structure in which other activity is permitted.

MANIPULATION

Let us consider now the growth of visually guided, intelligent manipulation during infancy, this being the first step towards the hand becoming capable of using tools. The first stages of human reaching have been beautifully described by Twitchell (1965). These first stages consist principally in the appearance and eventual recession of a set of reflex responses that must clearly relate to man's primate origin. At birth, but usually gone by the end of the second month, there is a "traction response" of the arm and hand, a proprioceptively-elicited hand flexion produced by the stretch of shoulder adductors and arm flexors. It is produced only by stretch and not by contact or visual presentation. At about 4 weeks, the "grasp reflex" proper reaches its full strength. Initially it involves the catching and holding of the object contacted. A distally-moving contact stimulus between forefinger and thumb initially evokes abduction of those two digits. Later the reflex spreads to the other fingers and to the whole hand. The grasp reflex can be produced only by contact: not by visual means nor by the proprioception related to the traction reflex. The third pattern to appear is not present until approximately the fourth month and is called by Twitchell the "instinctive grasping reaction". I would prefer to call it the groping reaction because this feature of the response is perhaps the most interesting part of it. A light contact on the ulnar or radial side of the hand produces a groping reaction of the hand with either supination or pronation that orients the hunting hand towards the stimulus. When contact is made, the groping reaction now contains the grasping reflex. The hand touches and closes on the object but the grasping reflex, as it can properly be called at this stage, is held in reserve while groping runs its course and the object is found. Although Twitchell notes that contact sets off the instinctive grasping reaction, Alt (1968) has shown in our laboratory that the instinctive grasp reaction can also be elicited by visual presentation of an object as well. Finally, there is a less organized pattern of response, the so-called avoidance reaction, which is produced by a stimulus moving on the outer surface of the hand in the direction of the body. The reaction consists of the hand drawing away from the proximally-moving tactile stimulus on the ulnar surface.

The growth of visually guided voluntary use of the hands has been described by Piaget (1952) and by White, Castle, and Held (1964) as dependent upon the development of a sensorimotor schema which is constructed of inputs that are visual and kinesthetic, being the products of feedback from prior action. Held (1966) and Hein (1966) have shown in their beautiful experiments on the effects of deprivation of action in kittens and in young monkeys that action is necessary for the development of visual control of the kinesthetic and proprioceptive elements involved in reaching for an object. There are disagreements in the literature as to which specific kinds of feedback are important for the development of a sensorimotor schema, but it should be emphasized that these disagreements are relatively minor. For example, Piaget (1952) emphasizes that, in the development of a guiding-reaching schema, the infant's visual scanning of his reaching hand and of the object being reached is essential. Alt (1968) has shown the likelihood of there being certain preadaptative structures in the visual manipulative space of the infant that make such scanning back and forth unnecessary. But the point to be emphasized is that the opportunity for reaching provides instances of afferentation and reafferentation out of which a more elaborated space for the hand and eye is built.

In this context we should note that voluntary reaching does not begin until after the recession of most of the instinctive manipulatory activity. Perhaps the feedback from more reflexive activity is required for sufficient schemata to become established, or perhaps a different mechanism comes into play; we simply do not know the answer to this point. The first stages of voluntary reaching are quite unlike a prepared manipulatory reflex. Typically the child first orients himself to a presented object with a fixed gaze and a gradual raising of the limbs. It is as if, under visual guidance, the manipulatory system is activated. Occasionally the child may give a swipe outwards; a careful cinematic analysis of this swipe indicates the extent to which it is accurately aimed towards the object. As Alt (1968) remarks, there must be visual guidance of the ballistic swipe for it to come so close to the object.

It is characteristic of the swiping movement that the hand often closes in a fisted fashion before it reaches the object. As the child becomes able to move his hand more slowly and less ballistically towards the object, it remains wide open—almost as if by oppositional contrast to inhibit the premature tendency to close the hand in rejection. Also during this stage the active reaching is now embedded in a longer intentional sequence involving the retrieval of the object to the mouth. The terminal mouthing now becomes a very important element in the reaching sequence and, as one can see in Fig. 8, in the 7-month-old the mouth may open at the initiation of a visually guided reach and remain open virtually throughout the reach until the object is brought up to it. Our film analysis shows that during this reaching—some time between the launching of the hands in the direction of the object and the final grasping of the object—the eyes may close until the fingers touch the object and a visually guided correction grasp is applied.

Very soon after this more prolonged act of reaching to obtain an object for the mouth, the child is able to free the response from this single terminus. A heavy object that produces kinesthetic reaction when lifted may lead the child to a repetitive banging response with the object. Or the child may lift the object towards the mouth but then, if it is visually interesting, hold it before the eyes. A bit later he may lift the object and drop it to the ground. As the child becomes competent at using objects in these various ways, the components of the act begin to be differentiated, with more marked pauses between the modular components. A close cinematic analysis of the reaching movements of three infants aged 7, 14, and 20 months carried out by Bruner and Kahneman indicates that, as the infant becomes more skilful in his reaching, the initial reach, the closing on the object, the grasping of the object, and the retrieval each begin to develop a uniformity of time. They require approximately 300 milliseconds with a 150-millisecond pause in between. A child's hand goes up when there is a slight pause, goes out followed by a slight pause, goes in on the object with a pause, comes back. The act can be interrupted at each of the pauses or, more accurately, it can be recombined or redirected at each of the pauses. By 14 months, the process of modularization is such that the time required for the child to reach for an object either near or far, and with

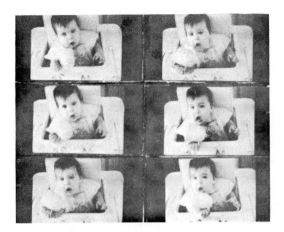

FIG. 8. Anticipatory mouth-opening and mouth-aiming during cup lift in 7-month-old baby.

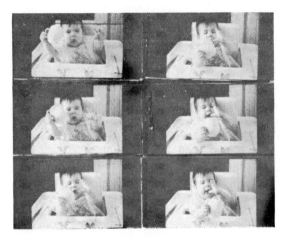

FIG. 9. Baby attempts to capture a cup with two hands and excludes vision in the process.

one hand or both, becomes approximately the same. We have been struck by the fact that the initial pounce reach of the infant seems to be a unified whole, much like an infant's initial holophrase in language, and that it gradually differentiates into detachable parts in much the same way as the initial holophrase breaks down into individual lexemes. It is as if the initial behaviour for differentiating into parts could be then recombined into new skilled forms.

It is interesting to note that, during the first $1\frac{1}{2}$ years, there are constraints on the recombinability of different features of reaching that follow the first appearance of visually guided reaching around 4 months of age. One such constraint is in the cooperation of the two hands. We are in process of investigating how the two hands cooperate in different tasks. In one of these studies, by Bruner, Simenson, and Lyons, the child has the task of raising a transparent sliding panel that covers a desirable toy in order to retrieve the toy. It is a task that requires the cooperation of the two hands, and the 7-month-old has great difficulty holding the panel up with one hand while reaching underneath with the other. Indeed, the first compromise solutions to the problem consist of pushing the panel up with both hands, then attempting to free one hand in order to slip it under the panel. One notes how often the infant fails because the two hands operate in concert.

In another study being carried out by the same investigators, children are handed, in quick succession and either at the midline or to one side, one object, then another object, then a third, a fourth, and so on. Typically the 6 or 7-month-old child takes the object with one hand and, if another object is offered to him on the same side as the hand in which he is holding the first object, he will drop that one and grasp the new one. By 8 or 9 months he is capable of taking an object with one hand and, when the second object is offered, he grasps it in the other hand; but if a third object is placed before him, he will now drop one that he is holding in order to grasp the new one. It is not until about 12 or 13 months that most infants are able to use one hand for holding the objects that are gathered by the other hand.

Part of the child's difficulty is in coping with the manual midline. In a study of detour reaching being conducted by Bruner, Kaye, and Lyons one notes what difficulty the child has in reaching across the midline. In this experiment an object is placed behind a screen which is contralateral to the hand being used. The child typically reaches for the object with the hand which is ipsilateral to it or ipsilateral to the barrier between the hand and the object. Consequently he has great difficulty in getting the object, even though a small movement of the idle contralateral hand could easily retrieve it.

These studies are particularly relevant to the early tool-using of the infant, which is represented by the first use of a cup for drinking. For example, the 7-month-old has considerable difficulty in joining both hands on a cup that has been lifted by a single hand. Figure 9 shows a sequence in which the infant attempts, but fails, to grasp the cup with both hands until finally she closes her eyes in order to achieve the joining by kinesthetic means. In Fig. 10 reaching consists of a pounce from slightly above the visual line. Such a reach by the 7-month-old has no place for detours. Finally by 14 months reaching movements can almost be described as successively Cartesian—a spreading apart

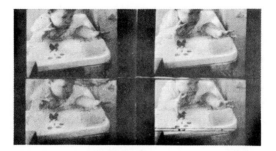

FIG. 10. Pounce-reach of 7-month-old baby.

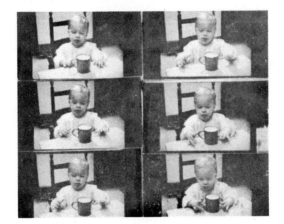

FIG. 11. The "successively Cartesian" reach of a 14-month-old baby.

laterally of the hands and arms from the resting position, then a reaching straight out with both hands moving parallel to the midline or sagittal plane until the hands are extended to about the distance of the object, and then a closing in of the hands on the object (Fig. 11). Each of these differentiated segments of behaviour is separated by a pause. Correction is possible within each of the sectors, and a pause can be extended, thereby delaying the next sector of activity.

CONCLUSIONS

To conclude, I should like to reiterate the points made earlier about learning mechanisms. Differentiation is everywhere to be seen during the first stages of growth. It is a differentiation into segments that moves towards a modular form capable of being combined into larger-scale acts of which there are, to use an expression from linguistics, privileges of occurrence and place-holders. Skill, as Lashley (1951) remarked, has a grammatical property about it. As behaviour becomes more flexible it also develops substitutional rules—several alternative responses can now be substituted within a given position in a goal-directed activity. The integration of behaviour is increasingly governed by the atemporal principle of fulfilment and intention. At first the intention or goal is symbolized by an external segment of behaviour such as an out-stretched hand or an open mouth or a continued rhythmic activity of the sucking mechanism that is, so to speak, idling. In time, intention can be carried out without these external supports. It is this that consti-tutes what earlier was referred to as internalization. One notes also that the recombinability of early behaviour is notably constrained in the number of degrees of freedom permitted. The hands operate inde-pendently at the outset; only gradually can they enter into a com-plementary relationship.

It is striking that the conventional mechanisms of learning—the fixation of individual responses to reinforcement—are not much in evidence in the first stages of growth. The task during this period is to develop the componentry necessary for differentiated, adaptive and subtle interaction with the environment. At the outset the child has many prepared preadaptive innate patterns on which he can rely. These become voluntarized and differentiated with time. As they move towards recombinability they gradually achieve increasing adaptive power over the idiosyncracies of the human environment.

REFERENCES

ALT, J. 1968. The use of vision in early reaching. Unpublished Honors thesis, Dept. of Psychology, Harvard University.

BERNSTEIN, N. 1967. *The coordination and regulation of movement.* Pergamon, New York.

BRUNER, J. S., OLVER, R. R., and GREENFIELD, P. M. 1966. *Studies in cognitive growth.* Wiley, New York.

COGHILL, G. E. 1929. *Anatomy and the problem of behavior.* Macmillan, New York.

HEIN, A. 1966. Acquisition of eye-limb coordination. *Proceedings of the XVIIIth International Congress of Psychology*, Symposium 30, Moscow. Pp. 197–202.

HELD, R. 1966. Plasticity in sensorimotor coordination. *Proceedings of the XVIIIth International Congress of Psychology*, Symposium 30, Moscow. Pp. 27–34.

HOLST, E. VON and MITTELSTAEDT, H. 1950. Das Reafferenzprinzip. *Naturwissenschaften* **37**, 464–476.

KRON, R. E., STEIN, M., and GODDARD, K. E. 1963. A method of measuring sucking behavior of newborn infants. *Psychosom. Med.* **25**, 181–191.

LASHLEY, K. S. 1951. The problem of serial order in behavior. In L. A. Jeffress (Ed.), *Cerebral mechanisms in behavior: the Hixon symposium*. Wiley, New York. Pp. 112–146.

PIAGET, J. 1952. *The origins of intelligence in children*. International Universities Press, New York.

SAMEROFF, A. J. 1965. An experimental study of the response components of sucking in the human newborn. Unpublished doctoral dissertation, Yale University.

SPERRY, R. W. 1950. Neural basis of the spontaneous optokinetic response produced by visual inversion. *J. comp. physiol. Psychol.* **43**, 482–489.

TWITCHELL, T. E. 1965. The automatic grasping responses of infants. *Neuropsychologia* **3**, 247–259.

VYGOTSKY, L. S. 1962. *Thought and language*. Wiley and MIT Press, New York.

WHITE, B. L., CASTLE, P., and HELD, R. 1964. Observations of the development of visually-directed reaching. *Child Devel.* **36**, 349–364.

Discussion

From Ballistic to Continuously Guided Movement

BRUNER: I have always found puzzling the relationship of congruence between the head and the eyes, and the body and the eyes; it is characteristic of eye movements that they are ballistic in nature. There is suppression of vision as the eye is thrown from one position to another. Now as we watch this further in our studies of the development of stability in the platform of the eyes, that is, in adjustments of the head, we find that the head also is initially used in a ballistic fashion. In adults, of course, head movements are not so rapid. In adults, as an object is moved through the visual field, the subject follows for about 15 to 30 degrees with his eyes. Then, if the object continues to move further than this very rapidly, the head moves usually by about 15 to 30 degrees depending on the speed of the object. A regular head-eye saccade results. It's a very graded kind of movement with the eyes moving to catch up for the eye range. With an infant who is held by supporting him under the arm, when an object moves about 30 degrees, you also get this displacement of the eyes. Beyond that, he will then fling his head around in the same ballistic way in which his eye moves. This is an infantile pattern in the relationship between the head and eyes that is soon outgrown.

What the infant gradually learns is to go from a ballistic fling of the head that matches his eye movement to one in which he has continuously guided movement. Progress in this depends to a considerable extent upon his ability to support his own head and trunk. The position in which the child practises this, or is tested, is very important in determining the grading of his movement. I suspect there is a whole range of movements at this particular stage of life that are determined by the way in which the child is handled: the way he is made to sit, the opportunities provided for turning with and without support. Such factors might make a considerable difference to the growth of the child's confidence in his own use of his body, head and eyes. A theorem in any theory of toys may have to do with their role in providing the child with opportunities for learning just these kinds of head-eye-body functions.

Foss: Something which must be related to this is Gregory's finding (R. L. Gregory, 1958. *Nature*, **182,** 1214) that, if one looks at a smoothly moving light in a dark room, eye movements are saccadic but if one points to it while it is moving, then they are smooth.

Bruner: Yes, in the latter case you are yoking two systems together. If you simply follow your own hand with your eyes, the tracking movement is smooth. Follow somebody else's hand and it is saccadic again.

Role of Learning in Early Head-Eye-Body Functions
Levine: Bruner, you made a statement that the infantile stimulation area may be related to learning mechanisms. I did not succeed in linking the work you have described with that statement, and I wonder if you would do this.

Bruner: The kinds of thing I discussed, place-holding operations, differentiation and so forth, strike me as first order candidates for learning mechanisms at this particular stage. I am purposely avoiding jumping in one big leap to notions like reinforcement and to the development of fairly minute aspects of behaviour which might be dealt with in terms of the development of operants, although as you can see we are using an operant technology. I would like to get a description of some of the big motor mechanisms, the motor processes that seem to be involved in learning. I tend strongly to favour the view that the young infant is trying out hypotheses. He generates hypotheses which come, not randomly, but out of the order that is intrinsic in his musculature and central nervous system. He then tries these out and shapes them to the environment through learning both how to anticipate and how to intercalate these forms of behaviour into a hierarchical sequence.

PAPOUŠEK: I should like to make two points, the first on eye closing. We are studying the potential learning which occurs very soon after birth when the baby makes eye movements. When he hits his eyes or nose or face it's as if closing of the eyes is a protective mechanism. Maybe it's innate, maybe it's learned during this early period, I don't know. But I think that in our studies we should pay attention to it as a possible form of learning. Actually we had to restrict this kind of activity in our new-borns because it was very unfavourable for our experiments.

The second point is that head movement is, in fact, not a simple motor pattern. There are many segments involved like eye movements, differentiated mouth contracting, movement of the trunk or of the whole body. These different patterns are subject, in different situations, to varying sequential co-ordination and integration. In our experiments with premature babies, where we saw this ability to integrate all these partial patterns of behaviour, we also found that disintegration can occur when the infant is exposed to a very difficult task. We saw this disintegration especially in conflict situations connected with discrimination of two segments and the showing of two different responses. There are situations in which the baby puts its eyes to one side and its head to the other side; or, with the head in the middle, it turns the trunk to one or other side and there is inability to give a responsive movement with the head.

BRUNER: By the time we usually start to study babies, at 5 or 6 weeks, they've got all that mastered. In spite of the fact that we had the stimuli appearing from different angles, we have never seen a baby put his head in one direction and his eyes in the other. But such mastery no doubt had to be learned in the preceding stages.

HAMBURG: It seems to me that one general trend in these observations is to move us in the direction of viewing the human infant as a searching, exploring, novelty-seeking, sense-making, predicting, problem-solving organism.

Author's Note

In the time since the above section was written, considerable advances have been made in the research reported therein. The reader is referred to the following references.

BRUNER, J. S. 1968. *Processes of Cognitive Growth: Infancy.* (Vol. III, Heinz Werner Lecture Series.) Clark University Press with Barre Publishers, Worcester, Mass.

BRUNER, J. S. 1969. Eye, hand and mind. In D. Elkind and J. H. Flavell (Eds.) *Studies in Cognitive Development: Essays in Honor of Jean Piaget.* Oxford University Press, New York. Pp. 223–235.

BRUNER, J. S. 1970. Origins of problem solving strategies in skill acquisition. *Cognitive Psychology.* In press.

BRUNER, J. S. The growth and structure of skill. C.A.S.D.S.—Ciba Foundation study group on "Mechanisms of Motor Skill Development", 1968. In press.

BRUNER, J. S. and BRUNER, B. M. 1968. On voluntary action and its hierarchical structure. *Int. J. Psychol.* **3, 4,** 239–255.

The Functions of Conditioning Stimulation in Human Neonates and Infants

HANUŠ PAPOUŠEK[1] AND PAULA BERNSTEIN[2]

Research Institute for the Care of Mother and Child, Prague

The University of Denver

INTRODUCTION

THE TITLE OF this paper contains two notions that call for introductory comment: the earliest period of human postnatal life, and the stimulation involved in the process of conditioning.

The deductions which will be presented are all based upon observations made on human infants during the first 6 months of life, that is, in the preverbal stage of development. Although the methodological approach to this period is unusually difficult we chose to work on it for several reasons. We hoped that, soon after birth, we would be able to see the so-called "higher" mental functions emerging in their simple basic form, before rapid maturation and the impact of the environment have made them so very complicated. Empirical observations amply support the belief that, from the point of view of further mental growth, early infancy is a very sensitive period of development. There is, however, a great lack of experimental data which could reveal what are the critically important kinds and amounts of stimulation, probably inherent in mothering, that are necessary for effective cognitive development. It appeared to us that a possible way of elucidating these problems would be by studying the infant's capacities both for processing stimulation coming from the environment and for developing new behavioural responses to it.

[1] The author wishes to thank his research assistant Jarmila Melicharová and the staff of the research unit for their devoted cooperation.

[2] Part of the experimental work, carried out in Denver, was supported by a faculty research grant from the University of Denver. This support is gratefully acknowledged.

As this paper is concerned with the role of conditioning stimulation, we shall be discussing the effects of stimuli which derive, not from their physical or chemical properties, but from their relation to other events bearing upon the organism, as they typically do in any learning situation. Although, in laboratories, research workers usually try to manipulate the experimental stimulus as an isolated informational unit, we must recognize that any stimulus is always transmitted to the central nervous system as part of a larger total informational input. It can be accompanied, preceded, or followed by other external or internal changes with different degrees of relevance for the organism. Under these conditions it can acquire entirely new qualities which give to the organism information about these other changes.

Logically any stimulus is a potential conditioning stimulus. The significance of a new functional relationship between a stimulus and other relevant events depends upon the probability with which this stimulus appears to be related to them. The relation of one particular informational unit to the rest of the total informational input may be very complicated. Since more cognitive processes can be involved in processing the informational input and in conceptualizing adequate responses than those usually discussed in theories of conditioning, it may not seem appropriate here to use the terminology of conditioning. We do so, nevertheless, because at least during the preverbal stage of human development, conditioning is probably the most important form of learning. In any case, all the observations and ideas to be presented here were culled from various sorts of conditioning experiment.

In our experiments the physical qualities of conditioning stimulation were kept stable, as were the other experimental conditions, while detailed observations were made of individual differences in behavioural responses. We then attempted to analyse the factors that could determine such differences.

Studying human neonates and young infants, we very soon realized that, even in carefully controlled experimental situations, the predictability of the conditioned responses was rather low. An attempt to evaluate the effects of such factors as age, sex, or nutrition solved only part of this problem. The remaining variability between, or within, individual subjects led us to the kind of problem that is usually discussed in contemporary learning theories under the heading of "intervening variables". We paid particular attention to the question of cognitive mediation, which represents a crucial problem not only for learning theories but also for the general theory of motivation.

This problem is seldom discussed with regard to the period of early postnatal development and almost never on the basis of adequate experimental data. That is why we dare to present our contribution. Our theoretical interpretation of some of the experimental data is intended merely as a hypothetical springboard for future studies. We are at that stage in our work when an active experimenter takes the position of an overseer or prophet, in order to explore the most fruitful direction for the next step in research.

Our material comes partly from studies carried out in Prague within a broader investigation of individual differences in the higher nervous functions of infants. Those parts of the experiments which required new methods were designed at the University of Denver during the stay of the first author there; the experiments themselves were carried out both in Denver and in Prague. The details of the various conditioning procedures employed will be given along with the presentation of their results.

Observations were made on healthy full-term neonates and infants up to 6 months of age living either in a special research unit in Prague or in a nursery in Denver. It was a matter of basic importance that, for the studies of individual differences carried out in Prague, subjects could be reared at a research unit where the caretaking regimes and feeding schedules were comparable and where the infants were with their mothers or trained "substitute mothers". We made sure that the social or medical reasons prompting parents to seek admission for their infants were not connected with poor health or with any risk of abnormal development.

Head turning was the specific motor response observed. Head movements mature very early. They are fully functional at the moment of birth and can easily be observed or analysed in respect of intensity and latency. They can be used for different conditioning or learning procedures, since a head turn can become an instrumental act for reaching the source of food, for observing some visual stimulation, or for avoiding unpleasant stimulation.

Using standard experimental conditions, and with an acceptably uniform system of caretaking for all infants, we tried to discover how much variability would appear independently of environmental factors. The logical sequence of analysing differences between different groups of subjects, between individual subjects in each group, and between individual trials for each subject gave us material for commenting upon four major problems. These will now be summarized under the headings of maturation, innate individual differences, general behavioural states, and cognitive mediators.

MATURATION

We know that the rate of somatic growth is highest of all during the first 6 months of an infant's life. We assumed, therefore, that the same may be true with regard to mental growth and learning functions. In the literature, however, we could not find reliable data on this question. From animal studies, for example, the reports were contradictory (Pantsheková, 1956): some indicated that conditioning was easier in neonates, others that it was easier in adults; still others could not find any difference.

In very young human infants conditioning methods have been used for testing the maturation of sensory organs or for studying the first occurrence of conditioned responses as, for example, in the studies of Denisová and Figurin (1929), Ripin and Hetzer (1930), and Marquis (1931). It is clear that methodological difficulties have obstructed more detailed study of such problems. For instance, the utilization of sucking as the motor response for conditioning became inconvenient for maturational studies because the regressive changes that take place in sucking movements are in contrast to the development of conditioning capacity. Moreover, with increasing age, anticipatory sucking movements gradually disappear, being non-functional (Papoušek, 1960).

Some of the maturational changes that appeared in our study of the conditioning of head turning (Papoušek, 1967) are shown in Fig. 1. In three different age groups of infants, conditioned head turning to the

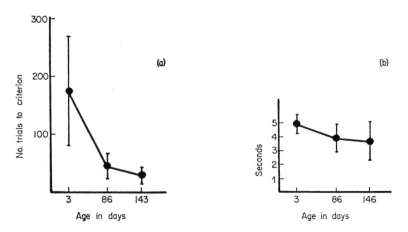

FIG. 1. Age differences in head turn conditioning: (a) rate of conditioning; (b) mean CR latencies.

left side was established to the criterion of 5 successive positive responses out of 10 trials per session. The conditioned stimulus was the sound of an electric bell coming from the midline; the unconditioned stimulus was milk presented from the left through a nipple.

Figure 1*a* indicates an increase in conditionability during the first 6 months of life, particularly during the first 3 months. However, a marked variability within groups shows that individual differences are great, and that they are present in infants from birth. Figure 1*b* presents the developmental changes in the latency of the conditioned response. The latency becomes significantly shorter. Again, there is a marked variability within each group, including the neonates. In neonates a significant correlation between conditioned response latency and rate of conditioning ($r = 0.68, p < 0.01$) may indicate that the variability observed within groups is not accidental, but dependent upon some determinant other than maturation.

A larger body of data, including more age groups, in which age differences were analysed in greater detail, revealed that in such young infants one month's difference in age was already associated with a significant difference in the rate of conditioning. Equivalent results obtained with a conditioned eye-blink technique in the same subjects confirmed the general validity of this finding (Janoš *et al.*, 1963). Age differences have also appeared in qualitative parameters, for instance in the course of acquisition curves reported elsewhere by Papoušek (1967).

Maturation can manifest itself in responses to conditioning stimulation in different ways. In one case it can be a simple matter of the absence or presence of responses, according to whether the structural system necessary for making a response has or has not become sufficiently mature and functional. Many examples of this can be found in different developmental tests. In another case the manifestation of maturation can depend upon a shift of the limits within which the stimulus-response relation is optimal and outside of which stimuli are either ineffective, subliminal, or supraliminal with perhaps even nociceptive effects. In the literature there is not enough information on this aspect of maturation, although in the Pavlovian literature the term "supraliminal inhibition" is well known, and general statements about the developmental fragility of higher nervous processes during early ontogenesis are not infrequent. We have reported elsewhere certain changes in affective responses and in the general behavioural state of infants during experiments which might support these assumptions concerning the manifestations of maturation. The problem is, however, still an open one requiring more attention.

So far it can be assumed that the degree of maturation is one of the factors determining responses to conditioning stimulation, and that this factor plays a particularly important role in early infancy. It is not the only organismic determinant, since within a group of subjects of the same postconceptional age there exists a marked inter-individual variability in responses to conditioning stimulation applied under comparable conditions. Because such variability can be observed as early as the neonatal phase, it leads us to the problem of innate individual differences.

INNATE INDIVIDUAL DIFFERENCES

It should be clearly understood that, when using the term "innate differences", we are not trying to oversimplify the problem of heredity versus environment. Like many authors today, we believe that the development of behaviour in man is a multifactorial function where genetic endowment and learning are in mutual interaction. We also realize that, even in neonates, response variability can be determined by numerous factors. We shall discuss later those factors which lead to variation over short periods of time such as from trial to trial. We shall now consider the possibility that, besides the genetically fixed peculiarities in response repertoire which can characterize individuals, environmental influences can be significant as well. A typical fixed and innate difference that dichotomizes all experiments is the biological difference in sex. Its relation to learning abilities has been studied many times from different standpoints without any general conclusions. No evidence of sexual differences was found in any of our groups of infants from birth to 6 months, either in rate of conditioning or in latency of response. We also examined whether the environmental factors of nutrition and of season had any influence on our results.

Seasonal differences were not significant when performances were compared either between the first and the second halves of the calendar year, or between spring and summer on the one hand and autumn and winter on the other. Although feeding schedules were very similar for all subjects, differences nevertheless existed in the total amount of calories consumed per day and in the length of nursing periods. Therefore the mean caloric quotient (daily intake in calories per kilogram of body weight) was correlated with the conditioning parameters. The correlation was significant in neonates ($r = 0.69$, $p < 0.05$) and in 86-day-old infants ($r = 0.63$, $p < 0.02$) indicating quicker conditioning in infants with a lower daily intake of milk. In older infants the correlation was insignificant. A breast-to-cow milk ratio was calculated as well in order to test for the influence of breast milk, but no significant correlation was evident between this ratio and the parameters of conditioning. The interpretation of the relationship between caloric intake and rate of conditioning in groups of younger infants is rather difficult, since the experiments were not designed to solve this problem. The results probably reflect the excitatory effect of a mild degree of hunger. Such hunger was due to the fact that, in order to maintain adequate sucking at the mother's breast, we had to make a slight reduction in the amount of formula used for the additional feeding period. This effect would therefore be only temporary.

In general, then, having ruled out a number of factors, our exploratory analysis of possible determinants of inter-individual differences in conditioning performance did not contradict the hypothesis that these differences were partly determined by factors of genetic endowment.

So far we have been talking about differences between different age groups of infants and about inter-individual differences within each group. We also observed distinct intra-individual differences in each infant. In the older children we were struck by the discrepancy between the uniformity of experimental conditions, which could hardly have been improved upon, and the diversity of elicited responses, which could hardly be less predictable. It soon became obvious that more attention ought to be paid to at least two more determinants: the general behavioural state and the cognitive mediators.

THE GENERAL BEHAVIOURAL STATE

The phenomenon of fluctuating level of vigilance has been studied most in a neurophysiological context, independently of the problems of learning. In learning experiments, subjects are typically observed in the waking state, and the readiness to respond is considered to be a function of preceding experience, internal drives, and the qualities of stimulation. With infants, however, the situation is strikingly different. Fluctuations in the general behavioural state are frequent, and it is sometimes difficult to detect the differences between sleep and waking. Moreover, the conditioning stimulation itself can frequently elicit changes in the general state.

Mutual interaction between conditioning stimulation and vigilance level is encountered in the Pavlovian theory of conditioning. Pavlov explained changes in vigilance as changes in the interaction between the processes of central excitation and central inhibition, these being due to the excitatory or inhibitory effects of different stimuli transmitted to the brain cortex. Another of Pavlov's concepts was that the cortical cells respond to increasing stimulus intensities with increasing excitation only within a certain limit. Beyond this point the conditioning stimulus produces a "protecting inhibition" which reduces reflex magnitude and prevents damage from overstimulation. The limit of tolerance is dependent upon various factors, including maturation. Pavlov also described several phases in the transition from a waking state, where stimulus-response relations are optimal, to the state of sleep. Situations in which the same conditioning stimulation may elicit at one moment a strong response, and at another moment a weaker one or no response at all, could be explained in terms of this theory by reference to the general behavioural state. The notion of "protecting inhibition" also explains why the general behavioural state can be affected by conditioning stimulation at an age when the functional capacity of cortical cells is, due to insufficient maturation, still very low.

These assumptions, of course, cannot be accepted fully until ontogenetic neurophysiology produces satisfactory experimental evidence. Some progress in understanding the physiology of sleep has already been made. Methods have been worked out for observing, analysing, and categorizing sleep patterns in neonates and infants, and basic data have been collected on both the peculiarities of and developmental changes in the course of sleep in early ontogeny (Dreyfus–Brisac, 1967; Parmelee et al., 1961; Prechtl and Lenard, 1969). Unfortunately, the situation regarding the analysis of waking states is less favourable. This is partly due to the fact that, during sleep, both mental processes and motor activity are reduced to a basic minimum; this makes the recording and interpretation of the reduced repertoire of behavioural indicators much simpler, and sensitive electrophysiological techniques are not obstructed by as many artefacts as during waking.

In our own conditioning experiments, in order to discover the influence of the general state on the course of the conditioned responses or vice versa, we used observational coding of motor behaviour and vocalization, stabilimetric recording of total motor activity, and pneumatic recording of respiration.

It should be kept in mind that the main purpose of our studies was not the analysis of behavioural states. Nevertheless, we can demonstrate several facts worth mentioning. First, we found that during a relatively short experimental session (10–12 minutes), fluctuations between behavioural states at the opposite extremes occurred relatively frequently,

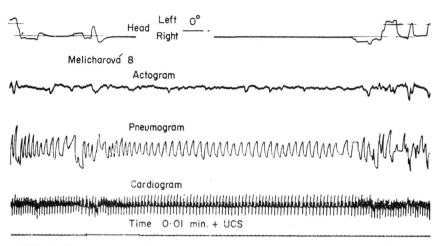

FIG. 2. Changes in behavioural state observed during operant conditioning.

particularly in the youngest subjects. Such microcycles last only a few minutes. An example is shown on a polygraphic record in Fig. 2.

We soon found that these microcycles did not appear accidentally, but that they were dependent upon the course of conditioning. The dependence was mutual: conditioning stimulation, under certain conditions, could cause dramatic changes in the behavioural state, while the behavioural state influenced the course of the conditioned responses. This interrelation can be demonstrated in two examples from our material.

First, we analysed (Fig. 3) the influence of different waking states preceding the conditioning stimulation upon the course of the condi-

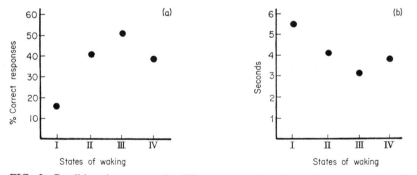

FIG. 3. Conditioned responses in different states of waking: (a) frequency of CR; (b) latency of CR.

tioned response. Four states of wakefulness were distinguished, according to the behavioural indicators shown in Table I.

TABLE I. THE BEHAVIOURAL INDICATORS OF FOUR STATES OF WAKEFULNESS IN YOUNG INFANTS

State I:	Regular breathing, no other movements or vocalization, eyes open.
State II:	Irregular breathing, quiet movements of eyes, head, or distal parts of extremities, no vocalization.
State III:	Vivid movements of all extremities or trunk and/or vocalization other than fussing or crying.
State IV:	Uncoordinated gross movements and/or fussing or crying.

Significant differences appeared in the frequency of conditioned responses to stimuli applied in different states ($N = 4,287$, $p < 0.01$) and in the latencies of correct responses ($N = 1,521$, $p < 0.001$). Transition from sleep to state IV is sometimes considered to be a function of a continual increase in excitability between these two extreme states. We found, however, that both for frequency and latency of conditioned responses, the means in the different states ranked from I to IV show, not a linear relationship, but an inverted-U function. Obviously, the opposite pole to deep sleep is represented by states II or III, whereas states I and IV should be considered as two different types of deviation from the optimal waking state.

The second example (Fig. 4) shows the effect of the inhibitory conditioned stimulus upon the level of conditioning performance. In this case conditioned responses of head turning were established to two different acoustic stimuli, A and B. Stimulus A was then applied without reinforcement until the response to it was extinguished, whereas stimulus B was always reinforced. After extinction, although stimulus A elicited no conditioned response, it was not irrelevant in the way that it had been before the beginning of conditioning. It had an inhibitory effect that appeared in two forms: as a prolongation of the latencies of responses following stimulus B and as a change in the general behavioural state. The effect of an inhibitory stimulus upon the general state is the same as was shown in Fig. 2.

In a previous report (Papoušek, 1967) I described the changes in behaviour associated with establishing a conditioned response in infants. With a certain regularity the course of conditioning was associated also

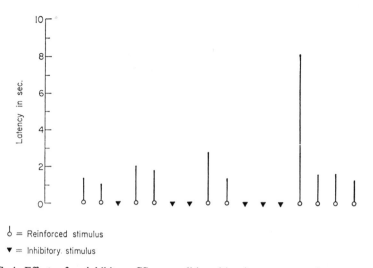

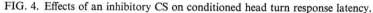

ↄ = Reinforced stimulus

▼ = Inhibitory stimulus

FIG. 4. Effects of an inhibitory CS on conditioned head turn response latency.

with fluctuations in the vigilance level. In the stage preceding the occurrence of the first conditioned responses, conditioning stimulation elicited increased general motor activity and concomitant vocal and facial responses that are usually accepted as signs of distress. In marked contrast, the first conditioned responses, particularly in neonates, were often followed by short periods of an inhibitory state that very much resembled what is usually described as a transitional state between wakefulness and sleep. This is probably one reason why younger infants are unable to carry out several correct responses consecutively during the initial stage of conditioning, and why the first conditioned responses appear in an isolated way. During extinction of the conditioned response, non-reinforced stimuli sometimes acquire a marked inhibitory effect, and if repeated several times consecutively they can lead, according to the behavioural indicators, to a decrease in vigilance and eventually to microcycles of real sleep.

Such phenomena raise again the question of the limited functional capacity of brain structures in immature organisms, to which we alluded in the section on maturation. A lower tolerance of the neural cells beyond which conditioning stimulation can elicit paradoxical effects is one of the possible hypothetical interpretations.

In our consideration of the determinants of behaviour it is important to realize that stimuli which were originally quite irrelevant, such as the different acoustic stimuli in our experimental situation, can acquire distinct excitatory or inhibitory qualities once they become conditioning stimuli. This brings us to the problem of cognitive mediational processes which are closely related to the functions of conditioning stimulation.

COGNITIVE MEDIATION

Over the history of learning theory the role of cognitive processes has been viewed in a number of different ways. Radical behaviourists adopted a negative attutide to the idea of there being any mediation between stimulus and response. Most contemporary theories, however, take into account intervening variables within the organism and pay attention to the mechanisms of mental processing of stimulation.

From the developmental point of view an interesting hypothetical model for the development of an ability to form concepts was presented by J. McV. Hunt (1966) in his paper on intrinsic motivation. For this purpose he applied the principle of the servo-control T–O–T–E system, giving a good example of it in the regulation of body temperature in the neonate. As a homeothermic organism the neonate has a genetically coded plan of the span within which his body temperature must be kept in order to ensure survival. He also has organs for testing the temperature and organs that can change the caloric output. If his testing organs signal a change of temperature beyond the limits of the given span (step T), a command is given to the operational organs to start operations that will restore the right temperature (step O). The effect of the operations is tested again (step T), and when the temperature has been restored operations can be stopped (step E). Modern neurophysiology (e.g. Ruch et al., 1965) has produced evidence that, in the basic functioning of the central nervous system, mechanisms are included which act on the principle of servo-control systems to enable a higher degree of control over responses.

In the hypothetical model we use in our own studies, the notion of categorization and conceptualization in cognitive mediation between stimulus and response plays an important part. We consider any stimulus to be part of a whole constellation of signals coming to the central nervous system from its external and internal environment. Together with the signals from the systems of feedback control and memory, they form the so-called "total input". This total input undergoes constant changes. The physiological balance between organism and environment is maintained by the ability of the organisms to organize responses to environmental changes. Responses, also, consist of constellations of many partial muscular or hormonal responses, together with informational signals transmitted to the systems of feedback control and memory.

A certain repertoire of responses is innate. In terms of our model let us assume that there exist some innate, genetically coded, matrices with standards for evaluating the total input and for organizing innate patterns of behavioural responses necessary for maintaining the physiological balance whenever it is disturbed. We may call these "primary matrices". In other words, primary matrices ensure unconditioned responses to unconditioned stimuli. Such matrices can be postulated for maintaining the different conditions necessary for survival. They act as physiological thermostats, homeostats, hormonostats, etc.

Let us assume, further, that these matrices are open systems into which new informational units can continually enter, for instance through learning. Thus, an organism can learn that a certain constellation of signals can, with a certain probability, announce in advance disturbances of physiological balance. It can also learn that certain, originally irrelevant, behavioural responses can prevent or minimize such disturbances. In this way secondary matrices, and eventually matrices of higher orders, are formed. A conditioned response to a conditioned stimulus would be a simple example of the functioning of a secondary matrix. Secondary matrices provide the organism with an ability to predict relevant environmental changes and to ensure physiological balance in advance. Referring back to the example of thermoregulation in the neonate we can understand that, with more experience, the organism can also respond to stimuli signalling environmental events that lead to changes in temperature. We can see, too, that the concept of adaptive operations can include learned behaviour that either facilitates the restoration of the right temperature or minimizes the danger of the change in temperature. For example, when an adult has read the weather forecast he may change into warmer clothes or turn on his air conditioner.

Since the total input can contain an enormous number of signals (imagine only the variety of colours or movements that must be analysed), the logical requirement for its analysis is the use of classes or categories. Similarly, since the relationship between different relevant signals can vary according to certain complicated principles or rules, the analysis of the total input must also involve an ability to decode the rules. On the output side we have to consider a similar conceptualization. Even a simple motor response involves many synergic and antagonistic muscle fibres, and can be accompanied by different humoral, autonomic, or affective responses. Usually our responses are represented by complicated chains of different behavioural patterns, elicited by a great constellation of well organized signals or categories of elementary signals. According to our concept these basic cognitive processes should already be functional in neonates. These assumptions, then, would allow us to construct a theoretical model for interpreting our data and for interpreting an infant's behaviour in general. Until now, however, there has been a lack of experimental data to support an hypothesis of this sort.

Our interest in cognitive mediation was further stimulated by our own empirical experience with young infants. In observing our subjects closely in conditioning experiments, and by recording their facial and affective responses, we gained the impression that in their conditioned behaviour more complicated cognitive processes were involved than just the summing of experience from trial to trial. The infants seemed to look as though they were solving problems, experimenting, seeking a correct solution. From 3 months onwards we could often see in their faces responses resembling adult expressions of concentration, surprise, disappointment, tension or release, pleasure or displeasure. This was particularly evident in experiments on conditioning discrimination. Here we often saw the infants using something like "strategies" in responding to the conditioning stimuli.

In our discrimination experiments two acoustic stimuli were differentially reinforced by the presentation of milk from different sides. The sound of an electric bell was associated with reinforcement from the left, the sound of a buzzer with reinforcement from the right. Each session consisted of 10 trials. When a subject had reached the criterion of 6 consecutively correct responses, 3 to the bell and 3 to the buzzer (the stimuli being in random order), the sides of reinforcement were reversed.

These experimental procedures resembled problem-solving situations. Although the bell and buzzer signals were used in random order, the infants' head turns occurred in certain regular patterns which could be labelled as follows:

(i) the milk was expected to come from the side on which it had been presented in the preceding trial;

(ii) the milk was expected from the side on which it had been presented more frequently in the two preceding trials;

(iii) the milk was expected to come consecutively from the left and from the right, and vice versa;

(iv) the solution was to turn always to one side and to correct the response if the milk was not soon presented on that side.

This is not a complete list of the "strategies", only of those most frequently observed. We ought also to add that there were subjects in whom we could not detect any regular patterns: their behaviour looked chaotic. Furthermore, it so happened that the randomized signals were sometimes accidentally incongruent with the strategy or expectancy of the subject. Incongruency, as compared with congruency, elicited different behavioural patterns. With incongruency infants usually showed signs of displeasure or distress: their motor activity increased and often they started fussing or crying.

The idea that during the preverbal stage of development an infant may be able to detect certain rules in environmental events and to adjust his behaviour in accordance with those rules raises the question of the relationship between speech and cognitive processes. One might object to the idea on the ground that, in man, cognitive processes develop only because speech enables him to use the abstract symbols necessary for thinking. Logically, however, an opposite assumption is also possible—that it is precisely because man has such a high innate ability to categorize and conceptualize that he is able to form and use verbal symbols and develop speech as an important tool for still more effective thinking operations.

Before an infant starts speaking he is already able to differentiate between familiar and unfamiliar faces. If we realize that a face consists of an innumerable number of signals in constantly changing combinations, we have to admit some capacity in the infant to use cues for decoding those fluctuating combinations and for abstracting their constant aspects. According to Koltzová (1967), the first signs of abstracting appear in the phenomenon of "generalization", when the infant makes a conditioned response not only to the conditioning stimulus but also to other stimuli that are similar to it. As to conceptualization, however, it was difficult, without experimental evidence, to predict the degree to which this could occur during the preverbal period.

After various preliminary attempts we decided to study these problems in infants with the help of conditioned head turning, employing operant procedures. Caron (1967) had described an interesting modification of our head turning method in which the infant's head turn was reinforced with visual reward applied from the mid-line, so that the turn was an instrumental act only for "switching on" the reward; the head turned back to the neutral position during reinforcement. Using this modification we rewarded the subjects with coloured lights—five pairs of white, yellow, green, blue, and red 6-volt bulbs, blinking in random order—placed in the mid-line in front of the subjects.

For our observations we chose 4-month-old infants whose parents were mostly university students. Operant conditioning occurred in two 5-minute blocks in one session per day. A variety of experiments were done employing different schedules of reward for reinforcing the head turns. Thus in the first series of experiments every turn to the given side exceeding 30° of rotation was reinforced. In the other series every second turn or every third turn to the same side was reinforced; or the subjects had to turn regularly once to the left and once to the right, or twice to the left and once to the right in order to reach the reward. The most complicated task so far has been to turn twice to the left and three times to the right to be rewarded. No instruction was given.

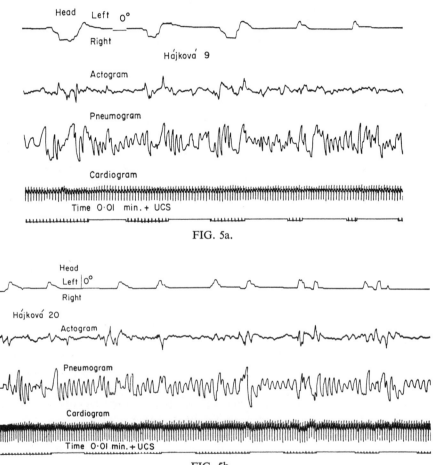

FIG. 5a.

FIG. 5b.

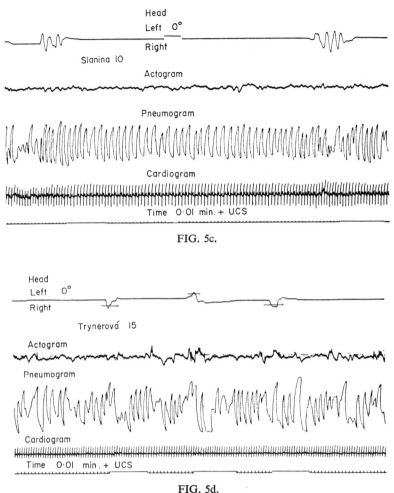

FIG. 5c.

FIG. 5d.

FIG. 5. Modification of spontaneous head turning by reinforcement of turns exceeding 30° according to different schedules: (a) every left turn; (b) every second left turn; (c) every third right turn; (d) left and right turns in regular alternation.

Figure 5 shows that the infants were able to adapt their responses in accordance with the schedule of reinforcement in situations where every second or third turn to one side was rewarded, or where left and right turns in a 1:1 ratio were rewarded. Alternating reward in a 2:2 or 2:3 ratio presented too difficult a problem. Nevertheless, couples and triads of head turns were formed in a way that never appeared in preconditioning blocks so that, in individual subjects, the change in the patterns of head turning was significant. For a statistical analysis of whole samples of subjects, however, several methodological difficulties must still be surmounted before we can reach the standardization necessary for comparison. Attaining the strategies is a more difficult task for the infants than one would predict, and rigid criteria for achievement can sometimes puzzle the subject. For instance, in order to obtain the reward the subject must turn three times to the left at the chosen criterion of 30° of rotation; he does make three turns to the left but one of them may be weaker than the chosen criterion. Again, he carries out a couple of turns instead of a triad, but he may correct the response by carrying out a new triad rather than by adding one more turn to make the couple a triad. In such situations, individual treatment that can facilitate the process of learning interferes with the experimental standardization.

Nevertheless, as a preliminary conclusion we can say that a method was found for studying the formation of behavioural strategies in human infants during the preverbal period, and that evidence was obtained of the apparent mastery of several types of simple strategy applied by the experimenter.

In respect to our working hypothesis, it was very interesting to see the effects of eventual incongruency between the strategy to be attained and the subject's response. The incongruency led to increased searching movements of the eyes and head, locomotor movements, and affective behaviour, as if the incongruency were a trigger signal for a powerful alarm response related to the cognitive functions from which the validity of the used matrices was being tested. It was as though correcting operations were being organized that involved the mobilization of orienting or experimenting behaviours and the activation of different mechanisms to ensure better evaluation of the total informational input and of the effectiveness of responses. Congruency, on the contrary, was often accompanied by signs of release and pleasure. Sometimes we even had the impression that successful solving of the problem elicited more pleasure in the subject than did the reward.

A final word on those mechanisms which ensure different aspects of the physiological balance between organism and environment. Should we not include in our theoretical model the notion of a more general mechanism that maintains a balance in the organism-environment relation in the area of mental processes? Such a balance is achieved when there is optimal analysis of the informational input and when there is optimal conceptualization and adjustment of responses.

Such a mechanism would probably be one of the most important mechanisms of motivation. Here we may be getting too far from the facts and into the realm of theory, and perhaps even of faith. But we thought that this question of the basic motivational mechanism might be an interesting topic for discussion.

REFERENCES

CARON, R. F. 1967. Visual reinforcement of head-turning in young infants. *J. exp. Child Psychol.* **5**, 489–511.

DENISOVÁ, M. P. and FIGURIN, N. L. 1929. The question of the first associated appetitional reflexes in infants. (Rus.) *Vopr. genet. Refleksol. Pedol. Mladen.* **1**, 81–88.

DREYFUS-BRISAC, C. 1967. Ontogenèse du sommeil chez le prématuré humain: étude polygraphique. In A. Minkowski (Ed.), *Regional development of the brain in early life.* Blackwell, Oxford.

HUNT, J. McV. 1966. Intrinsic motivation and its role in psychological development. In D. Levine (Ed.), *Nebraska symposium on motivation, 1965.* University of Nebraska Press, Lincoln.

JANOŠ, O., PAPOUŠEK, H., and DITTRICHOVÁ, J. 1963. The influence of age upon various aspects of higher nervous activity in the first months of life. (Czech) *Activ. nerv. super.* **4**, 407–410.

KOLTZOVÁ, M. M. 1967. *Generalization as a function of brain.* (Rus.) Nauka, Leningrad.

MARQUIS, D. P. 1931. Can conditioned responses be established in the newborn infant? *J. gen. Psychol.* **39**, 479–492.

PANTSHEKOVÁ, E. F. 1956. The development of conditioned reflexes in white rats during ontogeny. (Rus.) *Zh. vys. nerv. Deiat.* **6**, 312–318.

PAPOUŠEK, H. 1960. Conditioned alimentary reflexes in infants. I. Experimental conditioned sucking reflexes. (Czech) *Cesk. Pediat.* **15**, 861–872.

PAPOUŠEK, H. 1967. Experimental studies of appetitional behavior in human newborns and infants. In H. W. Stevenson, E. H. Hess, and H. L. Rheingold (Eds.), *Early behavior: comparative and developmental approaches.* Wiley, New York. Pp. 249–278.

PARMELEE, A. H., SCHULZ, H. R., and DISBROW, M. A. 1961. Sleep patterns of the newborn. *J. Pediat.* **58**, 241.

PRECHTL, H. F. R. and LENARD, H. G. 1969. Verhaltensphysiologie des neugeborenen. *Fortschr. d. Pädologie.* 2, in press.

RIPIN, R. and HETZER, H. 1930. Fruhestes Lernen des Säuglings in der Ernährungssituation. *Z. Psychol.* **118**, 82–127.

RUCH, T. C., PATTON, H. D., WOODBURY, J. W., and TOWE, A. R. 1965. *Neurophysiology.* Saunders, Philadelphia and London.

Discussion

Matching and Concept of Drive

KAGAN: I agree that congruency and incongruency are important issues for the young infant. In my own work I have measured reactions to visual stimuli in terms of such responses as fixation-time, smiling and cardiac deceleration. If a 4-month baby is shown, over a series of trials, a human face for which he has a schema, these responses have high magnitudes on the first trial and then decrease. If, on the other hand, the same baby is shown a completely novel stimulus, these same variables often show peak values on trials 2 and 3 because there is no schema for them. After a trial or two the child has built up a partial schema, and then there is pleasure in matching. Matching is the essential process here. What I don't understand is why Papoušek, in explaining this kind of thing, wants to bring in mechanisms of motivation; these imply the concept of "drive". Suppose we just say that matching is a characteristic of the organism. There is no drive to match. We do not say that hydrochloric acid has a drive to combine with sodium hydroxide, but acknowledge that it is in the nature of these substances to act in this way.

PAPOUŠEK: I mentioned motivation because that's the way these things are often explained in the literature. But the fact is that we lack terms which are not contaminated with longstanding conceptual implications. Perhaps instead of saying that there is a drive, we could say that there are genetically coded matrices, primary matrices for different functions each of which accounts for such things as hormonostats, homeostats, thermostats and so on. The question is whether there is not a more general matrix which filters the total sensory input from the point of view of functioning.

KAGAN: The newborn is attracted to a contour because of the physiology of the visual system. Similarly, the infant maintains attention to a discrepancy until it is resolved because he has no choice.

BRUNER: I agree with this, but I would like to add one thing. I wonder whether Kagan would be willing to give up the concept of drive altogether, including for hunger. In a hungry baby you find again and again that a novel stimulus will inhibit sucking. You certainly don't want to treat orientation towards stimuli as some crude cognitive thing which keeps a hungry baby from sucking. One wonders, therefore, whether it might not be a good idea to get rid of concepts of drive and motivation altogether at this particular level of development, and to talk instead about the kinds of thing which in fact produce certain types of behaviour. The hydraulic imagery deriving from the 19th century, of the baby being pumped up with hunger or pumped up with some kind of perceptual incongruity—the notion that the pipes get full of pressure —doesn't do any service for us at all, especially when dealing with infants. I'd like to get rid of the notion of drive altogether.

LEVINE: In terms of Sokolov's model (E. N. Sokolov. 1960. *The central nervous system and behaviour.* Transactions of the Third Conference, Josiah Macy Found.) you seem to be dealing with a process where, before there is a match, you get these kinds of behaviour which look like orienting responses. I just don't see the whole notion of "drive" fitting into this orienting and habituation response.

BATESON: I object to the term "orientation" being used when we are dealing with anticipatory responses. We use the term when an animal responds to something novel, not when it shows appetitive behaviour. The concept of "expectancy" seems to me to be quite different from that of "orientation" in the Sokolov model.

PAPOUŠEK: Sokolov's model was outlined in respect to neurophysiological findings. In the realm of hypotheses we might find more convenient models in information theory. In some respects the structural model of exafference and reafference used by von Holst and Mittelstaedt might be more helpful. We are obviously not far enough to be able to find a model which will enable interpretation of all the recent observations on the development of behaviour or provide an explanation of the development of voluntary actions. Therefore until a new concept brings a new terminology we need general terms that are less compromised. But do we have them?

Developmental Changes in Early Learning

LEVINE: Is there a developmental pattern to the early changes in problem solving? Does it start at a certain age and is it related to the development of the central nervous system?

PAPOUŠEK: I would like to study these questions but it will be a very difficult task. We have not yet been able to find a good way of standardizing the whole situation.

Although we were able to shape the behavioural patterns we studied, at that early stage of development they were very fragile. As soon as we started the regular experimental procedure under standardized conditions we hit problems. In my paper I mentioned an example of how the setting up of rigid standardized criteria for conditioning can upset an infant's conceptualizing: you remember there were two different ways by which an infant could try to complete an incomplete trial response, one of which was unsatisfactory. We have to solve the problems of standardization before we can start comparing age groups. So far, my impression is that at the age of 4 months we are close to the very beginning of the ability to solve the problems represented by our experiments.

DENENBERG: Do you get equal retention of conditioning with your various groups, or is there a differential retention rate when you reestablish the response?

PAPOUŠEK: We have not studied retention as such, but we have noticed a pretraining effect when reestablishing the conditioned response after its extinction. In addition, the fact that we do not run experiments on Saturdays and Sundays has given us enough evidence of retention across 2-day intervals in learning. We know from our former experience, however, that 3 or 4 week intervals in learning do result in extinction of a learned response.

DENENBERG: Is there a linear relationship between 3 days and 86 days in terms of original learning?

PAPOUŠEK: The curve showing the relationship would be of the asymptotic type. The developmental changes in the course of learning are, however, not confined to quantitative changes. We have also been able to demonstrate qualitative changes: for example, the acquisition curves of 3-month infants show a rather different pattern from those of neonates.

BATESON: I'm a little bothered by the way you talk about maturation. What you have is a change of behaviour with age, which may suggest purely endogenous changes. However, when you look more critically at the situation, you might find specific types of experience which co-vary with age. It seems to me that in your case, when your babies are not in your experimental set-up, they are having all sorts of practice at home. They are getting practice in operant and classical conditioning, presumably with their mothers, and the improved performance that you find may to a certain extent reflect the kind of experience that they are having at home. Do you want to rule this out?

PAPOUŠEK: Under no circumstances do I want to simplify the problem of heredity-environment. All the babies we studied, however, came from a rather comparable environmental background and we still found individual differences and some common trends in changes with age. It's difficult, therefore, not to think in terms of maturation because we see in babies effects which are very obviously the results of endogenous changes, for instance in the development of vocalization.

Head Turning as an Avoidance Response

AINSWORTH: Both in Brackbill's experiment on conditioning the smiling response (Y. Brackbill. 1958. *Child Develpm.*, **29**, 115) and in Rheingold's experiment on conditioning the babbling response (H. L. Rheingold *et al.* 1959. *J. comp. physiol. Psychol.*, **52**, 68) the infants showed signs of distress during extinction. At any rate, there was refusal to look at the experimenter who had previously done the reinforcing: there was aversion of the head. In your head turning experiments did you find any similar kind of response during the extinction trials?

PAPOUŠEK: Turning away rather than towards the stimulus can often be seen during extinction; also in situations where infants cannot solve some problem or learn something, or where their expectancy has been violated. Such phenomena may, however, be interpreted in more than one way. Some may regard them as signs of frustration, others as signs of oversatiation.

AINSWORTH: This looks like a very primitive kind of defence. At the end of the first year you see this quite conspicuously with certain infants in a separation situation. Instead of giving way to distress they seem to resort to some kind of defence and, when the mother goes back into the room, instead of looking at her or greeting her, they avert the head or turn away.

SCHAFFER: You see this also in behaviour to strangers. Whereas an infant experiencing minimal fear may show intense and prolonged visual fixation in order (presumably) to assimilate the unfamiliar sensations, the infant who is overwhelmed by the fear will avert his head and so cut out the painful experience.

The T–O–T–E Model

FOSS: The T–O–T–E model (G. A. Miller *et al.* 1960. *Plans and the structure of behaviour.* Holt, New York) seems to me to have three interesting implications. First, when the test is made against the criterion, do you think it possible that the orientation response involves switching in a new lot of criteria against which the tests have to be made? Presumably some of these criteria have to be learned, and this suggests two stages in learning: the learning of new criteria and the learning of operations, that is, learning to make the match with the criterion. The second point is that the T–O–T–E model implies that the operations are built up hierarchically. Thirdly, since the T–O–T–Es depend on a feedback loop, it should be possible to interfere with the feedback so that the match has to be made in a different way. I have in mind here the tests which were made of von Holst's earlier model of "reafference" where the "efferent copy" was cancelled. When you suggest using the T–O–T–E model, do you want to accept these implications or not?

PAPOUŠEK: These interesting comments can only serve to initiate further steps in our research; I cannot answer them in terms of our previous studies. When we finished our original project we found that in fact we were at the very beginning of new problems. The T–O–T–E system is too simple to be universally applicable, but it does help in understanding the functioning of different homeostatic mechanisms. A complex living organism is, of course, very different from a simple technical device, and the higher levels of control in the hierarchy are probably built up according to specific laws that are valid only for living organisms. However, I do not dare to use hypothetical models that are too complicated before we have more evidence of neurophysiological support for them.

Some Response Measures that show Relations between Social Class and the Course of Cognitive Development in Infancy

JEROME KAGAN

Harvard University

WE HAVE BEEN conducting a longitudinal study of 160 first-born Caucasian children who reside in the Boston–Cambridge area. The project was initiated in an attempt to gain information on three issues. The first is concerned with islands of continuity during the first 3 years of life and the possibility that there may be sex differences in the profile of continuity for selected psychological variables.

A second question inquires into the antecedents of a dimension that we have called conceptual tempo. Earlier work with 6- to 10-year-old children had indicated that there were stable individual differences in decision-time when the child was confronted with a problem that led to response uncertainty. Typically, a child was presented with a match-to-sample task in which only one of several possible answers was correct. We were interested in how quickly the child decided on a solution hypothesis. It is hoped that the present study will provide an early preview of this tendency during the early school years to make fast or slow decisions. One hypothesis being tested is that rate of habituation of attention during the first year indexes a disposition to fast versus slow processing of information which shares variance with the decision-time variable.

The third question concerns differential rates of cognitive development as a function of different child rearing practices associated with social class. The sample includes lower middle class, middle class, and upper middle class families. The lower middle class parents did not complete high school and the fathers were in unskilled occupations. The middle class parents completed high school or a few years of college.

The upper middle class parents were college graduates and the fathers were employed in professional or semi-professional positions.

The children were observed in the laboratory at 4, 8, 13, and 27 months of age and observed in their homes at 4 and 27 months. In the laboratory the children were exposed to representations of human faces, human forms, and transformations of human speech. The major variables that were quantified were as follows: duration of fixation of the visual stimuli, orientation to the source of sound, smiling, vocalization, and magnitude of cardiac deceleration to the onset of stimulation. We might note briefly that magnitude of cardiac deceleration during an initial attentional epoch is an especially interesting and potentially important response. Recent empirical work indicates that surprise is one of the major determinants of large decelerations in an infant. In one study, a group of 3-month-old infants were allowed to study a novel mobile at home for 30 minutes a day for 4 weeks. These infants were then brought to the laboratory and exposed to the stimulus they saw at home as well as to three transformations they had never seen. Control infants saw all four stimuli for the first time at 4 months. Among the girls, the largest cardiac decelerations occurred to the transformations, not to the familiar mobile they had seen at home. The control infants displayed equivalent decelerations to all four stimuli.

Some impression of preliminary results is gained if we consider, briefly, the relation of social class to some of the indices. Let us start by considering the relation of fixation-time to social class as a function of age of child. In order to appreciate the results it is necessary first to discuss the changing determinants of fixation-time during the first two years.

During the first weeks of life, stimuli that have a high rate of change elicit the longest fixation-times, and we estimate that this dimension is maximally effective during the first 60 to 90 days. Very young infants show longer fixations to moving than to static stimuli, and to designs with high black-white contour contrast than to those that have homogeneous hue.

The salience of rate of change, produced either by high contour or movement, becomes subordinate to discrepancy, beginning at 12 weeks. At this time degree of discrepancy between a stimulus and an acquired schema becomes a major determinant of fixation-time. Duration of sustained attention seems to be a curvilinear function of degree of discrepancy of an event from a schema. The discrepancy hypothesis states that events that are moderately discrepant from a scheme (alterations in the arrangement, number or form of the distinctive elements), elicit longer fixations than either events that are minimally discrepant from it or events that bear no relation to it. Time does not allow me to summarize the empirical data supporting this hypothesis.

A third determinant of fixation-time appears at about 10 or 11 months and is prominent by age 2. It is defined by the density of hypotheses associated with a class of events. A growing child acquires both a more articulated schema as well as a set of associations and hypotheses. These are activated when he is exposed to an event that is discrepant from a schema. The activation of these hypotheses is accompanied by prolonged fixations because the child is trying to construct the familiar from the discrepant: he is trying to transform the discrepant event to the original that he knows. The more knowledge he has about a class of events, the longer he can work at this assimilative construction and the more prolonged his attention.

In summary, then, there are three factors which control duration of fixation in the infant and young child. High rate of change in physical parameters operates during the first 10 to 12 weeks, discrepancy is added at 3 months, and activation of meaningful hypotheses is added at about 10 months. These factors supplement each other, and an event that has all three characteristics should elicit a longer fixation-time from a 1-year-old than an event having only one or two of them.

These assumptions find support in the relation between fixation-time on the one hand and both age and social class on the other. The assumption that density of hypotheses to a discrepant event controls fixation-time at the end of the first year is supported by the increasing magnitude of correlation between educational level of the child's family and the infant's fixation-time to a set of four clay faces across the ages 4, 8, 13, and 27 months. There is no relation between parental educational level and fixation-time at 4 months for either sex. At 8, 13, and 27 months, however, the correlations become increasingly large (and significant), and always slightly higher for girls than for boys. Since upper middle class children are likely to be taught a richer set of symbolic structures surrounding faces than are lower middle class infants, the former should possess richer nests of hypotheses to the clay faces and display longer fixations. The increasing co-variation between social class and fixation-time is congruent with the idea that meaningful hypotheses are being activated during periods of fixation.

The relation of fixation-time to age also supports these ideas. There is a U-shaped relation between fixation-time to the clay faces and age. Fixation-times are high at 4 months, lowest at 8 months, and begin to climb again from 13 to 27 months. Independent data gathered by

Gordon Finley, now at the University of British Columbia, are corroborative. Finley studied three cross-sectional samples of 1-, 2-, and 3-year-old children, showing them chromatic paintings of male faces. One group of children were peasant Mayan Indians living on the Yucatan peninsula, the second was a middle class group from Cambridge. Fixation-times increased linearly with age. When we combined the data from our longitudinal study with that from Finley's subjects, we found an almost perfect U-shaped function relating fixation-time and age, with fixation-times going down from 4 to 12 months and increasing from 12 months to 36 months.

The relation of social class to magnitude of cardiac deceleration to the human faces yields a different age function. Cardiac deceleration is presumed to be elicited by surprise rather than by the activation of hypotheses. The children should be less surprised by the faces as they grow older because the 1- or 2-year-old child can assimilate the clay faces more readily than can the 4-month-old. Magnitude of cardiac deceleration to the faces showed a linear decrease from 4 to 27 months of age; the largest decelerations occurred at 4 months. Moreover, the upper middle class children showed larger decelerations than did the lower middle class infants at 4 months. Home observations of parent-child interaction indicated more face-to-face contact between the infant and the mother among the upper middle class than among the lower middle class families. The more frequent face contact should lead to a better schema for the face and, therefore, more surprise to a clay mask at 4 months.

It is interesting to note that babbling showed no relation to class during the first year. Only when the children were able to speak meaningful sentences at 27 months did we find a positive correlation with educational level of the family. It is also important to note that, although fixation-time and cardiac deceleration are positively related, babbling is independent of both of these variables. Vocalization under 1 year behaves as an independent vector. We regard babbling during the first year as an index of excitement, with multiple determinants Babbling occurs both when the child becomes restless, and also when he is excited by a stimulus.

Finally, we might say a few words about the smile. Smiling was relatively infrequent and had to be analysed nonparametrically. About 60 per cent of our infants showed some smiling to the clay faces at 4 months, and at 8 and 13 months it was even less frequent. There was no correlation between smiling and social class at 4 or 8 months. However, to the speech stimuli at 13 months there was a positive relationship between smiling and social class. In this situation the child sits in a high chair, with his mother to the right of him, and a speaker baffle emits 20-second epochs of speech. The tape recording contains four sets of sentences: nonsense read with low inflection or high inflection and meaningful speech read with low or high inflection. Upper middle class children were more likely to smile at this "speech" than were lower middle class children.

In summary, each of our major variables (fixation-time, vocalization, smiling, and cardiac deceleration) displayed different functions with age and with social class. We plan to use multivariate analyses in an attempt to gain a better understanding of the fragile and dynamic processes that we call "attention".

Discussion

Significance of Social Class Differences

PRECHTL: I do not doubt that the different behaviours you study are related to class differences. Unfortunately, obstetrical risk is also correlated very highly with class differences. Have you looked at this?

KAGAN: Yes. No child was taken for study if examination of his hospital record showed any sign of prematurity, anoxia, etc. Children were included in our samples only if they were passed by the doctor as healthy.

SCHAFFER: Social class is a very global concept; one needs to enquire what variables within it are operative to produce your results. As Prechtl has indicated, maternal behaviour variables are obviously involved. There is a set of relationships here that require to be isolated. Have you any ideas on this?

KAGAN: Yes. We find, for example, that lower middle class parents engage in less face-to-face distinctive vocalization with their children during non-feeding times. The upper middle class mother will lean over her daughter and play vocal games with her much more than will the lower middle class mother. Moss (1967. *Merrill-Palmer Quarterly*, **13**, 19) finds the same thing. Class, however, is not an explanatory variable; for us it is only an effective way to maximize differences in mother–child interaction patterns.

AINSWORTH: Having selected your sample to maximize the differences, you would probably get something even more clear-cut if you then classified the terms of your observations.

BRUNER: There is another thing you might look at. If your peak correlations are about 0.40, you are accounting for less than 20 per cent of the variance. When you're accounting for that little variance, one of the ways in which you can get a better view of what's going on is to use a co-variance design, pulling out the variance due to other factors. This will keep your effects from being swamped by other unwanted sources of variance.

KAGAN: We are planning to perform multivariate discriminative analyses, because one must study the dependent variables simultaneously. The single variable analysis of variance is inadequate to assess complex processes defined by many variables.

Cardiac Deceleration and Acceleration

PRECHTL: I wonder if the cardiac deceleration you measure is not a remote phenomenon deriving from holding the breath, which is a usual response to surprise.

KAGAN: Occasionally it is. Sometimes, however, deceleration occurs without any change in the respiratory pattern.

PRECHTL: How was respiration monitored?

KAGAN: By a transducer around the chest.

PRECHTL: Measurement of transthoracic impedance would probably be better because this indicates the minute volume of air exchange by imposing a current through the chest.

HAMBURG: Do you find any conditions under which you get a cardiac acceleration?

KAGAN: Yes, acceleration is likely to occur if the child becomes startled by the stimulus, or if he should make a trunk-twisting movement. The child who does neither shows no change in heart rate.

HAMBURG: Do you find that on the occasions when a child gets grossly upset there is an acceleration?

KAGAN: Yes, this happens if the child at 8 months should become frightened by one of the clay masks.

BRUNER: Does the child at this age reach for the masks?

KAGAN: Not very much, but by 13 months there is more reaching. There are individual differences which stabilize with increasing age. For example, the most attentive 4-month olds are the ones that tend to lean forward at 13 months to touch the mask.

BRUNER: Do they attenuate somewhat on the cardiac deceleration, because reaching does give rise to some acceleration?

KAGAN: No. They look then decelerate and then lean forward. There is a positive correlation of 0·40 between leaning forward and deceleration on a trial.

Aversive Head Turning

FREEDMAN: Do you find turning away of the head at 4 months?

KAGAN: A small group of children, about 10 per cent, show such aversive behaviour. One child I studied seemed to be disturbed. After two or three trials he would refuse to look at the stimulus, though he did not cry. But the infants who turn away at 4 months do not do so at 13 months.

Sex Differences

KAGAN: Let me mention another aspect of the data which is interesting because the same pattern comes up in two other studies. Terence Moore (1967. *Human Development*, **10**, 88) found that vocalization on the Griffiths Infant Scale at 6 months predicted cognitive development for girls, but not for boys. There were no mean differences in the babbling of boys and girls at 6 months, but individual differences in babbling among girls predicted later vocabulary; this was not the case for the boys. Nancy Bayley (Cameron *et al.* 1967. *Science*, **157**, 331) reported a similar finding. In our study the babies were in a very structured situation, looking at the clay mask. We measured total time babbling to the faces. Girls who babbled to the faces at 4 months oriented to a sound source at 8 months; this relation did not occur for boys.

Identifying Early Response Dispositions

HAMBURG: Kagan, you mention that, in analysing your observations in the very early period, you are looking for a preview in the first year of life of a response disposition in the area of decision making. This is very interesting. What are you finding that might enable you to identify that?

KAGAN: The variable we study is time taken to reach a decision. On tasks that contain response uncertainty some children show fast decision-times, others show slow decision-times. We call the former impulsive, the latter reflective. We are seeking to determine if this response disposition can be predicted during the first year of life. Since one cannot give infants problems with response uncertainty, one searches for a response that may reflect the same dimension that is mediating the decision-time process. One candidate is rate of habituation of attention to visual stimuli during the first year. We believe that infants who show rapid habituation of interest will be more likely to become impulsive than reflective children. Data on 70 boys studied at 4, 8, 13, and 27 months suggest that the infants who show rapid habituation of fixation-time to visual stimuli at 4 months and rapid shifting of foci of attention with toys at 8 months are likely, at 27 months, to have short epochs of involvement with objects and fast decision-times in situations having response uncertainty. When one examines the children at the extremes of these distributions, one is persuaded of the stability of this dimension. It is not clear whether biological factors contribute to this continuity.

HAMBURG: I find this quite fascinating. There is obviously scope for much more discussion on the role of postnatal stimulation in all this. A question I should like to see answered is whether you can identify, very early in life, certain consistent individual differences in response to one or another aspect of stimulation, for example its intensity, mode, or duration that will categorize the baby. Responses of special interest to study in the infant would be those that might interact in interesting ways with characteristics of the mother. There is a need for much more consideration of research designs that are deeply interactional as between certain specified categories of the mother's behaviour and those of the infant.

Phenotypic and Genotypic Variation, Early Stimulation and Cognitive Development

GENERAL DISCUSSION

Biological Advantage of Genotypic Variation in a Population
GINSBURG: In order to consider the significance of individual differences in relation to questions about biological function and the adaptive evolution of behaviour, I will summarize some points that are covered in extenso elsewhere (B. E. Ginsburg. 1966. *Soc. Serv. Rev.*, **40**, 121; B. E. Ginsburg. 1968. In D. Glass (Ed.), *Genetics*, Biology and Behavior Series. The Rockefeller University Press and Russell Sage Foundation).

The typical phenotype characterizing a population is a statistical amalgam of diverse genotypes and of both manifest and latent phenotypic variability. One can study this in several ways. One is to take a genetically randomized population from nature, or from random-bred laboratory mice, and pull it apart by selection with respect to criteria such as the early sensitive periods for the kinds of behaviour that Levine, Denenberg and others have been studying. If one begins with a population of laboratory strains of mice that are already differentiated into several pedigrees through genetic inbreeding and selection, one finds that the sensitive period for producing the greatest outcome of early handling paradigms in the preweaning period varies greatly among different segments of the population. The direction and magnitude of the effects on various tests for outcome are also different. This means, in an evolutionary sense, that a population taken either from nature or from a laboratory has retained a variety of different genetic styles of response. One then speculates why these should have been retained. For example, some genotypes, as a result of such early stresses as living in a crowded environment, will become more pacific, others will become more aggressive. The former will tolerate crowding, the latter will space out and enhance the probability of their finding more favourable niches. Again, some individuals will have their "personalities" changed by

261

early stress and some will have them changed by stress later on; some will change in one direction, some will change in another. The style of response that develops is determined by the biological predisposition of the individual. This is variable within the population but it can move the style of response in one direction or another depending upon the environmental circumstances. It is clearly adaptive for a population to have these varying styles of response in its biological repertoire. Now a human being may be very different from a mouse in that he can learn much more, and there is less coding in the biological substratum. His emotional development may, however, be subject to the same mechanisms that obtain for the mouse.

BRUNER: The phenotype variation for a particular genotype might be even more variable in human beings.

GINSBURG: Yes. The trouble is that, in characterizing populations, we tend to homogenize these variations by talking only about the central tendencies, forgetting about how the genetic minorities vote. These genetic minorities can be extremely important if the selective circumstances change. A potential for flexibility such that, in the same externally applied circumstances, varying styles of response have different kinds of outcome is probably among the most adaptive features that a population can have within its genetic repertoire.

I would now like to pass to a point about phenotypic buffering. Except in the case of identical twins, everybody is obviously individually different from everybody else, and these differences extend to behaviour. Now the genetically based differences in styles of response are usually assimilated to a normative phenotype. Genetic systems subjected to the ordinary laws of population genetics are essentially conservative. The population does not exhibit the range of variability that is potentially there in the genotype. In artificial selection experiments with mammals, lasting from three to seven generations, one can pull out genetic variations very quickly and exaggerate them very effectively. The buffering of an established population against a seething potential for variability has been an evolutionary product. The norm depends upon the selective demands made by the environment in which the population lives. In a mouse population, for example, we have speculated that one genotype may lead to a tendency to space out whereas another may result in an ability to tolerate other individuals. Clearly the former genotype would be favoured if spacing out were the most adaptive condition, whereas the latter would be favoured in an environment where crowding had to be tolerated.

BATESON: You seem to imply one very clear prediction, which is that any inbred strain of any animals, because it is less genetically variable, will be less fitted for a natural environment than any outbred strain.

GINSBURG: Yes, that's true on the whole. However, there are populations, and the wolf is an example, where there is significant inbreeding in nature. Within any one pack the animals probably have a relatively small genetic repertoire. In such cases, however, one usually also finds that there are a series of semi-isolated populations, each having some genetic exchange with the others. The total gene pool is then differentially partitioned among the groups. The total population complex still retains the usual kinds of flexibility but any one sub-population does not. The human species has probably conformed to this model until very recently.

Genetic and Environmental Factors in Human Cognitive Development

BRUNER: Genetic flexibility within the total population is, I think, of major importance for understanding individual differences in cognitive functioning in the human, and how they originate and develop. It is one of the reasons for the differences in outcome when different individuals have similar encounters with the environment. Encounters with the environment ought to be regarded as opportunities that permit the realization of functions which are potentially present. The potential is due to genetic factors, but environmental stimulation is required in order to set a particular function going and to permit it to develop. Let us take the example of learning the structure of space. It is inconceivable that we learn the structure of space; there has got to be some way in which it is already represented in the nervous system. I know that Freedman can give us an interesting example of this.

FREEDMAN: I observed an infant week by week from 1 to 6 months of age. She was blind from rubella. She had complete cataracts on her lenses but she could perceive bright light. Nystagmus developed at the end of the first month, as it usually does in these infants, so that the eyes moved constantly. The exception was when the mother bent over her and talked to her: then the nystagmus stopped and the eyes converged and went towards the source of the sound. A similar thing happened if, standing beside her as she lay passively on her back, I waved at her: the nystagmus would stop and she would turn towards the source of the wind. In other words, somehow there was a sense of where the stimulus was coming from, without there having been any visual practice.

BRUNER: In contrast to this, I don't think that the child develops a corresponding postural model for space, which is critical for getting locomotion going, unless he has an opportunity to interact with the environment by means of responses which, on the reafference side, are going to provide a model that corresponds to the reality. Now it's quite apparent, from studies on body posture and postural models, that there is an option for creating a locomotor space which is either predominantly visual or predominantly body-postural. In position tests employing a tilting chair, some people depend tremendously on the stimulation that comes from the vestibular mechanism, others depend mainly on the visual field. Bearing in mind what Ginsburg said about the different ways in which a genotype can express itself through phenotypic options depending upon encounters, I begin to wonder whether this isn't all part of what we would speak of as normal variability in the population.

I am trying here to fit together three things into what seems to be a crucially important package. First, we have innate capacities; second, these lead to encounters with the environment; third, these encounters bring out phenotypic variability within the species.

HAMBURG: Ginsburg's point about the immense genetic variability in a population is extremely important. There is another aspect of this variability that I should like to mention. To put it crudely, no species, let alone the individual, is wise enough to know what environmental changes may come to pass. Some of the genetic variability that is of little value in a contemporary environment may turn out to be of great importance in a different environment. For example, if radiation levels go up much more, it might be that genes which provide some kind of biochemical buffering against radiation would take on enormous importance in respect to our contemporary species. This whole problem, it seems to me, ought to be very much on our minds today when, since industrialization, the rates of change in some important aspects of the environment are greater than they ever have been.

The genetic background for learning capacities is very relevant here. In the primate order there is a prolongation of the period of immaturity from about 3 or 4 years in many of the old-world monkeys to roughly double that in the great apes. In chimps it takes about 10 years to reach full maturity, and in man it is of course still longer. On the face of it this would appear to have some disadvantages, and in the short-term it certainly does. For example, it is apparent from primate field-studies that there are constraints imposed upon the range of territory that can be covered daily by the mother, and therefore by the group as well, due to the presence of a more or less helpless infant clinging to the mother. There are also reproductive constraints. Most primates, having repro-duced, don't do so again until lactation has been completed. It would seem, therefore, that they could both move faster and further and also have more young if they didn't have these helpless creaturesa round for a long time. One has to ask, therefore, what kind of selective advantage could offset short-term constraints of this kind. It seems to me and to many others that one of the major advantages must be that this prolonged period of immaturity is a period when, through the protection afforded by the adults, the young have a prolonged opportunity for learning. Now the learning that can be accomplished in the higher primates, the great ability to integrate simple components into more complex ones in long sequences, can be oriented to the specific requirements of a given environment whatever its characteristics may be. The water is here or there, the shelter is here or there, the food sources are here or there, and the predators are of one kind or another. Adaptation can be made to a very diverse array of environments as a result of the shaping of behaviour in this long protective period of immaturity. It seems probable that, in human evolution, natural selection has favoured behaviour patterns that are capable of dealing with highly varied environments.

FREEDMAN: In the light of Ginsburg's paper, and bearing in mind the Headstart Programme in the United States, I should like to know what Bruner now thinks about the desirability of priming the cognitive pump within a certain age range if it is to be able to operate at full-flush thereafter.

BRUNER: The fact is that we don't yet have much evidence about what it is in the early period that might be producing our non-specific learning capacities. When one sees the decline in culturally deprived children around age 3, one supposes there must have been something during the early period that produced it. We think it is something to do with living in a very shut-up, non-predictable, kind of environment. We hoped that the Headstart Programme might stimulate all of us to do more research into what conditions produce those declines and what might be done to ameliorate them. As yet there is only fragmentary evidence about these conditions.

What appears to me to be the most promising kind of evidence on the sorts of thing that make a difference is coming out of the type of work that Ainsworth and David reported to us here. That's where we find the biggest cultural differences. Martin Richards (personal communication) made exquisite observations of the types of pattern of interaction that occur in really bad slum migrant Negro families in New Jersey. He found that there was practically no interaction between infants and their mothers of a structural kind that related to the ongoing activities and state of the infant. There seemed to be long periods during the day when both the adults and the children in the house, which was usually half-dark, were inactive and apathetic. In his view this was partly due to malnutrition: most infants were grossly underweight for their ages and were retarded regarding the basic motor milestones. Nevertheless, likely as not, the huge deficiencies in interaction were probably working their way down to affecting the kinds of things that Papoušek and I have been talking about here. Within the child care package there was an absence of the learning opportunities of the more complicated sorts that we study in our laboratories. I would hope that, in the future, there will be much more of a push towards doing this kind of research in natural settings so that we can make comparisons between the effects of different cultural backgrounds.

GINSBURG: In some kibbutzim in Israel and in some collectives in the Soviet Union, although infants spend some time with their parents, they are raised mostly in children's homes or in nursery situations. In these settings, ethnic differences, genealogical differences, class differences and so on are, for the most part, disregarded. I gather that, if the communal rearing begins at about 3 years of age, the differences to be expected later are not wiped out nearly as much as when the experience begins in infancy (reports by Smilansky, The Henrietta Szold Foundation, Jerusalem). The difficulty is in interpreting these findings. One can still take a nativist view. With respect to environmental variables, the work of Bloom (B. S. Bloom. 1964. *Stability and change in human characteristics*. Wiley, New York) suggests that about 50 per cent of the child's later ability is determined and manifest by the age of about 4 or 5. If you go back to the actual statistics on which this assertion is based, it appears to me that about 50 per cent of the variance has been exhibited by that age. This would suggest that alternative interpretations along developmental genetic lines are possible. The interpretation of all these findings seems to me to be critically important in furthering our theoretical concepts about child development, which are now being translated—perhaps too quickly—into practical measures.

BRUNER: I reinterpret Bloom's data in terms of Stoutford's "theory of intervening opportunities". The general concept is that, where the individual has an opportunity for contact with sources of change or sources of amelioration of function, the individual, having had one intervention, is likely to increase the number of interventions that follow. That is to say, one such opportunity leads to a following opportunity. What it amounts to is that the opportunities, if not provided early on, are not going to multiply as you go further along. This is what constrains the variability.

There is another thing that interests me in relation to all this. One would assume that, in any particular functioning system that is going to develop, there probably are at the outset certain highly general skills which are almost protopathic with respect to what later is to be the epicritic area. For example, one of the things that is required in order for there to be problem solving is a certain amount of early training in the maintenance of attention across distractive stimuli. It is inconceivable that a person is going to be a good problem solver unless he can stick at the task on the way up. Köhler (1925. *The mentality of apes.* Routledge and Kegan Paul, London), for example, in describing episodes of tool use in apes, comments that an ape cannot sustain a chain of activity which would really allow for the elaboration of tool use. Human beings obviously have the capacity for doing this, but there is nevertheless variability in it. In the hyperexcitability syndrome, for example, that Prechtl has described, there are diffuse discharges in the nervous system which prevent the individual from sticking to a task for very long. Another kind of factor which might affect the development of this capacity has to do with early training. It is obviously desirable that this should permit a child to learn how to keep his response invariant across transformations in the state of the environment. Now if it turned out that such learning tends to occur only at some crucial stage early in the life cycle, and if a child was not then given the opportunity to practise attentional control, then the opportunity for further expansion of capacities would become reduced. Moreover, it would become reduced in a multiplicated fashion because, if once you fail to develop such basic skills as are necessary to use the intellectual technology of human culture, then your opportunity for achieving full realization through the amplifiers of the culture is grossly reduced. In that sense, there would be a vast reduction in the later possibilities of variability in a given individual, because of the limitations that were set at the stock root stage.

It may help to look at instances of this through genetic-coloured glasses. My impression from looking at some of the literature on "true infantile autism", or Kanner's syndrome, is that these are kids who can attend tremendously to things happening for a long time, but who really don't have the ability to scan and make connections. May there not be something here that is in part biological; may not attention mechanisms in themselves constitute a biological genetic problem for investigation?

A Combined Biological and Psychosocial Approach to the Study of Behavioural Development

CHAIRMAN'S CONCLUDING OBSERVATIONS

DAVID A. HAMBURG

Stanford University

As THIS STUDY group has progressed, participants have commented repeatedly on its unusual value. Perhaps the major thrust of these reactions has been in appreciation of the informative challenging quality provided by the diversity of the participants. Information and ideas from many sources in biological and behavioural science make all of us stretch beyond the usual boundaries of our interests. At the same time, we have recognized the complexity in finding meaningful points of conjunction among different approaches, let alone achieving a comprehensive interpretation.

In these closing remarks I could not hope to summarize, and certainly not to integrate, the richness and variety of this study group. I hope instead to capture the interdisciplinary behavioural spirit of the occasion by sketching an emerging research area of considerable potential importance.

The Influence of Early Hormonal and Socio-environmental Stimulation upon the Development of Aggressive Behaviour

Research in this problem area has recently linked work with rodents, nonhuman primates, and man; more generally it has linked biological and psychosocial variables in a fruitful way. In examining this research, I am taking as my point of departure Levine's discussion. (p. 50) of the model provided by the effects of early administration of testosterone on subsequent behaviour in rodents (S. Levine and R. Mullins. 1966. *Science*, **152**, no. 3729, 1585). The findings about these effects, to which he has contributed so significantly, have provided the main impetus for the model he has constructed here of the mechanism by which the Levine–Denenberg type of stimulation might affect the brain (via adrenocortical activation) and hence affect subsequent behaviour.

The effects of early hormonal variation upon brain organization and later behaviour have constituted one of the exciting scientific frontiers of the past decade (C. H. Phoenix, R. W. Goy, and W. C. Young. 1967. In L. Martini and W. F. Ganong (Eds.), *Neuroendocrinology*, p. 163. Academic Press, New York). For example, treatment of newborn female rats with male sex hormone (testosterone) results in lifelong abolition of female sex behaviour and in an exaggeration of male behaviour patterns, particularly various forms of aggression (C. A. Barraclough, 1967. In L. Martini and W. F. Ganong (Eds.), *Neuro-endocrinology*, p. 61. Academic Press, New York). During the past few years, such work has been extended to primates, utilizing the familiar laboratory species, Rhesus macaque (R. W. Goy. 1968. In R. Michael (Ed.), *Endocrinology and Human Behaviour*, p. 12. Oxford University Press, London). Investigators have given testosterone to pregnant monkeys, spanning roughly the second quarter of gestation. Though it is difficult to maintain pregnancy under these conditions, they have produced abnormal female offspring who have some anatomical and behavioural characteristics of the male type. Their work was based on the earlier finding of sex differences in the behaviour in infant monkeys, the males being more aggressive. Reliable behavioural norms have been established, documenting these sex differences in behaviour during infancy. Indeed, they are apparent almost as soon as the infants are capable of any sustained activity. In the hormone experiments, the social behaviour of the untreated female offspring did not differ importantly from that described for normal females, but the behaviour of the treated females (male sex hormone was given to the mother in pregnancy) much more closely resembled that of males. The masculinized females threatened, initiated play, and engaged in rough-and-tumble play patterns more frequently than the controls. Like the normal males, these masculinized females also withdrew less often from the initiations, threats and approaches of other subjects. So far, 8 such female monkeys exposed to male sex hormone *in utero* have been observed to adult status. To what extent does this shift towards male behaviour endure? As adults, they continue to be quite high in threat behaviour towards other monkeys, though the other aggressive characteristics have diminished somewhat under the laboratory conditions in which they have been studied so far.

These findings raise the basic question as to how such an effect might be produced. There is evidence that, in rodents, testosterone is taken up in the brain, particularly in the hypothalamus. It is conceivable that we have here some differentiation, in the biological sense, of circuits in the hypothalamus, or hypothalamic-limbic circuits, which then mediate future aggressive behaviour. Would this mean that a fixed behaviour pattern was being set by the brain's exposure to the hormone during this sensitive period of development; or would it mean that some general orientation, some temperamental disposition, was influenced by the early androgen? I would think the latter is more likely to be the case, in view of the great dependence of primate species upon learning. It seems likely that the hormone exposure would affect the ease of learning aggressive patterns, the readiness for learning such patterns, rather than elicit virtually reflexive patterns which become permanently set or fixed. I can imagine that the early hormone exposure lowers the threshold of response to certain stimuli that elicit fighting; or that it makes more rewarding certain patterns of action such as large muscle movements that are so critical in agonistic encounters. The general point is that this approach involves interaction of genes and hormones with the learning process.

Experimental methods for analysing the deployment of attention in the developing primate should be helpful here. It would be interesting to expose isolation-reared monkeys to different kinds of stimuli in order to determine whether they have preferences within the sphere of aggressive behaviour. If various types of visual input were provided, it is possible that some types would elicit more sustained attention than others. Infant monkeys might work harder for the opportunity of seeing some types of pictures than others. In view of the well established sex differences in aggressive behaviour (observed both in the field and in experimental primate research), it would be reasonable to predict that males, if exposed to a variety of play patterns, would spend more time than females in viewing rough-and-tumble play.

The sort of experiment I have just sketched has not yet been done with specific reference to aggressive behaviour, though we hope to pursue this line of inquiry at Stanford. We are encouraged in the promise of this approach by a recent experiment (G. P. Sackett. 1966. *Science*, **154**, 1468). Though Sackett was not primarily concerned with aggressive behaviour, his findings are interesting in this context. He raised monkeys in a total isolation chamber for the first 9 months of life, during which he exposed them to various types of visual input from coloured slides. These slides depicted monkeys in various activities and also depicted various nonmonkey stimuli. Among the various categories presented, it is quite interesting that monkey pictures elicited much more interest than nonmonkey pictures. Moreover, pictures of monkeys threatening were especially potent in eliciting behavioural responses. Between $2\frac{1}{2}$ and 4 months of age, threat pictures yielded a particularly high frequency of disturbance. Recently, Sackett (personal communication) has repeated this experiment using motion picture films and has obtained similar results. These findings suggest that there is a sensitive period in early development during which the infant monkey is exceedingly responsive to the threatening facial expression which is characteristic of the species. Given a predisposition of this sort, it is not difficult to imagine how the infant in the natural environment would learn a great deal about threat and attack behaviour. Through the processes of observational learning, which appear to be so important in primate development, it seems highly probable that once the infant monkey's attention is powerfully drawn to threat stimuli, he would rapidly go on to learn both the conditions under which threat and attack patterns are likely to occur and the behaviour that is useful in ameliorating them. It is at least plausible that the exposure of brain to testosterone *in utero* might have a bearing on the differentiation of circuits that will ultimately mediate response dispositions like those occurring to the threat stimulus in infancy.

The monkey experiments on early testosterone have recently been followed up by an investigation of girls who had been exposed to androgens *in utero*; that is, their developing brains in fetal life came in contact with chemical compounds similar to the male sex hormone. (J. Money and A. A. Ehrhardt. 1968. In R. Michael (Ed.), *Endocrinology and Human Behaviour*, p. 32. Oxford University Press, London). A total of 22 such girls have been studied, mostly in the 10- to 12-year age range. Those with striking anatomical abnormalities had undergone surgical correction shortly after birth. The categories used for analysis of sex differences in behaviour were (1) energy expenditure level, particularly as represented by the organized movements of vigorous, outdoor, athletic activity; (2) play, toy and sports preferences (i.e. male type preferences); (3) clothing preferences (i.e. male type preferences); (4) maternalism (i.e. behaviours that involve rehearsal of maternal roles, as in playing with dolls); (5) career ambition; (6) body image (especially as reflected in drawings of persons); (7) perceptual erotic arousal (especially oriented to visual arousal, which Kinsey reported to be more characteristic of males). Via interviews and projective tests, information was obtained from each girl and from at least one parent in each of the 7 behavioural categories. The results indicated that the early-androgenized girls, as contrasted with a control group, tended to be described by self and others as tomboys, to engage in much rough-and-tumble play, and to prefer toys ordinarily associated with boys. This is a provocative study that will require replication and additional controls. Though not definitive, these observations raise an important question and illustrate a line of inquiry which has led from basic research on the biology of sex differentiation to an important human problem.

Another biological situation has recently arisen which is of interest in the present context. The XYY syndrome is characterized by the presence of an extra Y chromosome (S. Kessler and R. Moos, 1969. *J. Psychiat. Res.*, in press). In man, the Y chromosome, though shrivelled in appearance, is strongly determining of male characteristics. Indeed, individuals have been discovered who have several X chromosomes and one Y, yet they are males. It is highly plausible that the Y chromosome is important for the synthesis of testosterone. In any event, it has been established during the past few years that XYY individuals are exceptionally tall. It has also been suggested, on the basis of somewhat limited evidence, that they tend to be hyper-aggressive. If so, it would be a matter of great interest to determine whether these individuals also have unusually high levels of circulating testosterone or other androgens. In studying problems of this kind, we must bear in mind that the correlation, if any, between androgen levels and aggressive behaviour need not be contemporary, but rather might well be developmental. In other words, a high level of androgen secretion at an earlier point in life might affect the brain in such a way that the individual would be predisposed toward the development of aggressive behaviour subsequently. In such a case, it seems overwhelmingly probable that the hormonal effects would interact with conditions of the social environment during the years of growth and development.

From the standpoint of human development, this poses very difficult problems. The possibility that variations in early androgen exposure might influence the interests or preferences of the growing child in respect to aggressive and sexual behaviour is particularly intriguing because it would make a crucial link between biological and psychosocial processes (D. A. Hamburg and D. T. Lunde. 1966. In E. Maccoby (Ed.), *The Development of Sex Differences*, p. 1. Stanford University Press). Unfortunately, it is exceedingly difficult to get the vital information in man. In order to do this, it would be very helpful to determine the hormonal situation during pregnancy. (O. Green. 1965. *Pediatric Clinics of North America*, **12**, 615). What are the points of entry for determining the exposure of brain to testosterone during fetal life? With the methods that have become available quite recently, it is possible to measure testosterone and other androgens in tiny amounts in the blood and urine of the mother. The more difficult questions concern the way in which the mother's androgen situation is affecting the fetus. In some countries it has been possible to utilize the circumstance of therapeutic abortion for important research on this problem. In Sweden, where therapeutic abortions may be performed at mid-pregnancy by cesarean section, it has been possible to perfuse the fetus and so to get a dynamic picture of steroid metabolism in the early developing organism. While this does not solve any problems of later behaviour, it does help to understand what may be learned from the mother about the situation in the fetus. In due course, it may well become possible to get a picture of fetal endocrine activity by measuring testosterone and its metabolites in the blood and urine of the mother throughout pregnancy. There is a rapid transfer of steroids across the placenta from fetus to mother. The fetus uses the maternal urinary route of excretion. Thus, some leverage may be obtained by the discovery of so called unique metabolites; that is, metabolites made only or chiefly by the fetus. When such metabolites appear in the urine of the mother, there is a high probability that they are coming from the fetus. One interesting lead in this connection is the tendency of the human fetus to make 16-hydroxylated steroids. (J. Reynolds. 1966. *J. clin. Endocr. Metab.*, **26**, 1251). Perhaps other distinctive features of steroid metabolism will be discovered in the next few years. However, this is a very difficult area in which progress has been understandably slow.

I do not want to leave the impression that I believe aggressive behaviour to be solely or even mainly determined by such hormonal effects. Current primate research is providing abundant and growing evidence of the importance of early social environment for later behaviour. Some recent work from the Wisconsin laboratory on monkeys reared in total isolation is interesting in this connection. Mitchell (G. D. Mitchell. 1966. Ph.D. Thesis, University of Wisconsin) has done follow-up studies on monkeys reared in total isolation for 6 months and also on monkeys reared in total isolation for 12 months. At $3\frac{1}{2}$ years of age, and again at $4\frac{1}{2}$ years of age, they showed serious disturbances in the aggressive sphere. For instance, they were unable to establish a stable dominance hierarchy. This is not surprising in view of the serious, pervasive deficits that occur in social behaviour under conditions of isolation rearing. Perhaps the most striking observation in this work is that aggressive behaviour, at least under the conditions studied in this laboratory, actually became more extreme with the passage of time. The $3\frac{1}{2}$-year-old monkeys were more aggressive in attacking other animals than they had been at an earlier age, and the $4\frac{1}{2}$-year-old monkeys were more aggressive still. This aggressive behaviour includes "suicidal attacks" on adult males and includes severe attacks by females on infants. These latter two categories of attack are particularly remarkable in view of the fact that they are virtually non-existent under natural conditions, as highlighted by recent field studies (S. L. Washburn and D. A. Hamburg. 1968. In P. Jay (Ed.), *Primates: Studies in Adaptation and Variability*, p. 458. Holt, Rinehart and Winston, New York). Evidently, growing up under conditions of total social isolation produces truly remarkable, bizarre effects on the development of aggressive behaviour. In a similar vein, a recent report from the Wisconsin laboratories indicates that experience with a hostile mother during the first few months of a rhesus monkey's life tends to produce hyper-aggressive behaviour 4 years later. (G. P. Sackett. 1967. *J. comp. physiol. Psychol.*, **64**, 363).

The adaptive significance of observational learning in natural environments has been emerging from recent field studies of primate behaviour. In circumstances of food-getting, mating, and infant care (D. A. Hamburg. 1969. In B. Foss (Ed.), *Determinants of Infant Behaviour*, vol. IV, p. 3. Methuen, London), there is growing evidence of an observation-imitation-practice sequence. Infants show these sequences commonly in relation to older animals, from whom they evidently learn a great deal early in life. Experimental work has also shown that the observing monkey is able to learn from errors of the observed animal as well as from his successes—that is, from the consequences of his actions.

Similar considerations must apply to the development of aggressive behaviour. From the field studies of primates under natural conditions, it appears likely that aggressive patterns of interaction are largely acquired through observational learning. In many species, particularly those which spend a great deal of time on the ground, aggressive play is prominent during the growing years. Most species show clear differences, with males spending more time in aggressive activities. There is preliminary evidence that, in some species, the adolescent male becomes a particularly keen observer of adult males. From our own field work, this appears particularly intriguing in chimpanzees and certainly deserves further study. Both chimpanzees and gorillas have elaborate aggressive displays in adult life. These are much more highly developed in males than in females. Interestingly, rudimentary aggressive displays are undertaken in infancy much more prominently in male than in female animals.

It appears then that observational learning in a social context is an important part of the primate evolutionary heritage and has an important bearing on the development of aggressive patterns. This view is pertinent to the recent studies on observational learning of aggressive behaviour in human subjects. In research with pre-school children, a remarkable set of findings has recently highlighted the susceptibility of children to learning aggressive patterns by viewing models who act aggressively. (A. Bandura. 1965. In L. Berkowitz (Ed.), *Advances in Experimental Social Psychology*, vol. 2, p. 1. Academic Press, New York). For example, in one experiment, pre-school children were exposed to an aggressive model attacking a target object for 10 minutes in a laboratory situation, while a control group experienced the same situation without an aggressive model. When the children were tested in the same situation 6 months later, the former were much more aggressive towards the target object than the latter—that is, a mere 10-minute exposure had an effect of enhancing physical aggressiveness in the same situation 6 months later.

Psychosocial variables of this sort must be exceedingly important in the development of aggressive behaviour. Even from a biological perspective, these variables must be given much weight. The distinguished ethologist, Robert Hinde, has recently emphasized that a developmental approach which takes account of the social context of early learning has a great bearing on the problem of aggression. (R. Hinde, 1967, 2nd March. *New Society*, 302). In general, it appears reasonable that biological predispositions to the learning of aggressive patterns and exposure to specific social learning situations must interact to produce the great individual differences in aggressiveness that are observed during later life. Early hormone effects may well influence the young organism's disposition towards various classes of stimuli in the social environment. My reason for sketching this area of research has been to illustrate a way in which the search for factors governing the early development of behaviour naturally leads to the conjunction of biological and psychosocial approaches. That is why the great diversity of interests represented in this study group, sharing a common interest in the scientific study of behavioural development, has proved so stimulating and valuable for all of us these past few days.

It remains only for me to thank participants for excellent contributions. I would also like to thank Dr. Wolstenholme and the Ciba

Foundation for their fine hospitality, and the staff of the Centre. We must surely thank Dr. Ambrose for making it all possible. We wish him every success in the important venture of establishing the new Centre for Advanced Study in the Developmental Sciences.

Author Index

Numbers in italics refer to pages where References are listed at the end of each article.

A

Abood, L. G., 81, *88*
Abraham, K., 133, *162*
Ader, R., 8, *8*
Ainsworth, M. D. S., 3, *8*, 135, 156, 161, *162*
Alt, J., 219, 220, *224*
Ambrose, J. A., 98, 194, 199
Appell, G., 171, *183*
Austin, G. A., *247*

B

Bandura, A., 276
Barraclough, C. A., 270
Barrett, A. M., 47, *53*
Bateson, P. P. G., 109, 114, 115, 117, 118, 120, 121, 122, *123*
Bayley, N., 259
Bernstein, N., 207, *224*
Binks, C., 117, *124*
Bloom, B. S., 266
Boggan, W., 81, *89*
Bohus, B., 48, *53*
Bovard, E. W., 6, *8*
Brackbill, Y., 199, 251
Brady, J. V., 48, *54*
Brody, S., 134, *162*
Broekhuysen, G. J., 111, *125*
Brumaghim, J. T., 51, *53*
Bruner, J. S., 205, *224*, *247*
Brush, F. R., 49, *54*

C

Caldwell, B. M., 133, *162*
Cameron, J., 259

C (continued)

Campbell, B. A., 121, *123*
Campbell, G. L., 97, 117, *123*
Caron, R. F., 243, *247*
Castle, P., 219, *225*
Chevalier, J. A., 3, 6, *9*, 50, *54*
Coghill, G. E., 209, *224*
Conner, R. L., 48, 49, *55*
Cooper, R. M., 82, *89*
Cowen, J. S., 79, 81, 82, *88*, *89*
Cross, H., 70

D

Davenport, R. K., 70
David, M., 171, *183*
Davidson, J. M., 47, *53*
Denenberg, V. H., 4, 5, 7, *8*, 22, 23, 24, 25, 26, 27, 29, 30, 31, 32, 33, *34*, 48, 50, 51, 53, *53*, *54*, 85, *88*, 101
Denisová, M. P., 232, *247*
De Wied, D., 49, *53*, 59
Disbrow, M. A., 236, *247*
Dittrichová, J., 233, *247*
Dreyfus-Brisac, C., 236, *247*

E

Eiduson, S., 50, *54*
Emlen, J. T., 116, *124*
Endröczi, E., 48, *53*, *54*

F

Fabricius, E., 113, 116, *123*
Feekes, F., 111, *125*
Figurin, N. L., 232, *247*
Fischer, G. J., 117, *123*
Fisher, A. E., 77, *88*

279

Subject Index